PRAISE FOR *GLOBEQUAKE*

"Having worked in government and the church, Wallace Henley understands that our government cannot experience healing unless its people are healed first. Scripture warns what happens to people and nations that forget God. *Globequake* looks at current events and puts them in the context of the larger prophetic picture. Even if America is too far gone to be saved, believers are not. *Globequake* reminds us of the only road 'home.'"

—CAL THOMAS, SYNDICATED AND *USA TODAY* COLUMNIST AND FOX NEWS CONTRIBUTOR

"As an aide to a U.S. president, and a teaching pastor at one of the nation's largest churches, Wallace Henley has one of the most diverse experiences of leadership of any Christian leader writing today. His grasp of Scripture, understanding of human nature, and familiarity with the intricacies of leadership are obvious and apparent in every paragraph."

—GARY THOMAS, AUTHOR OF *SACRED MARRIAGE*, *EVERY BODY MATTERS*, AND OTHER CHRISTIAN LIVING BESTSELLERS

"At a time when fear, desperation, and chaos seem to stare at us wherever we turn in a world shaken by upheavals of historic proportions, Dr. Henley sends a message of joy, hope, and assurance for all who believe in the unshakeable promises of God. Why seek the promises of politicians and central bankers when the Creator has one that never fails? This book is refreshing and comforting, a 'must read' for all who are shaken by the Globequake of events unfolding around us."

—ERNEST LIANG, PHD, DIRECTOR, CENTER FOR CHRISTIANITY IN BUSINESS, HOUSTON BAPTIST UNIVERSITY

"The message of this book is insightful and powerful. It shows how to build unshakeable churches, solid families, truth-based educational systems, principled government, and sustainable and successful companies in the midst of global turbulence. This book will benefit many people around the world."

—SONG CAO, PHD, P̶ ̶ ̶ ̶ ̶ ̶ ̶ ̶ ̶ ̶ ̶GY CORPORATION; AND PRESIDENT, (̶ ̶ ̶ ̶ ̶ ̶ ̶OCIATION

"Wallace Henley masterfu̶ ̶ ̶ ̶ ̶ ̶ ̶ ̶ ̶ld 'Quakes' with change and unrest, ̶ ̶ ̶ ̶ ̶ ̶ ̶ ̶imely book helps explain the confusi̶ ̶ ̶ ̶ ̶ ̶ ̶ ̶mportantly, what to do about it!"

—GARI MEACHAM, AUTHOR OF *TRULY FED* AND *SPIRIT HUNGER*, PRESIDENT AND FOUNDER OF TRULY FED MINISTRIES.

"More than any person I know, my good friend and associate, Dr. Wallace Henley, keeps a finger on the pulse of this nation and world. His experiences in journalism, government and the church afford him a unique insight and discerning grasp of cultural shifts and changes, the aftershocks of which can shake our society to its very core. *Globequake* is a ready survivor's handbook for a crumbling world, with answers and hope grounded in the Book of the Unshakable Kingdom and in the One who still has the whole world in His hands."

—DR. ED YOUNG, SENIOR PASTOR, SECOND BAPTIST CHURCH, HOUSTON, TEXAS

"Wallace Henley is uniquely gifted to observe global shifts. He is that rare animal, a thinking man's pastor, a churchman who does not see everything through a coloured and restricted religious lens. His brush strokes are majestic, sweeping and broad, as they traverse human history. He comments incisively on events that call out for a spiritual perspective of hope in time of change, rather than the doom and gloom philosophy of so many religious leaders. Like the Apostle Paul, Henley throws his anchor deep into the bedrock of God's Eternal Purpose."

—J. RON HIBBERT, LONDON, ENGLAND, WORLD MISSIONS DIRECTOR, BRITISH ASSEMBLIES OF GOD

"Wallace Henley brings to the table a unique background which allows him to paint a picture of our past, present, and future. His vocational diversity gives him a unique viewpoint that few can rival. With the instructive capability of a professor, the critical eye of a reporter, the instincts of a White House aide, and the loving care of a pastor, he details the chaos with which all of us are far too familiar. It is one thing to point out the issues of the world. It is quite another to do so with hope and love for the God who works through the very events that shatter our lives. *Globequake* will lead you to experience the uncertainty of life and the certainty of the Creator."

—ROGER WERNETTE, AUTHOR OF WHOLEHEARTED AND EXECUTIVE DIRECTOR OF THE GATHERING OF MEN, HOUSTON

"This book is a masterpiece. At a time when 'everything that can be shaken will get shaken' we need deep-seated convictions and supernatural wisdom to steer our way through the tremors we experience and the upheavals to come. Through his personal experience in government, church life, business, education and family, Wallace Henley is well positioned to give us direction on how to navigate through the unparalleled challenges we as Christians face. Don't miss reading about the 'Globequake' before it hits!"

—MARKUS KOCH, MELBOURNE, AUSTRALIA, CHIEF EXECUTIVE OFFICER, DANIELS CORPORATION

"As a leadership speaker and consultant in twenty-one nations, not to mention his work as a teaching pastor and author, Wallace Henley knows what's going on in the world. He has seen a lot of turbulence, a lot of disaster, a lot of evil. And, he realizes that those of us who are paying attention are anxiously questioning our futures and the futures of our children and our businesses as well. *Globequake* is the answer we need. In the book, Henley employs the teachings of the Bible to focus, reassure, and calm our minds in this world gone chaotic. His looking back—both insightfully and powerfully—will allow us to move forward, to live in and act with hope."

—SIMON T. BAILEY, AUTHOR OF *THE VUJA DE MOMENT*, AND *RELEASE YOUR BRILLIANCE*; AND CORPORATE LEADERSHIP SPEAKER

"*Globequake* is powerful and compelling! I consider Wallace Henley one of today's most prolific and scholarly writers. He has a long, varied, and successful life and ministry that elicits love and respect from those who know him."

—JOHN EDMUND HAGGAI, AUTHOR, FOUNDER AND CHAIRMAN, HAGGAI INSTITUTE

GLOBE QUAKE

LIVING IN THE **UNSHAKEABLE KINGDOM** WHILE THE WORLD FALLS APART

WALLACE HENLEY

THOMAS NELSON
Since 1798

NASHVILLE   DALLAS   MEXICO CITY   RIO DE JANEIRO

Published in Nashville, Tennessee, by Thomas Nelson. Thomas Nelson is a registered trademark of Thomas Nelson, Inc.

Author is represented by the literary agency of Alive Communications, Inc., 7680 Goddard Street, Suite 200, Colorado Springs, CO 80920, www.alivecommunications. com.

Thomas Nelson, Inc., titles may be purchased in bulk for educational, business, fund-raising, or sales promotional use. For information, please e-mail SpecialMarkets@ThomasNelson.com.

Unless otherwise noted, Scripture quotations are taken from NEW AMERICAN STANDARD BIBLE®, © The Lockman Foundation 1960, 1962, 1963, 1968, 1971, 1972, 1973, 1975, 1977, 1995. Used by permission.

Scripture quotations marked NLT are taken from *Holy Bible*, New Living Translation, copyright © 1996. Used by permission of Tyndale House Publishers, Inc., Wheaton, Illinois 60189. All rights reserved.

Scripture quotations marked AMPLIFIED BIBLE are from the Amplified® Bible, © 1954, 1958, 1962, 1964, 1965, 1987 by The Lockman Foundation. Used by permission. (www.Lockman.org)

Scripture quotations marked KJV are from the KING JAMES VERSION.

Scripture quotations marked NKJV are from THE NEW KING JAMES VERSION. © 1982 by Thomas Nelson, Inc. Used by permission. All rights reserved.

Scripture quotations marked NIV are from the Holy Bible, New International Version®, NIV®. Copyright © 1973, 1978, 1984 by Biblica, Inc.™ Used by permission of Zondervan. All rights reserved worldwide. www.zondervan.com

Library of Congress Cataloging-in-Publication Data

Henley, Wallace.
  Globequake : living in the unshakeable kingdom while the world falls apart / Wallace Henley.
    p. cm.
  Includes bibliographical references (p.   ) and index.
  ISBN 978-1-59555-501-4
1. Change (Psychology)--Religious aspects--Christianity. 2. Change--Religious aspects--Christianity. I. Title.
  BV4599.5.C44H46 2012
  269--dc23

2012000566

Printed in the United States of America

12 13 14 15 16 QG 6 5 4 3 2 1

CONTENTS

To
Dr. John Edmund Haggai
Dr. Ed Young
Chuck Colson
Kingdom men, unshakeable leaders, beloved friends, inspiring mentors

PREFACE

This book begins with crisis and ends with hope. My purpose is to help people grappling with change and upheaval understand how to find safety, sanity, and stability in the midst of the turmoil and find their way to genuine hope.

You may be somewhere along that route.

In 2009, leaders at Houston Baptist University asked me to conduct a conference on the impact of worldwide change on business and the marketplace. A team of experts helped me dig deep into the contemporary issues faced by business leaders. As I reviewed the findings and prepared for the conference, I realized the intensity of change impacts not just business, but every aspect of our lives and the spheres with which we engage daily. That was one reason I wrote the book you are reading right now.

The second motivation was the approach of my seventieth birthday. I was born on the eve of a Globequake, on December 5, 1941, two days before Pearl Harbor. During my later school years, communism was crawling over the planet, and it appeared my generation wouldn't live into adulthood because of the constant threat of nuclear war. As a young newspaper reporter, I covered the civil rights revolution in Birmingham, Alabama, and other parts of the nation. A few years later I was standing on the lawn of the White House, watching my boss, President Richard Nixon, leave for

China. Three decades later I stood on the lawn of the church where I serve as a pastor to welcome three hundred students from China for a three-week immersion program at our church, which would include an introduction to the Bible. I suddenly realized the coming of those students from what we had always called "Communist China" was a fruit from the seed sowed in the moment in which I had played a small part thirty-five years earlier!

That's just a sampling of the change I've lived through.

As a pastor, I see the impact on people daily. I've counseled with hundreds of hurting, confused, distressed people. In recent years, however, the needs have deepened, bewilderment has intensified, and the problems have become much more complex.

I believe the answer for people living in our turbulent times is found in God, His Word, and His kingdom. My prayer is that you will see that the end of the journey for the person anchored to Him is the realization and consummation of hope—no matter how hard the shaking along the route.

PART 1

THE GLOBEQUAKE

The things on earth will be shaken,
so that only eternal things will be left.
—Hebrews 12:27 NLT

CHAPTER 1

THE GLOBEQUAKE AND THE NEW NORMAL

The shaking is here to stay

"Our political leaders are lying to us. All commodities are skyrocketing and have been for months. It's not just oil, but metals for manufacturing, labor costs, and everything else necessary to do business. It's beginning to kill us!"

The words erupted suddenly from the executive, like magma building for centuries in the throat of a volcano. I could feel the throbbing anxiety in the usually solid business leader. I knew he had survived—even thrived—through several disturbances in his long career. But somehow it was different this time.

As a pastor I had heard the desperation and fear in the voices of many people in all stages and spheres of life as they sought comfort and hope. I've been listening to people pour out their heartbreak and worries for forty years, but as in the case of the businessman, the tension has reached a new pitch.

Multitudes now are emotionally like people caught on camera as an earthquake of record-breaking proportions struck a Japanese city in early 2011. Men and women working in a skyscraper were filmed dashing out of the tall building. They had to dodge the steel and stone crashing down from the swaying high-rise. Their heads pivoted and their eyes looked desperately as they wondered, *Is there safety anywhere?*

It appears people everywhere seek security amid the instability of a world gone wild. Our planet is in a state of cataclysm, blasted with worldwide turbulence.

It's a Globequake.

Individuals across the globe sense something big is shaping. Is it global collapse? Fiery wars along the civilizational "fault lines" that Samuel Huntington wrote about in the 1990s?[1] Worldwide depression? Mass starvation? Ecological chaos? *The end of the world?*

People everywhere are asking,

- "What's going on?"
- "What can I do?"

Down deep in all this roiling turbulence people are trying to go about their lives, maintain solid marriages, raise and educate their children, and do their jobs.

All they know is gut anxiety.

It's as if the tectonic plates of society and culture are being torn apart and reshaped right under our feet. "The social threat to the American way of life" is "dire," wrote Rich Lowry.[2] Voices in many nations around the world would say the same for their societies.

GOOD NEWS

The good news is that behind the gut-wrenching uncertainties about the future are wonderful, strong certainties given by the Lord of history. In this book we will discover answers to the troubling questions through solid biblical truth that can be applied to bring stability to us and our institutions. What you will read here unites *orthodoxy* (right belief) with *orthopraxy* (right practice) based on foundational truth on which people can ground their lives when the continents are shifting at what seems light-speed.

In this book I will offer answers to the troubling questions through unchanging biblical principals you and I can apply to bring stability to ourselves, our families, and all our institutions. Everyone can build on these foundational truths. They are not just for one generation or culture, but are universal in the sweep of their guidance and hope.

In the Globequake turmoil we can either *react* with negative indignation or *proact* with positive insights. In the pages ahead you will discover the positive, exciting, stabilizing truths and principles that provide the insights by which we can be safe, sane, and stable amid worldwide disorder and be inspired with hope.

We are living through the spiritual, social, moral, philosophical, economic, political, and personal equivalent of the ancient geological tectonic shifts that brought drastic reshaping of vast landmasses. Like those redefining physical movements, the changes we are experiencing now are worldwide. Unlike the tectonic shifts of antiquity, in which the drift was inches a century, the changes rumbling throughout our worlds seem to be zipping at miles a second, with us riding on top!

The psalmist posed the question in the hearts and on the lips of multitudes today:

> *If the foundations are destroyed,*
> *What can the righteous do?*
> (Ps. 11:3)

SPINNING DOWN THE "RINGING GROOVES OF CHANGE"

Change, by definition, is initially a departure from a normative condition. After a while the new situation becomes the norm, until

5

change sweeps it away and drops something else in its place. However, under the Globequake conditions in which we now live, *rapid change and the resulting turmoil are the new normal.* "Let the great world spin forever down the ringing grooves of change," wrote Alfred, Lord Tennyson, Britain's poet laureate during Queen Victoria's reign. It appears he got his wish.

"The more things change, the more they stay the same," said nineteenth-century French writer Jean-Baptiste Alphonse Karr. That aphorism has been turned on its head in the Globequake age, and it now says, "The more things stay the same, the more they change." The status quo is an illusion. In one of the greatest literary images I've ever read, Alexander Solzhenitsyn wrote of the aging Stalin, "Death had already made its nest in him, and he refused to believe it."[3] Down deep in the thundering mass on which we go about our daily routines, boring rituals, and banal tasks, change has made its nest. The death of the world to which we've grown accustomed is just beneath our feet! No wonder political essayist Victor Davis Hanson wrote that "the natural order of the world is chaos, not calm."[4] Will Durant, writing in a more optimistic age, thought humans could dominate chaos by "mind and purpose."[5] But far from dominating chaos, humanity seems to be falling into "a systemic rise in worldwide unrest," wrote Peter Apps, political risk correspondent for Reuters.[6]

It's not just geopolitical systems trembling all the way to their foundations, but everything around us. The face of the world is being reshaped before our eyes, with new power centers emerging like islands suddenly thrust from the sea bottom by volcanic fury. "We are in the midst of a phase of history in which nations will be redefined and their futures fundamentally altered," said media mogul Rupert Murdoch in an internal memorandum to his staff.[7]

In my lifetime I have seen America and the West move through three eras:

1. *The Atlas Era*, when the Western alliance seemed to hold the world on its shoulders, leading the resistance to Nazi and then Communist threats to global freedom
2. *The Bacchus Era*, when, under the priesthood of people like Hugh Hefner and Timothy Leary, cultural elites, weary from shouldering the world, let themselves go, did their own thing, and retreated into the body and its cravings, taking masses with them[8]
3. *The Narcissus Era*, in which every wrinkle is a crevasse begging for cosmetic surgery, where every emotional flitter is a tornadic psychic upheaval, and where every Twittered and Facebook-inscribed self-narrative is epic literature

Under the Globequake, Western civilization has been dislodged from strong biblical moorings and shifted into nominal Christianity, then to the minimizing of Judeo-Christian influence, then to anti-biblical materialism, then into vague spirituality that tries to find anchorage in the sandy bottom of ancient paganism, and at last into a spiritual void that Islam and a host of other religious and philosophical systems are eager to fill. The Western nations have fallen into the deep rifts of *existentialism* (the only meaning is in the experience of the now), *nihilism* (there is no purpose or meaning in anything), and *hedonism* (since there's no purpose or meaning in anything, make life one vast party, then die).

We have arrived at the stage of history that Peter Drucker must have had in mind when he wrote on the eve of the twenty-first century, "Everybody has accepted by now that change is unavoidable. But that still implies that change is like death and taxes—it should be postponed as long as possible and no change would be vastly preferable. But in a period of upheaval, such as the one we are living in, change is the norm."[9]

What makes the turbulence of our time different from the

tremors and redefinitions of other eras? Can we really claim the contemporary turbulence is any more intense than that of any other time period? We will explore these questions in detail in chapters to come, but for now, let me submit to you three ways in which the current upheavals differ from those of other historic ages: scope, velocity, and magnitude.

Scope

For centuries, people have been talking about changing the world. In previous eras, the world they dreamed of changing was at best regional in scope. Hannibal could conquer only the small bit of the planet he could cover with his elephants. Genghis Khan may have fancied himself a world conqueror, but vast numbers of people living in his age were beyond the reach of his sword. Now, for the first time in history, it's possible to impact the whole world with change, which, in the Globequake era, is becoming viral and universal.

The alterations of the Globequake age are making borders irrelevant. In previous periods, attacking armies could be blocked at well-defended boundaries between nations, but electronic invasions render normal lines of defense useless and even meaningless. Regimes that don't want their societies to participate in the change can only try to block powerful marauders like Google, Facebook, Twitter, and other information systems, but they cannot prevent the leakage of news and opinion into their societies and the changes that inevitably occur.

Many have assumed the Internet would open closed nations to democracy. But authoritarian regimes are learning to use the Web to manipulate their populations through such strategies as propaganda-spreading blogs and to spy on opposition groups. The scope of change in today's world can be as ominous as it is promising. Powerful groups and individuals can spin the currents of change toward their own interests, and they can do it worldwide—*for the first time in history*.

Some even see a future in which computers become so dominant they take over the world. Professor Stephen Hawking has called for genetic engineering to develop human intelligence to outpace the growth of computer intelligence. "In contrast with our intellect, computers double their performance every 18 months," he told *Focus*, a German magazine. "So the danger is real they could develop intelligence and take over the world."[10]

Bill Joy, cofounder of Sun Microsystems, expresses a similar concern about the scope of change possibly looming for the world's future. By 2030, he says, engineers may be building machines a million times more powerful than today's computers. "I may be working to create tools which will enable the construction of the technology that may replace our species," worries Joy.[11]

The scope of the new normal of change is not merely electronic. In the industrialized nations especially, there is scarcely an institution not affected by what has become a continuum of change. Revered establishments that have preserved and propagated belief and value systems have toppled into the rifts opened by the Globequakes.

The scope is so broad it seems no one can escape the changes hurtling toward us in the Globequake age. Just about the time we adjust to one set of transitions, we are assaulted with more changes zipping at us faster than we can assimilate them.

Velocity

The accumulation of information is the fastest increasing quantity in the world.[12] Researchers at the University of California–Berkeley examined the "total production of all information channels in the world for two different years, 2000 and 2003."[13] In 2000, the total production of new information in a twelve-month period amounted to thirty-seven thousand times the information housed in the Library of Congress. By 2003, the accumulation of information was growing by 66 percent per year. The amount of scientific knowledge has been doubling every fifteen years since 1900.

Information alters existing realities and also creates new

phenomena. The velocity of information therefore accelerates change. The industrial age shows there are certain periods of mega-leaps, when technologies, systems, and processes morph seemingly overnight into radically new forms. Both an eighteenth-century balloon and the Wright Brothers' airplane enabled humans to fly, but the plane was a quantum leap into a new category.

Information is a primary catalyst of change. No previous historic period has experienced the velocity of the increase of information; therefore the contemporary period is unique—up to this point of history. This is why Globequake-level change is the new normal.

What about the future? Clearly if the velocity builds with its own momentum, the eras ahead will be marked by even more radical change. This raises a question of apocalyptic proportions: *At what point does the velocity overwhelm the vehicle?* An airplane, for example, has a maximum speed. Go beyond that and structural failure occurs. Systems break down. As the Berkeley study found, "the information about and from a process will grow faster than the process itself . . . and so as we progress, information will grow faster than whatever else is being produced."[14]

How will we contain it all? Jesus' words spoken twenty centuries ago have piercing relevancy for the Globequake age: "No one puts a patch of unshrunk cloth on an old garment; for the patch pulls away from the garment, and a worse tear results. Nor do people put new wine into old wineskins; otherwise the wineskins burst, and the wine pours out and the wineskins are ruined; but they put new wine into fresh wineskins, and both are preserved" (Matt. 9:16–17).

The gospel proclaimed by Jesus was truth so dynamic, so vibrant with life, that new structures were needed to convey it across society and history. The cry of the present Globequake age is for new "wineskins," new structures that can cope with the information coming at light-speed. Sadly, having rejected the way of Jesus, the old religion of humanism can't handle the flood either, and its leaders work their fingers raw trying to piece together new structures.

As we will see in the chapters ahead, once again the truth about Jesus and His kingdom is the "new wine" that will bring strength and vitality to the world in tumult. The structures of society must be renewed—they must become "new wineskins"—to receive the powerful principles that give them enduring calm and stability as they are being squeezed and torn by the Globequake. As the velocity of information builds, the accumulation of energy begins to impact the face of entire civilizations. Hardly an institution escapes the resulting magnitude of change.

Magnitude

The ancient tectonic plate movements in earth's geology and geography were immense in magnitude, altering the face of the whole planet. The changes now under way in the spiritual, social, political, economic, ethical, and philosophical continents of the world are just as huge. The upheaval that is the new norm in the present is redrawing the face of the world!

According to tectonic shift theory, in the earth's early history there was one vast supercontinent, Pangea. Cataclysms deep in the planet caused the plates on which the landmass rested to split, dividing massive chunks from one another and setting them adrift on the planet's surface.

In a sense, this is what is happening to the spiritual, intellectual, and sociopolitical systems of the world. There was once consensus holding whole civilizations together. For example, scholars have noted the similarities between the Ten Commandments and other law codes of nations surrounding the Hebrews. The Ten Commandments were revealed to Moses by God Himself in an act theologians call "special revelation." However, God's "general revelation" is written instinctively in every human being (Rom. 2:15), so it's no surprise there's a certain consensus among humans regarding murder, theft, adultery, and other moral issues on a near global scale.

Globequake forces, however, shatter the consensus. Moral relativism has devastated Western civilization. There is no longer a firm, inviolable consensus around a core belief system. When the consensus is destroyed, the Pangea of human belief and behavior is ripped apart. The world fragments into chaos similar to Israel in the time leading up to the judges, when every person "did what was right in his own eyes" (Judg. 17:6).

The fragmentation in the consensus about God has had an impact of great magnitude on many cultures. Under Globequake conditions, God has first been pushed off to the sidelines of the public square and, in the thought of many elites, shoved out of sight totally.

The magnitude of this act is immense in its destructive force. G. K. Chesterton wrote, "In the act of destroying the idea of Divine authority we have largely destroyed the idea of that human authority by which we do (an arithmetic) sum."[15] The destructive forces at the highest levels of magnitude radiate downward to the most detailed concerns of life. With the loss of reverence for God comes a loss of reverence for His creation—beginning with human life. Here the magnitude of the upheaval reaches truly tragic proportions, resulting, for example, in the abortion culture and the deaths of tens of millions of unborn babies.

THREE IMPACTS ON PEOPLE

The scope, velocity, and magnitude of the changes wrought by the Globequake impact us in three major ways:

1. We become increasingly insecure.

People have many reasons to feel insecure in the Globequake age. They worry about their marriages and other relationships, job security, care for their aging parents, and their own retirement, as well as a secure future for their children and grandchildren. On the national and world scale, there's concern about the availability of oil and other energy resources. Many worry about the declining quality of leadership in a period when churches, families, schools, government institutions, and businesses need the best.

And then there's always the weather. One chunk of the population fears climate change portends serious injury to the planet's ecosystem, which they believe to be fragile. Another hefty demographic worries that those who agonize over global warming and other environmental changes are laying the framework for more government control of industrial and commercial development, and the reduction of personal freedoms.

Many people are haunted by vague, unidentifiable anxiety, manufactured within their turbulent souls. We have managed to create an entire culture of insecurity. Both the real and the imagined threats of the Globequake age drive us deeply into ourselves in the effort to fend off the gremlins of fear and anxiety. The outcome is what we experience presently: self-absorption resulting in what Harvard sociologist Pitirim Sorokin called the "sensate" stage of a culture when feelings and emotions govern.[16] The more we view the world through the lens of our own emotions, the greater the threats to our security loom.

Christopher Orlet writes, "An overdose of self-esteem and self-promoting technology have combined to create a perfect storm of narcissism."[17] The more narcissistic we become, the more insecure we are, worrying about the ripples that will destroy the image we stare at relentlessly in the increasingly troubled waters of our world. Thus, there is a vicious cycle in which insecurity leads to a passion for self-preservation, which rushes into self-absorption, which results in more insecurity.

Under such pressure, the psyche begins to crumble. In the Globequake age, the heavy lifting of which only the spirit is capable has been cast upon the flimsy soul. The Greek word translated "soul" in the New Testament is *psuche*, from which we get *psyche* and a whole family of terms. Insecurity is felt most acutely in the soul, where we think and feel emotionally. If the condition persists, it affects the body with physical symptoms and drives people to the drugs and medications characteristic of our times. The best the weary, overtaxed soul can do is crank out counterfeit spirituality leading only to more disappointments, uncertainties, and desperate quests for security.

If we live in a state of insecurity long enough, after a while we drift into insanity.

2. Society loses its mind.

Insanity is at epidemic proportions. That was the conclusion of E. Fuller Torrey and Judy Miller in their 2002 book, *The Invisible Plague*.[18] From 1955 into the twenty-first century, many medications had become available, but the number of people diagnosed with mental illness had increased sixfold![19]

It's not just individuals, but whole nations can also lose touch with their identity and history. *What is the insanity that causes entire cultures to lose their minds and dive into the spiritual, moral, and intellectual fissures gouged by the Globequake?*

"Identity is an individual's or group's sense of self," wrote Samuel P. Huntington in *Who Are We?*, a study of contemporary America's identity crisis.[20] Identity is important, he adds, because it shapes our behavior. So people who rip apart high values covering them, their families, and nations suffer from sheer insanity. Their destructive behavior shows a loss of their own identity.

Insanity is "reason used without root, or reason in the void," wrote G. K. Chesterton.[21] "The man who begins to think without the proper first principles goes mad; he begins to think at the wrong end." Cultural, societal, and national insanity occurs when people destroy their roots and forget their first principles. The

Globequake tears out the root system and brings down the edifice of first principles. That's why whole societies lapse into insanity and lose their stability.

3. Instability shakes everything to the core.

One day in 1973 the reality of the world's instability flamed to searing focus in my mind. I had grown up and spent much of my young adulthood in a nation where you griped if you had to pay thirty-eight cents for a gallon of gas. But that morning as I pulled up to a pump, I was stunned when I saw the price for a gallon of gasoline had rocketed to fifty-eight cents. While I slept, something drastic had been afoot in the world. The tremors then were mild—we would eagerly pay fifty-eight cents for a gallon of gas today—but they portended greater instability and confusion to come.

In a much larger way, the devastating destabilization of the Globequake is its impact on the foundations on which all strength and order rest. So, in response to the psalmist's rhetorical question: *there is much the righteous can do in the midst of foundations crumbling under Globequake furor.* David gives us the foundational principle as, through the inspiration of the Holy Spirit, he begins answering his own question. The central fact we must keep in focus when the foundations are quivering beneath us is recorded in Psalm 11:4: "The LORD is in His holy temple; the LORD's throne is in heaven." Here are stability and confidence!

In a later chapter we will explore the unshakeable kingdom. Its strength is in the Person enthroned in the "holy temple." He is immovable and unchangeable not because He doesn't like change, but because He doesn't need it. At the core of all reality, and in the midst of the most catastrophic upheavals, there is One who is perfect and complete, dwelling in a temple no magnitude of quake can topple, on a throne from which He cannot be removed by any force or power.

There are three essential foundations on which the tremors focus their fury. The first is God Himself, the second is the foundation of truth, and the third is the foundation of humanity. The absolute and objective reality of God cannot be destroyed, but self-created human perceptions of God can be rattled to the very foundations. Since God and truth are inseparable, ultimate truth cannot be altered but, under intense tremors, can be distorted and confused. Because the human is created in the image of God, the foundational nature of humanity cannot be obliterated, but it can be twisted. If these foundations are destroyed in the subjective understanding and experience of human beings, what can we who seek to hold to God's holiness and purity amid the turbulence of our age do?

Plenty, as we will see in the pages ahead.

"THINGS WILL SETTLE DOWN"

"Things will settle down," my mother used to tell me. Pearl Harbor and America's entry into the world war came two days after my birth in 1941. My childhood was full of the global conflagration and its aftermath. Ten years later, divorce blitzed our home, and our family experienced personal tumult. When I was a teenager and young adult, the headlines were obsessed with the inevitability of global nuclear war.

Always my mother would say, "Things will settle down."

She's been gone a long time, but now I understand why she remained stable and hopeful, no matter how intense the quakes that rumbled through her life and world, and how she was able to steady our household.

Mother was the youngest of nine children. She and her widowed mom were left on a barren farm as my mother's older siblings went to the big city to try to find jobs to support themselves, their mother, and their little sister. There were times when my mom, at age six, had to milk the neighbor's cow so she and her own mother could survive. Later in life, my mom rode out the heart-rending turbulence of domestic violence and the divorce that destroyed her eighteen-year marriage. She was faced with the challenge of raising and educating my sister and me. But she couldn't be knocked down. She kept standing, no matter what. That's why I believed her when she said things would "settle down."

Now I see my mother didn't mean the tremors would stop. She knew they were the norm. One of the reasons my mother knew things would settle down was that she was old enough to see a big swath of history. She believed God was in charge of every moment. She knew all things "work together for good" for those called by God and set apart for His purposes—even if it took decades. (See Rom. 8:28–39.) She had an instinctive sense of how time works, and that formed her understanding of her narrow slice of history and an individual's experience within it.

Finally I figured it out. She wasn't telling me the external world would settle down, because the upheavals were the norm. Rather, my mother was saying *I* would settle down in the midst of the shaking by positioning myself on solid biblical truth, just as she had done.

"What can the righteous do?" For one thing, we must examine and incorporate into our worldview the Bible's revelation about how time functions and allow that truth to shape our perspective about the Globequake. As my mother demonstrated, you don't have to be an Albert Einstein or Stephen Hawking to get it!

CHAPTER 2

HOW TIME WORKS

The buildup to the Big One

To see why the present Globequake conditions are the new norm, we must grasp basic truth about how time works.

Comedian Red Foxx played Fred G. Sanford on the 1970s hit TV sitcom *Sanford and Son*. Sometimes to get himself out of a tight spot, Sanford would feign a heart attack, grabbing his chest and shouting to his deceased wife, "I'm coming, Elizabeth! This is the big one!"

History has heard a line like that many times from people who were certain the events of their era were ushering in the end of the world. When "the end" didn't come, there were three basic reactions:

1. Those who had been so certain tried to explain why their prediction was wrong.
2. Those who believed history was without direction or purpose thought their worldview was confirmed.
3. Those with beliefs based on major Eastern religions weren't surprised the cycles of history hadn't led to an end since time, they believed, is cyclical, not linear.

The difference between the way the Bible reveals time's nature and the view of Eastern religions is that they see history rolling *over* again and again, while the Bible shows time rolls *forward*, along a linear track. The wheels on the train cycle over the track, but the train moves toward a specific destination.

So, back to Fred G. Sanford. All those cycles of heart attacks and tremors *do* ultimately lead to the Big One. And for history, all the repeating patterns are building toward a climactic end. History is not a toy train running endlessly on an oval track. Time is moving more like a real train on a linear track leading from a point of beginning to a destination.

WHEN AND WHAT?

Jesus gave His followers some details about the end times one day when they walked together on the Mount of Olives. The awesome scene of Jerusalem's temple was spread before them as they peered westward from the slopes. The disciples were impressed with the great buildings, but Jesus saw far more. He spoke to the disciples about the ultimate plan of God. "Do you not see all these things?" He asked them. "Truly I say to you, not one stone here will be left upon another, which will not be torn down" (Matt. 24:2).

The disciples asked the questions people have asked subsequently down through the centuries: "Tell us, when will these things happen, and what will be the sign of Your coming, and of the end of the age?" (Matt. 24:3).

In Greek, "sign" is *semeion* and, in the Bible, refers usually to a supernatural indication or affirmation of something. The disciples were catching on that Jesus is the Messiah. They were grasping that all the prophetic sayings and events ultimately were about Him. They were even beginning to see He would leave them and then return.

Jesus began to answer the *what* and *when* questions like this:

See to it that no one misleads you. For many will come in My name, saying, "I am the Christ," and will mislead many. You will be hearing of wars and rumors of wars. See that you are not frightened, for those things must take place, but that is not yet the end. For nation will rise against nation, and kingdom against kingdom, and in various places there will be famines and earthquakes. (Matt. 24:4–7)

Prior to the end, says Jesus,

- false messiahs will come,
- many people will be misled,
- there will be wars and rumors of wars,
- cultural clashes will blaze, with people group (*ethne*) rising against people group,
- there will be many struggles between nations,
- famines will strike,
- earthquakes will shake worldwide,
- tribulations will abound, and
- Jesus' followers will be hated and persecuted.

But, said Jesus, "all these things are merely the *beginning* of birth pangs." The Greek word for "beginning," as used in Matthew 24:8, signifies a commencement of events leading to the fulfillment of a goal or purpose: "And then . . . they [the tribes of the earth] will see the Son of man coming on the clouds of the sky with power and great glory" (Matt. 24:30). Therefore the end times mark the initiation of a process leading to Jesus' second coming.

In the Globequake era we see the things that Jesus prophesied would characterize the end times all around us. Is it possible this time it's for real, that we are zooming toward the Big One?

THE "ENDS OF THE AGES"

The Holy Spirit, through Paul, leaves no doubt we are living in the "ends of the ages." In a sense, the Globequake rumbles with apocalyptic signs. Paul told the Corinthian Christians the things Old Testament Israel experienced in history "happened to them as an example, and they were written for our instruction, *upon whom the ends of the ages have come*" (1 Cor. 10:11, italics added).

Much has been made about ours being the terminal generation, but that has been true for all generations since the ascension of Jesus Christ. After all, the Corinthian Christians whom Paul addressed initially lived more than twenty centuries ago, yet theirs was as much the "ends of the ages" as ours.

"Ends" is the Greek word *telos*. The term refers to the aim or purpose of a string of events, spread across time. For example, Romans 10:4 states, "Christ is the *end* of the law for righteousness to everyone who believes" (italics added). God gave His Law through Moses at Sinai, centuries before the appearing of Christ. The ages in between encompassed the whole experience of Israel, including the crossing into the promised land, the establishment of Jerusalem and the temple as the center of worship, the exiles, the prophets, and the totality of Israel's interactions with God in the arena of history. But all of it was a buildup for the *telos* of Jesus Christ.

"Ages" is the Greek *aion*, from which we get, for example, the English word *eon*. *Aion* refers to "a point of time preceding another point of time, with a very long interval between," as well as "a unit of time as a particular stage or period of history."[1] To speak of the *telos* of the "ages" is to focus on the purpose of history.

What's the point of it all? People wonder whether there's any purpose to existence. Existentialists answer, "The present moment is all that matters." Nihilists disagree; "Nothing matters," they say. Hedonists agree with both: "There's no meaning in anything, and so the best we can do is wring all the pleasure we can from the existential moment, which is all we have!"

The Bible gives a different reply, one charged with dynamics and hope. Jesus states it clearly in Matthew 24:14: "This gospel of the kingdom shall be preached in the whole world as a testimony to all the nations, and then the end [*telos*] will come." The whole point of the ages of history is the advance of the kingdom, planted in the earth in the incarnation of Jesus Christ, growing in every historic period beneath the "soil," and ultimately to spring up like a vine of blessing that covers the whole planet! (See Mark 4:26–27.)

That brings us to the powerful word *apocalypse*. In New Testament Greek, the term refers to an "unveiling." History is the tantalizingly slow (to us) raising of the curtain whose finality will be the return of Jesus Christ and the complete rule of God's kingdom of righteousness, peace, and joy within the re-created world (Rom. 14:17).

Jesus' departure from the world was not a termination but a beginning. The moment He ascended, the curtain of cosmic history began coming up with Him. It has been slowly rising in every era since the completion of Jesus Christ's incarnate mission. And in every age, there is a cosmic struggle against the powers of darkness seeking to stand in the place of God's kingdom and push it aside. This is the spirit of *opposition* and *imposition*, the goals of antichrist, the "man of lawlessness" (1 John 4:3; 2 Thess. 2). The antichrist spirit appears across history (1 John 2:18) but will culminate in the ultimate Antichrist.[2]

Jesus' and Paul's teachings about the end are clear that it is both process and event. Somehow, for this to be true, time must be cyclical *and* linear, an apparent contradiction. However, as we probe the Bible's revelation about the nature of time, we see how time functions according to both dynamics.

HOW TIME WORKS

Long before Albert Einstein and his theory of relativity, and Professor Stephen Hawking and his complex book *A Brief History of Time*, the Bible revealed how time operates. The best way to study the nature of time is to probe the revelation given by its Creator.

First, the Bible presents time on two levels, described in two distinct Greek words, *kairos* and *chronos*. *Kairos* has these definitions:[3]

- a fixed and definite time, the time when things are brought to crisis, the decisive epoch waited for
- opportune or seasonable time
- the right time
- a limited period of time
- what time brings, the state of the times, the things and events of time

Chronos, by contrast, refers merely to the passage of time. Think of *chronos* as the tracks, history the train, and *kairos* the wheels spinning along the rails.

Light, as physics has shown, has the strange nature of being manifest both by particles and by waves. The Bible shows time has a similar quirkiness, being both linear and cyclical.

The *kairotic* aspect of time is revealed in the *pleroma*, or "fullness" of *chronos*. In the Bible's view, the ticktocks of a clock are building toward a *telos*, or goal-purpose. The end of time in the biblical view is not termination but arrival at the purpose toward which *chronos* leads. So, after centuries of types and shadows, and scores of messianic prophecies, "when the fullness of the time [the *pleroma* of *chronos*] came, God sent forth His Son" (Gal. 4:4). The coming of Jesus Christ into the world was the greatest of the kairotic events that will ever occur on the *chronos*-track.

Second, *kairos* events run in cyclical repetition across the line of *chronos*. "History repeats itself" is an idea based on this reality. Cyclical kairotic events are not the same in their detail, but they are the same in their general characteristics.

So, Jesus said, "The coming of the Son of Man will be just *like* the days of Noah" (Matt. 24:37, italics added). Jesus was not suggesting the end times will be an exact duplication of the daily routine of Noah. However, there will be similarity—eating, drinking, marrying, giving in marriage. The generally similar events and circumstances will keep turning on the rails, moving history forward to its destination.

Third, the kairotic events mount in intensity as they near the *telos* of *chronos*-time. Again, Jesus revealed that there would be many tribulations mounting up to the "great tribulation" (Matt. 24:9–29). Many antichrists will appear all along the track of *chronos* until the coming of one so completely controlled by this demonic spirit he is known as *the* Antichrist (1 John 2:18).

LINEAR-CYCLICAL

The Bible presents the *linear-cyclical* view of time. The train hurtles forward in a linear direction, but the wheels turn and turn. A train is therefore a linear-cyclical vehicle, moving straight but propelled by the spin of the wheels. Thus, kairotic events are the "spin" that keeps history—the train—moving on the straight tracks, which symbolize *chronos*-time. The Bible shows that historic patterns do repeat, but not endlessly. *Chronos* is moving in a linear direction toward a destination that God Himself has ordained.

So the events of our time *could* be the consummate kairotic occurrences. The Bible leaves that possibility open in all generations. Jesus said, "Of that day and hour no one knows, not even the angels of heaven, nor the Son, but the Father alone" (Matt. 24:36). Based on the biblical revelation of how time works, we must not dogmatically assert we are the *absolutely* terminal generation, but neither should we exclude the possibility we *may* be.

Harold Camping and others have tried to nail down the precise day and time of Christ's return, and they keep missing it. The reason is they gauge their predictions on *chronos*-time rather than *kairos*. Humans will not know the *chrono*logical exactness of the

Second Coming, but we can recognize the kairotic clues of His return. Jesus made this clear in Matthew 16:1–3:

> The Pharisees and Sadducees came up, and testing Jesus, they asked Him to show them a sign from heaven. But He replied to them, "When it is evening, you say, 'It will be fair weather, for the sky is red.' And in the morning, 'There will be a storm today, for the sky is red and threatening.' Do you know how to discern the appearance of the sky, but cannot discern the signs of the times [*kairos* in the Greek original]?"

The fourth time principle revealed in Scripture is that the Bible's disclosures about time and events occurring *within chronos* come from *outside chronos*, while *we* view them *within chronos*.

My favorite coffee mug illustrates this reality. The hefty cup is four and a half inches tall. Imagine you are a microbe living at the very bottom of that big mug. One day you decide to embark on the journey of a lifetime—all the way to the top of the cup. You will be of advanced age when you arrive at your destination and fulfill your goal of reaching the mug's rim. A human being is looking at the same mug and the same distances from outside the cup. It takes the one-cell creature its lifetime to reach the top, a mere two hours in human time.

This is the way God views the *chronos* we inhabit. The Bible puts it this way:

> The LORD looks from heaven;
> He sees all the sons of men;
> From His dwelling place He looks out
> On all the inhabitants of the earth,
> He who fashions the hearts of them all,
> He who understands all their works.
> (Ps. 33:13–15)

God is looking at *chronos*-time from outside, while we view it from within. Other passages reveal this same truth:

> *For a thousand years in Your sight*
> *Are like yesterday when it passes by,*
> *Or as a watch in the night.*
> (Ps. 90:4)

And the apostle Peter wrote, "With the Lord one day is like a thousand years, and a thousand years like one day" (2 Peter 3:8).

So, from our limited perspective of time, we ask,

- How far down the track of *chronos*-time is the train of history?
- Is there any indication the wheels of the train are spinning faster?
- What's different about this Globequake age than other periods of history when people thought the end was near?

We answer the last question first: *what's different about this Globequake age is that some of the global events prophesied in the Bible for the end times are possible for the first time in history.* Here are nine major signs of the times for the first time globally feasible. For the first time in history

1. global evangelization is possible and occurring because of rapid travel and communications (Matt. 24:14);
2. nations are aligning in opposition to Israel, as foretold long ago by the prophet Ezekiel (Ezek. 38);
3. global lawlessness is a reality because of the impact of media and instantly transmitted social forces (2 Thess. 2:1–12);
4. it is possible for revolution to leap from nation to nation because of the ability to broadcast inciting images instantly (Rev. 13:1; 17:15);

5. since the church was launched at Pentecost, apostasy in unimaginable proportions has spread into churches once faithful to the gospel (2 Thess. 2:1–3);

6. it is possible to bring whole civilizations into delusion because of global media (2 Thess. 2:11; 2 Tim. 3:1–8);

7. it is possible for markets worldwide to collapse in an instant because of the electronic economy (Rev. 18);

8. there are a globalization and an intensification of the persecution of the genuine church (Matt. 24:9; Rev. 12); and

9. the nature of war has shifted from conflicts between geopolitical entities to civilizational war (Matt. 24:6–7).

SEQUENCES AND CYCLES

Some students of history believe the tectonic changes come in predictable sequences and cycles. Karl Marx built his theories of social economics on the philosophical system laid out by Georg Hegel's concept of history.[4] At the heart of Hegel's thought is the idea that friction of opposing forces and contradictions build up until they produce major turning points in history. One set of ideas, values, and circumstances is overwhelmed by the contradictory and reactive forces on the opposite side, and in the collision, something new emerges from the synthesis of the colliding ideas and practices.

German historian-philosopher Oswald Spengler was more linear. Cultures follow a sequential pattern in which they arise, ripen, decay, and disappear forever. Hence, his 1918 book, *The Decline of the West*, sought to identify and reveal the forces that would bring the demise of Western culture.

Russian-born Pitirim Sorokin, founder of Harvard University's Department of Sociology, saw history's tectonic changes as moving in a three-part cycle of the ideational, the sensate, and the idealistic. During the ideational phase, a culture has a deeply spiritual sense of reality. But the contradictory force arises in the form of the sensate cycle, in which reality is essentially materialistic. Finally there is a resolving cycle, the idealistic stage, which combines the spiritualism of the ideational with the materialism of the sensate. Sorokin would see contemporary America as falling into the decadence of the sensate, which would lead to an idealistic era.

Historians William Strauss and Neil Howe advanced a more recent theory of cultural change in their "four turnings" theory. In their book *The Fourth Turning*, Strauss and Howe discuss the cycles they see redefining the historical landscape throughout time. The First Turning is an exuberant season in a society when institutions are growing stronger, individualism is fading, and a set of bold, new values displaces old ways of thinking and the organizations that promoted them. In the Second Turning a spiritual turbulence challenges the existing order of society. Culture seems to unravel at the seams during the Third Turning, which brings despair and gloominess as society's institutions crumble and individualism becomes dominant. Crisis is the atmosphere in a society during the Fourth Turning, marked by secular turbulence.[5]

A MYRIAD OF ANSWERS

Strauss and Howe, with the other writers who have noticed the change pattern in history, have a variety of answers for the causes of these shifts and redefinitions. The Bible, however, shows there are historic cycles and stages for nations and their institutions, *based on the people's interactions with God.*

The Bible's worldview is evident, for example, in the book of Judges, which shows a nine-stage historic cycle with the following elements:

1. *A period of the clear revelation of truth.* The culture is anchored to a solid belief system whose values form the consensus for the key institutions providing the society's infrastructure.

   "The people served the LORD all the days of Joshua, and all the days of the elders who survived Joshua, who had seen all the great work of the LORD which He had done for Israel" (Judg. 2:7).

2. *A relapse of memory phase.* The old values regime dies, and new values regimes (to borrow a phrase from Strauss and Howe) implant new beliefs in the culture, displacing the truth on which the nation was built and causing it to be lost for a period. For ancient Israel, this occurred when people forgot God and His ways.

   "All that generation . . . were gathered to their fathers; and there arose another generation after them who did not know the LORD, nor yet the work which He had done for Israel" (Judg. 2:10).

3. *The stage of rebellion.* Wittingly and unwittingly important elites in the culture rebel against the founding vision, its underlying truths and values, and a majority of people in the society join them.

   "Then the sons of Israel did evil in the sight of the LORD and served the Baals, and they forsook the LORD" (Judg. 2:11–12).

4. *The period of the refiner's fire.* Having separated from its foundational truth, the society now experiences the outcomes and consequences consisting of trials and tribulations.

   "The anger of the LORD burned against Israel, and He gave them into the hands of plunderers who plundered them; and He sold them into the hands of their enemies around them, so that they could no longer stand before their enemies. Wherever they went, the hand of the LORD was against them for evil, as the LORD had spoken and as the LORD had sworn to them, so that they were severely distressed" (Judg. 2:14–15).

5. *The turn toward remembrance.* As difficulties mount, important voices in the culture call for an attempt to remember and rediscover the core values and truths that were lost, and the people remember to call on God.

"When the sons of Israel cried to the LORD, the LORD raised up a deliverer for the sons of Israel to deliver them." (Judg. 3:9).

6. *The season of repentance.* This is a turning back by the legitimizers and their institutions to the ancient truths and values on which the society was built and once flourished.

"The sons of Israel said to the LORD, 'We have sinned, do to us whatever seems good to You; only please deliver us this day.' So they put away the foreign gods from among them and served the LORD; and He could bear the misery of Israel no longer" (Judg. 10:15–16).

7. *The age of revival.* Now substantial numbers of people within a society join the turning of repentance and move back to the foundational beliefs and principles. This is reflected in the exuberance of the period of Deborah's judgeship:

Then Deborah and Barak the son of Abinoam sang on that day, saying,

> *"That the leaders led in Israel,*
> *That the people volunteered,*
> *Bless the LORD!*
> *Hear, O kings; give ear, O rulers!*
> *I—to the LORD, I will sing,*
> *I will sing praise to the LORD, the God of Israel."*
> (Judg. 5:1–3)

8. *The time of restoration.* The society's fundamental truths are again revered, there is a return of respect for institutions promoting the original values, and the culture is restored to its roots. This

is reflected also in the Song of Deborah, when she sings of the "gates," whose restoration symbolized authority and security:

Bless the LORD!
You who ride on white donkeys,
You who sit on rich carpets,
And you who travel on the road—sing!
At the sound of those who divide flocks among the watering places,
There they shall recount the righteous deeds of the LORD,
The righteous deeds for His peasantry in Israel.
Then the people of the LORD went down to the gates.
(Judg. 5:9–11)

9. *The period of rest.* The society is characterized for a time by stability, peace, productivity, and prosperity.
"Then the land had rest forty years" (Judg. 3:11).

The abandonment of truth and its values always launches whole societies through the rigors, the stresses, and the pandemonium seen in these stages. All the institutions riding along on the cultural "plate" undergoing tectonic shift are shaken and threatened.

By 1796, for example, the American founders could have been very concerned about the nation they sired. Powerful factions had developed within America. As the great upheavals of the eighteenth century began to set off global tremors, America "was often a nation at war with itself," wrote Jay Winik. To the disgust of the founders, as the nation "ventured farther away from the writing of the Constitution, the country was reinventing itself with each crisis it confronted—with wholly unpredictable consequences."[6]

The journey through cycles of redefinition seems at times to be apocalyptic. Apocalypse in the popular sense is scary only because it destroys all our preferred subjective interpretations of reality with stark objectivity. But from the Bible's perspective, for those in covenant with the Creator and Sustainer of the universe, the apocalypse is charged with hope and expectancy—so much so that Paul, for one, referred to the true apocalypse as the "blessed hope" (Titus 2:13).

Therefore this book will be honest about the hard challenges brought on by the Globequake, but it will look at reality through the lens of hope. As we've seen, historic change is so obvious that most who study history have felt obligated to try to explain it. The Globequake has happened before, and it is occurring again. *We've been here before.*

But just because we've been here before doesn't mean this time it might not be the Big One. The curtain may be going down on *chronos*, but the curtain of God's *kairos* is going up. While this present world fades from view, the rising veil reveals more and more of the kingdom that cannot be shaken or destroyed by the Globequake.

CHAPTER 3

THE UNSHAKEABLE KINGDOM
Still standing at the end of the day

The situation was pathetic and laughable.

As the summer of 1776 faded into autumn, the British had placed the largest expeditionary force they had ever sent anywhere in the American colonies. Thirty thousand well-trained, battle-ready troops were ready to take on the tattered American amateurs. Another five thousand Hessians were en route to join British General William Howe's forces. He also had the backing of seventy of the most feared warships in the world and hundreds of other craft that could wear down the colonists.[1]

George Washington, the Virginia farmer who commanded the colonial revolutionaries, did well to find ten thousand soldiers he could count on. The British would commit more and more troops throughout the eight and one-half years of the war. Even though the Americans would be joined by France, Washington's total force would never go beyond sixty thousand, and he would have to deal with a 20 percent desertion rate.[2]

Despite the almost insurmountable challenges, the American armies ultimately prevailed. Some historians think George Washington was the primary reason. "Whatever his failings as a general, Washington's moral strength held his army together," wrote biographer Ron Chernow.[3] When General Charles Lee retreated from a battle in June 1778, Washington himself took charge, turned around the retreating troops, and fought the British to a tie. Washington's young French military aide, the Marquis de Lafayette, watched it all and wrote that Washington's "presence stopped the retreat . . . brought order out of confusion, animated his troops, and led them to success."[4]

In the twentieth century it would be Britain that was apparently weak and ill prepared as the Nazis targeted the island nation. On June 4, 1940, as London and other cities were being battered by enemy bombs, Winston Churchill, the new prime minister, addressed Parliament. His words still ring: "We shall go on to the end. . . . We shall fight on the beaches, we shall fight on the landing grounds, we shall fight in the fields and in the streets, we shall fight in the hills."[5]

Churchill was depicted as an unrelenting bulldog who wouldn't surrender an inch of ground. Churchill's strength and stability anchored the nation, inspired its people to huge sacrifice, and gave them hope.

George Washington, Winston Churchill, and many other leaders across history have proved that when chaos is intense and doom certain, there must be an immovable center. Right at the core there must be a point so sturdy that those hurtling through terrifying change can lock on and find safety, sanity, and stability.

There is, then, no greater hope in the Globequake age than the truth revealed in Hebrews 11–12. Chapter 11 lists unshakeable people who anchored history and who shared the common bond of an unshakeable faith. It was not airy optimism, but solid stuff. "Faith is the *substance* of things hoped for, the evidence of things not seen," says Hebrews 11:1 (NKJV, italics added).

The Greek word appearing in verse 1 translated "substance" is *hupostasis*, referring to an underlying support on which something stands. For example, Paris's Eiffel Tower must bear immense windloads. Its skeleton consists of massive girders laced in an elegant arrangement. What's crucial, however, is the *hupostasis* beneath the ground. Construction started with the digging of four massive foundations, going down fifty-three feet. Concrete was then poured in, forming powerful solid blocks on which the four vertical piers of the Eiffel Tower stand.

No one would be so foolish as to say the tower has no foundations just because they cannot be seen. There's no other way to explain its ability to keep standing for decades. *The Eiffel Tower's looming presence over the Seine proves the existence of its foundations.* That's the point about the unshakeable people listed in Hebrews 11. Faith is not only the substance on which they keep standing, but also the evidence of the foundations invisible to the observer on the surface. That unshakeable people continue standing under great duress is testimony to the faith upholding them.

Hebrews 11 closes with a summation of some blasts of tribulation through which the unshakeable people it describes stood:

By faith the walls of Jericho fell down after they had been encircled for seven days. By faith Rahab the harlot did not perish along with those who were disobedient, after she had welcomed the spies in peace. And what more shall I say? For time will fail me if I tell of Gideon, Barak, Samson, Jephthah, of David and Samuel and the prophets, who by faith conquered kingdoms, performed acts of righteousness, obtained promises, shut the mouths of lions, quenched the power of fire, escaped the edge of the sword, from weakness were made strong, became mighty in war, put foreign armies to flight. Women received back their dead by resurrection; and others were tortured, not accepting their release, so that they might obtain a better resurrection; and others experienced mockings and scourgings, yes, also chains and imprisonment. They were stoned, they were sawn in two, they were tempted, they were put to death with the sword; they went about in sheepskins, in goatskins, being destitute, afflicted, ill-treated (men of whom the world was not worthy), wandering in deserts and mountains and caves and holes in the ground. (Heb. 11:30–38)

Foundations are no stronger than the soil in which they are embedded. God Himself is the rock in which the foundations of faith are laid. "I, the LORD, do not change," He says (Mal. 3:6). In the part of Texas where we live, the soil in some areas is called gumbo because of its tendency to shift. But the foundations of faith don't ride on a soupy base of mud. "The LORD is my rock!" shouts the psalmist (Ps. 18:2). If the base on which the foundation rests is unshifting, then the foundation is unshakeable, and the structure rising from it is stable.

Hebrews 11 presents a list of unshakeable people, and Hebrews 12 then speaks of the unshakeable kingdom of which such people are citizens and ambassadors. God says, "Yet once more I shake not only the earth, but also heaven." The passage continues,

Now this, "Yet once more," indicates the removal of those things that are being shaken, as of things that are made, that the things which cannot be shaken may remain. Therefore, since we are receiving a kingdom which cannot be shaken, let us have grace, by which we may serve God acceptably with reverence and godly fear. For our God is a consuming fire. (Heb. 12:27–29 NKJV)

Among the outcomes of the Globequake is "the removing of those things which can be shaken, as of created things" (Heb. 12:27). Time's tremors have littered the landscape with collapsed temples, shrines, scientific theories, philosophical systems, political ideas, social ideals, and whole cities of intellectual, emotional, and spiritual edifices where people thought they could find shelter when everything around them was shaking to pieces.

When I was twenty-nine, I worked in a world I thought to be indestructible. Every morning I would drive into Washington from the Virginia suburbs, park my car in a designated area, and walk a short distance through the gates of the White House. Inside that universe we were impregnable. Guards were everywhere. The presidential institution seemed too powerful to be brought down, no matter how great the chaos Washington might experience.

Harry Dent, my boss and friend, once apologized to President Nixon for a statement he had given to the press. "Don't worry, Harry," Nixon replied. "The people forget in six weeks."

From inside the White House compound and deep in the inner vault of the Oval Office, the powerful political giants and their ideas and behaviors seemed untouchable. Nothing could bring them down. Nixon would discover afresh that far from forgetting, one's political opponents collect the scraps of damaging information until they have enough to forge a wrecking ball to swing at the foundations of what appear to be indestructible institutions and shatter them.

Ultimately everything that can be shaken will be shaken and brought down. At the end of the day, all that is left standing is what is established on the eternally immovable.

THE IMMOVABLE STONE OF ETERNITY

Whatever rests on the foundation of the kingdom of God cannot be moved. Let tempests roar, continents shape and reshape, civilizations come and go, and mighty people strut their moment on the stage, the kingdom still stands, fixed on the immovable stone of eternity. People, nations, and institutions with footings in the kingdom of God are as enduring as it is.

The kingdom of God is the extension of His cosmic rule into the world of time, space, and matter. When the prophet Ezekiel and, much later, John saw visions of what Moses (Deut. 10:14) and the psalmist (Ps. 68:33) term the "highest heavens"—or, as Paul put it, the "third heaven"—the centerpiece was the throne and its glorious Occupant. (See also Ezek. 1; 2 Cor. 12:1–6.) A throne is a seat of authority, and the throne of heaven is the location of ultimate Authority. *Wherever God rules, there His kingdom is manifest.*

Ultimately Christ's kingdom rule will extend to everything. However, until Christ returns, there are vast areas not acknowledging God's kingship. The all-powerful God permits this because He is committed to the freedom of His image bearers.

Since the fall into sin, Satan and the powers of darkness have sought to hurl everything into deepening chaos. The Devil's aim is to make the world as hellish as the realm he will ultimately inhabit. Isaiah, through prophetic insight, had Lucifer in view when he wrote,

> *Is this the man who made the earth tremble,*
> *Who shook kingdoms,*
> *Who made the world like a wilderness*
> *And overthrew its cities,*
> *Who did not allow his prisoners to go home?*
> (Isa. 14:16–17)

"World," for the readers of the Septuagint—the Greek translation of the Old Testament—would have been *cosmos*. The verb form, *cosmeo*, refers to putting things in an orderly arrangement. The city—the *polis*—was the outcome of such order, a place where human beings could live, raise families, and do business in a secure environment. But Lucifer's aim was to scour the world until it was a barren desert and to reduce the cities to ash heaps.

When Allied troops penetrated German cities after World War II, they gave a name to the horrible landscape battered by years of guns and bombs. They called it the "rubble world." All that could be seen in the hearts of once elegant cities were piles of bricks and other jagged remnants of buildings, ash heaps where people tried to survive. Satan's goal is the opposite of cosmos, which is chaos, the reduction of earth and its cities to a rubble world condition.

God's kingdom restrains disorder, not through raw power but through genuine authority. Jesus is the incarnation of authority, and when people see Him as He really is, they happily and freely place themselves under His rule. We will explore more implications of the differences between power and authority in later chapters.

God made Adam and Eve His regents within natural creation. What they said was the way things would go. In this sense God is like a property owner who subleases his house. He wants the renters to be comfortable. "You are in charge; do whatever you like to my house," the owner says, assuming the leasers to be trustworthy. But the day comes when the property holder returns to the house he owns and finds it trashed beyond recognition. Through their choice of rebellion, Adam and Eve brought down the manifest reign of God's kingdom within the created domain and trashed God's beautiful world. (See Gen. 3.)

A rival system grew like an alien in earth's womb. Ultimately it would be symbolized by the Tower of Babel and by Babylon, the city of raw human power. (See Gen. 11; Isa. 14; and Rev. 14–18.) John, in his Revelation visions, saw the deeper meaning of Babylon as the world system organized without and in defiance of God. But the Owner has never relinquished the property. He will return and demand an accounting from those to whom He has given dominion. Until then, His kingdom is manifestly present in the world through those people and places where He is freely given authority.

"We are ambassadors for Christ," wrote Paul (2 Cor. 5:20). This was among the first Bible verses I learned as a child, but it would take many years for me to begin to comprehend the depths of the concept. Jonas Kouassi was my teacher. Jonas was at that time a member of the diplomatic corps of the government of the Ivory Coast, a country in West Africa. I spoke annually for a leadership conference in the huge church where he was an elder, and Jonas was usually my translator. Jonas understood the kingdom of God.

"An ambassador has extraterritoriality when he's serving in a foreign country," Jonas said. He explained two thrilling implications for our roles in this world as ambassadors for Christ and His kingdom. First, an ambassador on duty in an alien land remains under the authority of the nation and government of his homeland. He doesn't pledge to foreign flags. He obeys the commands of those who sent him, not the leaders of the country where he resides on assignment. Second, that means *the governing powers of the land where the ambassador is serving have no authority over him.*

Think about what this means for you and me as Christ's ambassadors. Three times Jesus referred to Satan as "the ruler of this world" (John 12:31; 14:30; 16:11). Later, John would write, "We know that we are of God, and that the whole world lies in the power of the evil one" (1 John 5:19). The Devil, as we have seen, has temporary power in the world we inhabit. However, if we are Christ's ambassadors, because of the principle of territoriality, the Devil has no authority over us!

There are only two ways the Prince of Darkness can get at us. Sometimes God will permit the Devil's influence to build our faith and teach us spiritual warfare. In this case think of the Devil and his demons as the *-ites* who fought Israel—the Amalekites, the Hivites, and all the others. (See, for example, Num. 14 and 2 Sam. 22:30–35.) God was training the Hebrews to occupy the promised land. The good news is that when God allows the Enemy to come up against us, God knows our limits and will make a way of escape when His purposes are achieved (1 Cor. 10:13).

Some behaviors had to be "shaken off" Simon Peter if he was going to be an effective ambassador for Christ. Peter's impetuous actions, his presumptuous attitude, and other rough edges had to be knocked off. "Simon, Simon," Jesus said to him one day, "Satan has demanded permission to sift you like wheat; but I have prayed for you, that your faith may not fail; and you, when once you have turned again, strengthen your brothers" (Luke 22:31–32).

Satan had to seek permission to "sift" Simon Peter because Peter was then under Christ's authority and had extraterritoriality. Jesus inferred the permission was going to be granted. When Peter's wrangle with the Devil was done, he was to use what he learned

Buddy

vet

4:00

to instruct and build up his fellow disciples. Satan used a serving maid to bring a surprise attack on Peter as he stood in Caiaphas's courtyard, watching the beginning of Jesus' ordeal that culminated on the cross—and ultimately the empty tomb. Peter denied knowing Christ, just as Jesus said he would. Immediately Peter remembered Jesus' earlier words, "and he went out and wept bitterly" (Matt. 26:75). That act of repentance restored Peter to his ambassadorial status and taught him vital lessons that would carry him through a challenging mission—all the way to his own martyrdom.

Peter was shaken so he could become unshakeable!

There is a second way we can be afflicted by Satan and his demons while on our ambassadorial assignment in this world despite our extraterritoriality. Sometimes, through the works of the flesh, we bring ourselves under the Devil's control. Some years ago a drunken Russian diplomat in Washington, DC, killed a person in a horrific car crash. His government waived his right of diplomatic immunity so he could be tried in an American court. When we come out from under Christ's authority and practice evil, our extraterritoriality is waived, and Satan has power over us until we repent. When we return to Christ and a godly lifestyle, we regain the status and privilege of extraterritoriality.

No wonder Peter wrote, "Be of sober spirit, be on the alert. Your adversary, the devil, prowls around like a roaring lion, seeking someone to devour. But resist him, firm in your faith, knowing that the same experiences of suffering are being accomplished by your brethren who are in the world" (1 Peter 5:8–9).

In contrast to Satan's domain of raw power, God's kingdom is "righteousness and peace and joy in the Holy Spirit" (Rom. 14:17). The Devil's regime is wickedness, conflict, and misery. God's is the kingdom of heaven, but Satan's is the kingdom of hell. The kingdom of God is the kingdom of light, but Satan's realm is the kingdom of darkness. God's kingdom is the cosmos where the childlike revel in their innocence, but the Devil's world is an arena of exploitation and guilt.

KINGDOM IMPACT IN THE WORLD

In the end, it's all God's, and He's coming to get it back and bring judgment against those who have marred its innocence and beauty— beginning with Lucifer and the armadas of fallen angels who carry out his assaults!

When will this happen? Jesus gives us key clues. "The kingdom of heaven," He says, "is like leaven, which a woman took and hid in three pecks of flour until it was all leavened" (Matt. 13:33). The Lord is telling us that once the kingdom is seeded, it is catalytic and transforms everything it touches. Ultimately all creation will be "leavened," changed into the nature of God's kingdom, just as a lump of dough takes on the nature of the fermented chunk a baker inserts to convert it to bread.

The kingdom entered the world in seed form in the incarnation of Jesus Christ. He casts a demon from a man one day and tells the gawking crowd, "If I cast out demons by the finger of God, then the kingdom of God has come upon you" (Luke 11:20).

Until then, there's a wonderful progression of kingdom impact within the world. The kingdom advance, says Jesus,

> is like a man who casts seed upon the soil; and he goes to bed at night and gets up by day, and the seed sprouts and grows— how, he himself does not know. The soil produces crops by itself; first the blade, then the head, then the mature grain in the head. But when the crop permits, he immediately puts in the sickle, because the harvest has come. (Mark 4:26–29)

This does not mean, however, that dreamy-eyed utopians and their institutions will bring in the kingdom in its completeness. Christ's followers through the ages can impact their domains with His kingdom, but only He can establish it fully and completely in the earth. This Christ will do in His second coming.

All this came home to me one bright April day when Irene and I visited the Normandy invasion beaches in France. We were at the vast American cemetery at Omaha Beach. I looked at the 9,300 graves and wept. My tears were not just for the fallen soldiers, but also for the realization of the nature of God's kingdom, which had suddenly become so clear. Christ's first coming was "Normandy," and His second coming is symbolized in the total defeat of the Nazis, their war machine, and their rule over Europe. Until then, we press on, taking territories for Christ and His kingdom, fighting the good fight, and "looking for and hastening the coming of the day of God" (2 Peter 3:12).

The day in which everything that can be shaken will lie in shambles is "the day of God." This is the day in view when Jesus says, "Just as the Father has life in Himself, even so He gave to the Son also to have life in Himself; and He gave Him authority to execute judgment, because He is the Son of Man" (John 5:26–27). It's also the day Paul writes about when he says, "Because of your stubbornness and unrepentant heart you are storing up wrath for yourself in the day of wrath and revelation of the righteous judgment of God" (Rom. 2:5). It will be a day when "God will judge the secrets of men through Christ Jesus" (Rom. 2:16). The shaking is so great that the question will be, "Who can endure the day of His coming? And who can stand when He appears?" (Mal. 3:2).

Even the strongest, most powerful people, their regimes, and their empires will crumble. The rumblings have already registered on the seismograph of history. The alliance that won the victory in Europe and the Pacific in 1945 would, in ensuing decades, fall apart. The Western powers would form themselves into NATO to defend Europe from its former ally against the Nazis, the Soviet Union, and the states it had swallowed up. China would disappear down the craw of communism. Even the Western nations would squabble over the Middle East and other issues.

At least twenty-one civilizations have shuddered and collapsed into the dustbins of history. There is only one kingdom that endures and cannot be shaken. In the next chapter, we will examine five reasons why God's kingdom is unshakeable and why the Globequake cannot bring it down.

That leads us to a vital personal question: *Can you say with confidence that you are a citizen of the unshakeable kingdom of God?* The answer can be determined only in relationship to its King, Jesus Christ. Founders of religions declare that salvation is found in their messages and systems. Jesus, however, is the *propositional Person*. A proposition is a request, invitation, or command that demands a decision and response. Jesus says, "*I* am the way, and the truth, and the life" (John 14:6, italics added). He does not assert that His philosophy, worldview, traditions, and rituals save us; He Himself saves us.

Kingdom citizenship is determined by the way we respond to Jesus' proposition. We become citizens of the unshakeable kingdom when we say yes to its King. That yes is the commitment of our lives to Him: to receive His gift of salvation and to embark on the adventure of being His disciple, or apprentice.

Prayer is the way we voice our yes to Him. A proposition calls for a specific response at a precise moment in time. Is this your moment? It can be right now, and you can pray something like this:

> *Father, I believe that Jesus Christ is Your only begotten Son,*
> *that You sent Him into the world to take the penalty of my sins*
> *and to show me how to live. I believe Jesus died on the cross and*
> *was raised on the third day. I now turn away from sin and a*
> *lifestyle characterized by sin. I turn to You and cast my eternal*
> *salvation on Jesus Christ. I receive Him at this moment as my*
> *Savior and confess Him as my Lord and King. I believe the Holy*
> *Spirit manifests Jesus in my heart and life and empowers me for*
> *the purpose and work for which You placed me in the world. I now*
> *receive the empowerment of the Holy Spirit for whatever You want*
> *me to do. I make this prayer in Jesus' name. Amen.*

CHAPTER 4

STANDING LIKE A STONE WALL

Five reasons the Globequake can't crack the kingdom

"There stands Jackson like a stone wall!"

General Barnard Elliott Bee had no idea he was giving Thomas Jonathan Jackson the name history would remember him by on that bloody day in 1861. Confederate troops were under heavy fire from Union armies. Despite the ponderous Virginia heat and searing barrages on July 21, 1861, Jackson was able to hold his unit together during the Battle of First Manassas in the American Civil War.

Other Confederate units were in disarray, fleeing Federal troops chasing them down Matthews Hill. Chaos and desperation were everywhere. General Bee galloped quickly to Jackson's position and was ordered to gather his soldiers behind Jackson's First Brigade. Bee had to ride into the throng of wildly running troops, halt their retreat, and head them toward Jackson's brigade. As the men thrashed and turned, it was at that point Bee made his famous cry. Not only would people forget Stonewall Jackson's real first name, but his unit would be forevermore known as the Stonewall Brigade.

Other generals, both North and South, had perched high where their troops could see them and had been mowed down. In fact, General Bee would be killed in that same battle. Stonewall

Jackson, however, proved warfare, like earthquakes and tornadoes, is capricious.

In a whirling windstorm, a whole block of buildings can be flattened and one lone structure left standing. Tornadoes blast a dozen houses off the map and skip a single dwelling on the same street. Bombing raids level a city but leave a church towering over heaps of debris, like the ruin of the Kaiser Wilhelm Memorial Church in Berlin or the huge dome of St. Paul's in London.

THE UNSHAKEABLE KINGDOM

So the Globequake will ravage everything before its shaking is over. All that is weak will collapse. Civilizations, nations, cultures, institutions, titles, properties, and wealth will all come down in spectacular crashes or weasel ignominiously into yawing rifts. When it's all over, only God's kingdom and everything established upon its sturdy foundations will be left standing.

There are at least five reasons the kingdom of God is unshakeable.

1. The kingdom is unshakeable because of the strength of its King.

Ezekiel was given a rare look at the throne of God Himself. The prophet wrote, "On that which resembled a throne, high up, was a figure with the appearance of a man" (Ezek. 1:26).

Scores of humans are disappointed to discover that the throne of the universe is not up for grabs and that its Occupant cannot be unseated. Karl Marx said his goal in life was to dethrone God as well as destroy capitalism. Marx was late to that game. Before history, Lucifer tried to shove God off the throne and was cast out of the kingdom of heaven (Isa. 14:12). The antichrist spirit, through its human agents in the earth, still tries to unseat the King of kings and the Lord of lords. We are told that "the LORD shall reign forever" (Ex. 15:18). Had the would-be dethroners taken that disclosure seriously, they would have saved themselves and history a lot of agony—and blood!

The psalmist picked up the theme under the Holy Spirit's inspiration and wrote,

> The LORD has established His throne in the heavens,
> And His sovereignty rules over all.
> (Ps. 103:19)

The King is the embodiment of the kingdom of heaven, and the throne is the eternally established seat of His authority over everything. Because the sovereign Lord cannot be unseated, nor His throne toppled, the kingdom arising from Him cannot be shaken.

2. The kingdom is unshakeable because it is an eternal continuum.

Human regimes in a fallen world are cyclical, rising and falling, but God's reign is an eternal continuum. This implies that, while God's kingdom reign is timeless, it is not static. A *continuum* means certain conditions are consistent throughout a sequence, though they may manifest themselves in varying forms.

How can the changeless God dwell in a sequential environment, which implies a past, present, and future, even though it's a continuum? As we noted elsewhere, some theologians have concluded that God develops and grows with the sequential events of His creation. God is not omniscient, some of them teach, but has to respond, like everyone else, to each historical situation as it looms suddenly before Him. In this sense God is like a road builder who has to brake unexpectedly when he zooms into a tight curve on the very road he designed and constructed. This is a *reactive* deity, who has to respond to change. The true God, however, is *proactive* with respect to historic transitions and Globequake-level upheavals with the world He created.

"Your throne is established from of old; / You are from everlasting," said the psalmist (Ps. 93:2). "From" denotes sequence, movement from one place or time to another. Micah 5:2 describes the Messiah as One whose "goings forth are from long ago, / From the days of eternity."

God's movement, however, is not a jerky journey into sudden change. Think of a person who observes a mouse in a maze. The tricky passages are built into a topless box, three feet by three feet square and three feet tall. The watching human stands above, looking down into the whole labyrinth. For the mouse the trip is sudden turns, unexpected barriers, and unseen obstacles. The observer, however, is unaffected by the conditions down in the maze. The human who watches from above sees the whole path of the journey, which is in the past, present, and future experience of the mouse. The human is not a disinterested spectator, but desires the mouse to discover and enjoy the chunk of cheese whose aroma fills the box and tugs the little creature onward. The observer is outside the time-context of the mouse, but can enter the little animal's time and space by sticking in his hand and removing a barrier or actually picking up the mouse and setting it on a more direct course to the cheese at the center of the maze.

Similarly, God is outside time and sees the whole of history. Sin is not a sudden swerve resulting in frantic emergency meetings of heaven's high council to come up with a quick plan to address the problem. Rather, Christ is "the Lamb slain from the foundation of the world" (Rev. 13:8 KJV). Jesus Christ as the world's only Savior also points to the fact that God, though not bound to earthly sequences, can enter into the world's past, present, and future to make provision for the circumstances He observes from above time and space.

Change doesn't jolt the throne, its Occupant, or the kingdom established by His reign. The kingdom of God is therefore unshakeable.

3. The kingdom is unshakeable because its truth is absolute.

The primary ideas behind the Old Testament Hebrew word for *truth* are "firmness" and "stability."[1] Truth conforms to fact, which is absolute and irrefutable. God is the essence of all fact; therefore whatever is true aligns with His character:

> God is not a man, that He should lie,
> Nor a son of man, that He should repent.
> (Num. 23:19)

Thus, He is firm and stable in the factuality of His being and the authenticity of all that arises from Him. So Paul wrote that he was "a bond-servant of God and an apostle of Jesus Christ" for the sake of "the knowledge of the truth which is according to godliness, in the hope of eternal life, which God, *who cannot lie*, promised long ages ago" (Titus 1:1–2, italics added).

The Globequake, however, has created two intellect-stifling conditions with respect to truth—*equivalency* and *relativism*. Equivalency says that all ideas and their expressions are equally valid. Postmodern culture believes that truth is relative. The very act of holding an opinion makes the notion true. Since there is no objective truth factual all by itself, whatever is known must be true because it's true to the person who does the knowing.

This makes contemporary culture like the bizarre Wonderland visited by Alice, the central character in Lewis Carroll's *Alice in Wonderland*. The story includes an episode in which a group of animals gets sopping wet. "The first question was, of course, how to get dry again," wrote Carroll. The Dodo bird suggested a race around the lake. The creatures would run until they were dry:

> There was no "One, two, three, and away," but they began running when they liked, and left off when they liked, so that it was not easy to know when the race was over. However, when they had been running half an hour or so, and were quite dry again, the Dodo suddenly called out "The race is over!" and they all crowded round it, panting, and asking, "But who has won?"[2]

The Dodo bird had the answer to that too: "*Everybody* has won, and all must have prizes."

In the topsy-turvy Globequake world, all truths are equally valid, and there is no absolute truth. Everybody's opinion "wins." Well, almost everybody. Professor Allan Bloom, in his book *The Closing of the American Mind*, identified the loser in the culture where nothing is absolute except the claim that nothing is absolute. "The true believer is the real danger" in such an environment, he said. In cultures of relativism and equivalency, a person "is not to . . . really be right; rather . . . not to think you are right at all."[3]

The ancient Greeks, however, knew there was something utterly and completely "right," an absolute truth, at the heart of the universe. They called it the Logos, the expression of the core reality that is the structural center, the central nervous system, the brain of the cosmos. John gave the stunning revelation that the Logos, who had been present with God from before the beginning and through whom everything that exists was made, became flesh in the person of Jesus Christ (John 1:1–14).

Christ, therefore, is the incarnation of Truth. He is the holder of all authority, the King of the kingdom. If the Logos is Truth in the absolute, if such Truth is embodied in Christ, and if Christ is the King of the kingdom of God, then the Truth established by the kingdom is absolute!

4. The kingdom is unshakeable because of its universal and enduring relevancy.

If the truth arising from God's kingdom is absolute, there are no limits to its relevancy. Kingdom truth is true in all cultures, and it is enduring in all eras of history. Kingdom truth is relevant for a bushman in the Australian Outback, a professor at the Harvard Business School, and all others.

The ultimate statement of relevancy is in Hebrews 13:8, which says Jesus Christ "is the same yesterday and today and forever." Is He really? Is there historical evidence of the constancy of Jesus' relevance and that of His kingdom? There are major criteria by which we can test the proposition of the continuing relevancy of Jesus Christ and His kingdom.

SCIENTIFIC RELEVANCY: Modern science would not exist without the biblical worldview. Physicist-theologian Stanley Jaki wrote,

> The scientific quest found fertile soil only when this faith in a personal, rational Creator had truly permeated a whole culture. . . . It was that faith which provided, in sufficient measure, confidence in the rationality of the universe, trust in progress, and appreciation of the quantitative method, all indispensable ingredients of the scientific quest.[4]

SOCIAL RELEVANCY: One of the most surprising verifications of the relevancy of God's kingdom for whole societies comes from a self-identified atheist, Matthew Parris. He tells of returning to the African nation he knew as a boy as Nyasaland, called today Malawi. There Parris observed the work of mainly Christian charities in relieving the hardships of Malawi's people. Such services, Parris wrote,

> inspired me, renewing my flagging faith in development charities. But travelling in Malawi refreshed another belief, too: one I've been trying to banish all my life, but an observation I've been unable to avoid since my African childhood. It confounds my ideological beliefs, stubbornly refuses to fit my world view, and has embarrassed my growing belief that there is no God.

Parris said, even though he's a "confirmed atheist," he has become convinced "of the enormous contribution that Christian evangelism makes in Africa: distinct from the work of secular NGOs, government projects and international aid efforts." These are insufficient, Parris wrote, because they do not bring personal transformation.

"In Africa Christianity changes people's hearts," he said. "It brings a spiritual transformation. The rebirth is real. The change is good."[5]

ECONOMIC RELEVANCY: Researchers today "are re-examining whether there might be a link between religious belief and economic performance," reported Joshua Burek in the *Christian Science Monitor*. Burek cited studies seeking the answer to that question:

- In a 2003 study of nearly sixty countries, "Harvard researchers Robert Barro and Rachel McCleary found certain religious beliefs did contribute to economic growth. Notably, they concluded that a belief in hell was a slightly more potent economic spur than a belief in heaven."
- In 2004, "Niall Ferguson, a professor of history at Harvard University, examined the connections between faith and work ethic in light of divergent trends he found in the United States and Europe. Religious belief in North America has 'been amazingly resilient' amid big economic gains, he says, disputing the notion that wealthier countries necessarily become less religious."
- But abroad, Ferguson noted that "a decline in European working hours coincided with a decline in faith. 'Americans don't in fact do better work than Frenchmen,' he wrote. 'They just do *more* work. A lot more.' Between 1979 and 1999, the average US working year lengthened by nearly 4 percent. Yet in Germany, France, and Spain, that figure dropped by at least 10 percent. 'Europeans now seem to believe in holidays, not in holy days,' he adds. This divergence, Ferguson argues, coincides with a period of European de-Christianization, and American re-Christianization."[6]

POLITICAL RELEVANCY: The American founders disagreed on important issues, such as the strength of the federal government in relation to the states, when and how slavery should be abolished, and whether God was engaged in human history. However, they were in a general consensus that God exists and that principles given in the Bible are crucial for the formation of a nation. James Madison summed up this consensus when he said,

> We have staked the whole future of American civilization, not upon the power of government, far from it. We have staked the future of all of our political institutions upon the capacity of mankind of self-government; upon the capacity of each and all of us to govern ourselves, to control ourselves, to sustain ourselves according to the Ten Commandments of God.

Daniel Webster was convinced that "if we abide by the principles taught in the Bible, our country will go on prospering . . . but if we and our posterity neglect its instructions and authority, no man can tell how sudden a catastrophe may overwhelm us and bury all our glory in profound obscurity."[7]

5. The kingdom is unshakeable because it is based on the unbreakable covenant.

Democracies are based on the principle of social contract. John Locke's version of social contract theory influenced the American system. People unite to establish a state to promote their mutual well-being and form governments to secure the rights God has given. The social contract has proved effective—especially Locke's view—in structuring free societies.

However, not even the best and highest expressions of social contract can match the bond by which the kingdom of God is established in relation to human beings and their world. The kingdom of God is stable because it is based on immutable covenant, established by God Himself, and backed up by His character!

These contrasts help us understand why covenant is superior to even the best of contracts:

- Contracts have start dates and a point when the contractual agreement ends. Covenants endure.
- Contracts are based on law, while covenants rest on relationship and love.
- A contract covers only those aspects of a transaction or arrangement spelled out in writing. A covenant commits the whole person and all that he or she possesses.

A covenant binds two parties to an agreement. In ancient times, blood was the glue. Covenant makers would cut their hands and clasp one another, mingling their blood. The whole sacrificial system described in the Bible and culminating in the atonement of Jesus Christ is a blood covenant. It is initiated by God, who will not break His covenant with humanity under any conditions.

The kingdom of God rests on this unbreakable relationship, and that's a major reason it cannot be shaken. The promise of a kingdom based on covenant appears early in history. As Jacob speaks final blessings on his sons, who will form the tribes of Israel, he comes to Judah. The old man doesn't understand fully the historic impact of his words as he says,

> *The scepter will not depart from Judah,*
> *nor the ruler's staff from his descendants,*
> *until the coming of the one to whom it belongs,*
> *the one whom all nations will obey.*
> (Gen. 49:10 NLT)

Centuries later, the prophet Nathan, speaking for God, tells David, a member of the tribe of Judah, "Your house and your kingdom shall endure before Me forever; your throne shall be established forever" (2 Sam. 7:16). Thus, God says,

> *I have made a covenant with My chosen;*
> *I have sworn to David My servant,*

I will establish your seed forever
And build up your throne to all generations.
(Ps. 89:3–4)

Jesus Christ is the culmination of the kingdom covenant. When the angel tells Mary about the child she will bear, God's messenger says, "He will be great and will be called the Son of the Most High; and the Lord God will give Him the throne of His father David; and He will reign over the house of Jacob forever, and His kingdom will have no end" (Luke 1:32–33).

God's kingdom is unshakeable to the point that it has no end because it rests on the sturdy, unbreakable rock of God-established covenant. So how does the wonderful revelation of the unshakeable kingdom work out in the grit, grumble, and gruesomeness of everyday life? How do we actualize its reality to make the shaky worlds we inhabit places of safety, sanity, and stability?

CHAPTER 5

THE KINGDOM AND THE SPHERES
Getting God's world into your worlds

Our "worlds" are made for the kingdom of God as much as ships are made for the ocean.

Once I knew a man—we'll call him Salty, for his love of the sea—who built a forty-foot boat in his small heart-of-the-city backyard. I am a lover of sailing craft of all kinds, and Salty took me to see his creation. Great gaps of time would separate Salty's building spurts. The evening I saw the uncompleted vessel it needed hedge clippers more than a rigging knife. I was struck with the sadness of a boat out of water. It's like crown jewels without a human head and neck, a spoon without soup, or a throne without a kingdom.

KEY WORDS IN 2 CORINTHIANS 10

To put the powerful reality of the unshakeable kingdom to work in our everyday world, we must take it into our spheres. Paul laid down the broad principle in 2 Corinthians 10, applying it to the particular situation at the church in Corinth. While the context is important, we have much to learn from the general concept on which he built his case under the Holy Spirit's inspiration. Paul wrote,

> You are looking at things as they are outwardly. If anyone is confident in himself that he is Christ's, let him consider this again within himself, that just as he is Christ's, so also are we. For even if I boast somewhat further about our authority, which the Lord gave for building you up and not for destroying you, I will not be put to shame, for I do not wish to seem as if I would terrify you by my letters. For they say, "His letters are weighty and strong, but his personal presence is unimpressive and his speech contemptible." Let such a person consider this, that what we are in word by letters when absent, such persons we are also in deed when present.
>
> For we are not bold to class or compare ourselves with some of those who commend themselves; but when they measure themselves by themselves and compare themselves with themselves, they are without understanding. But we will not boast beyond our measure, but within the measure of the sphere which God apportioned to us as a measure, to reach even as far as you. For we are not overextending ourselves, as if we did not reach to you, for we were the first to come even as far as you in the gospel of Christ; not boasting beyond our measure, that is, in other men's labors, but with the hope that as your faith grows, we will be, within our sphere, enlarged even more by you, so as to preach the gospel even to the regions beyond you, and not to boast in what has been accomplished in the sphere of another. But HE WHO BOASTS IS TO BOAST IN THE LORD. For it is not he who commends himself that is approved, but he whom the Lord commends. (2 Cor. 10:7–18)

Embedded in the answers to the immediate concerns for Paul and the Corinthians is broader truth that will help us in the rigors of the Globequake-shaken world. These principles emerge as we examine three key words in the 2 Corinthians passage.

Province

A *province*, also translated "measure," is "a determined extent, a portion measured off."[1] The term carries the idea of legitimacy, a realm where an individual has legal right to exercise authority. *Province* is also "an outlying portion of an extended empire."[2]

First Kings 20:13–14 provides background as it tells us, "There came a prophet unto Ahab king of Israel, saying, Thus saith the LORD, Hast thou seen all this great multitude? behold, I will deliver it into thine hand this day; and thou shalt know that I am the LORD. And Ahab said, By whom? And he said, Thus saith the LORD, Even by the young men of the princes of the provinces" (KJV).

There are certain realms where you are "prince" or "princess." The "extended kingdom" is the kingdom of God. Ultimately it will cover the whole earth. John saw this in the Revelation visions and wrote of Christ's people, "You have made them to be a kingdom and priests to our God; and they will reign upon the earth" (Rev. 5:10).

Until then, there are provinces where the kingdom is manifest through His princes and princesses. That leads us to the next key word in 2 Corinthians 10:7–18.

Sphere

The realm where you are prince or princess is your sphere. In New Testament Greek, this word is "an area of activity, defined geographically and functionally."[3] The focus of *province* is authority, while *sphere* deals with function.

This can be illustrated through a constitutional monarchy, like the United Kingdom. All the British Commonwealth is the province of the king or queen. However, because the British monarchy is part of a larger constitutional system that grants legal authority to

Parliament, the king or queen functions within the sphere granted by the Constitution.

Further, wrote Paul, "we are ambassadors for Christ" (2 Cor. 5:20). An ambassador is sent with authority by his or her nation to a particular country.

As we will see, there is more than one sphere in which we function. In this book we will discuss six spheres:

1. The sphere of person
2. The sphere of church
3. The sphere of family
4. The sphere of education
5. The sphere of governance
6. The sphere of business-marketplace

In each of these we have the measure of authority necessary to carry out the function that God has assigned us.

Authority

Exousia, the Greek for "authority," means "the right to control or govern."[4]

The little word *right* shows the essential difference between authority and raw power. A right of authority is *given*, not *seized*. But where does the right come from? Authority moves from the higher to the lower. Over each higher tier there is another, even higher. The right of true authority keeps ascending until it reaches the throne of God. Thus, all authority comes from God. This is precisely what the Bible teaches.

For example, Jesus said, "All authority has been *given* to Me in heaven and on earth" (Matt. 28:18, italics added). Paul wrote, "There is no authority except from God" (Rom. 13:1). The authority in every sphere of human engagement comes from God. True authority is entrusted only to people under authority. Saul came out from under God's authority and lost his kingdom (1 Sam. 13:8–14). Bullies seize raw power and sustain it with their own strength.

When we operate in our spheres under the province of God's kingdom, we have genuine authority. True power—the Greek word is *dunamis*—flows from authentic authority. Rather than being destructive, the power resulting from genuine authority is edifying and positive.

VERTICAL SEPARATION VS. HORIZONTAL FLOW

Abraham Kuyper, a Dutch pastor who became Holland's prime minister in the early twentieth century, helped develop the concept of spheres. Kuyper understood the kingdom of God and its comprehensive authority in all spheres of human endeavor. "There is not a square inch in the whole domain of our human existence over which Christ, who is Sovereign over all, does not cry, 'Mine,'" said Kuyper.[5]

Sphere sovereignty was the idea developed around Kuyper's thought. Each institutional sphere stood on its own and had an authority separate from all other spheres. This led to *pillarization*, which saw the spheres as distinct towers, standing side by side, but not interacting. Some Dutch settlers in South Africa took the concept to an extreme and used it to justify the rigid racial separation known as *apartheid*. Pillarization led to fragmentation there and in Holland.

This distorted application, however, does not invalidate the Bible's revelation regarding provinces, spheres, and authority. Pillarization and fragmentation resulted from a misunderstanding of the spheres in relation to the kingdom of God.

Rather than think of stoic, stony pillars towering over a landscape in rigid isolation from one another, we must envision planets within a solar system. Here are some of the features:

A solar system consists of planets orbiting a star. Our sun symbolizes the center of the kingdom of God, which is the Lord in His brilliant glory, enthroned over everything.

In a solar system, each world exerts influence on the others. The gravitational forces within the solar system hold everything in balance. So, in a biblically based, kingdom-centered understanding of spheres, each contributes to the strength and stability of the others.

There is, therefore, both independency and interdependency within a solar system. The worlds are independent bodies, with their distinct elements and orbits, and yet they are interdependent for their survival, since orbital failure would produce deadly collisions. So the spheres of a culture are independent of one another. One cannot *control* the others, but all are interdependent for their own survival and the cohesion of the society. The breakdown of this orbital balance is producing the conflicts in contemporary American society, as well as that of others.

Rather than pillarization and fragmentation, the biblical view is *horizontal flow*. Each sphere brings the positive influence of its kingdom mission into the others. In horizontal flow, for example, the church enhances the governance sphere through a belief system and values supporting liberty, human dignity, and opportunity. The governance sphere protects the freedom of the church to worship and propagate its message. In a free market economy, the church propagates a belief system that produces economic prosperity through the sphere of the marketplace. In turn, the church shares in the abundance through its prospering people and has resources to carry out its mission of advancing the kingdom in all the spheres.

A report in *The Independent*, a British newspaper, described the nature of horizontal flow.[6] The writer, Alex Preston, told of sitting at his desk in the City—London's financial center—from which he could see the spire of a church. To him the steeple "represented something far from the grubby materialism of my day job."

The church also signified strength and stability for the marketplace. "The relationship between faith and finance runs deep," Preston wrote. "Quaker-run banks such as Barclays . . . survived when many of their peers crumbled during the crashes of the mid-1700s [in England] precisely because of the Christian ethics that underpinned their businesses."

When Globequake financial tremors erupted in 2008, "more evangelicals began to come out of the woodwork" of London's banks and brokerages. "The evangelical Christians had always been there but the uncertainty of the crisis made them feel more comfortable about revealing their faith," thought Marcus Nodder, a Christian leader quoted in the story. Preston went on to explore the many ministries now touching London's financial district. They range from Alpha Groups to informal gatherings within companies to lunchtime Bible studies in nearby churches.

The horizontal flow between the spheres of church and marketplace has touched even a skeptic like Preston, who worked for a decade in London's financial center. "Even if God doesn't exist," he wrote, "I've always thought the fundamental tenets of Christianity—charity, humility, forgiveness—are a pretty good moral basis for a human life. Especially a life spent in the City of London."

A model for horizontal flow between church and state is given through the prophet Zechariah. In a vision, he saw an angel, who roused Zechariah and said,

"What do you see?" And I said, "I see . . . a lampstand all of gold with its . . . seven lamps on it . . . also two olive trees by it, one on the right side of the bowl and the other on its left side." . . . Then I said to him, "What are these two olive trees on the right of the lampstand and on its left? . . . What are the two olive branches which are beside the two golden pipes, which empty the golden oil from themselves?" . . . Then he said, "These are the two anointed ones who are standing by the Lord of the whole earth." (Zech 4:1–3, 11–14)

These two "anointed ones" bring the "golden oil" of God's vitality and well-being. Who are they? The full context of Zechariah's book shows they are Joshua, the high priest, the spiritual leader in Zechariah's time, and Zerubbabel, the civil ruler. According to the Keil and Delitzsch *Commentary on the Old Testament*, "The two sons of oil can only be the two media, anointed with oil, through whom the spiritual and gracious gifts of God were conveyed to the church of the Lord, namely, the existing representatives of the priesthood and the regal government, who were at that time Joshua the high priest and the prince Zerubbabel."[7]

Profound principles embedded in this vision can bring clarity to the contemporary world.

First, the lampstand determines the position of the two trees—or spheres. The tabernacle helps us understand the significance of the lampstand, or golden candlestick, which is the menorah. The practical function of the golden candlestick, which stood in the Holy Place, was to give light inside the tent.

All of this foreshadowed Jesus Christ and the new covenant He would establish. In our solar system analogy, the lampstand would be the sun, the source of light. "While I am in the world, *I am the Light of the world*," Jesus told His followers (John 9:5, italics added). However, when the incarnate Christ left earth, His incarnate ministry remained in it in a new form, His body, the church. Anticipating this, Jesus told His disciples, "*You* are the light of the world" (Matt. 5:14, italics added).

The church, therefore, will be the agency within the province of the kingdom of God that will illumine all the other spheres. However, it will be the moon, not the sun. The church's light will arise not from itself but from God Himself. The church will reflect the light of the Lord in a dark world as the moon gives illumination in the depths of night. Thus, in Revelation, John saw lampstands at the center of each of the seven churches.

A vital principle is implied here. The church is not the lampstand;

it is a sphere. To forget this leads to the same type of abuses as those perpetrated by the medieval church, which saw itself as the only agency of the kingdom and thus superior to all other institutions. But in Zechariah's vision, the olive tree signifying the high priest stood *beside* the lampstand, as did the tree that represented Zerubbabel, the civil ruler.

The lampstand means Christ and His kingdom are the center of society. The kingdom of God, as we have seen, is the goal of history, and church and state have vital roles to play in the advance of the kingdom, each within the range of its distinctive kingdom mission, as we will show below. That leads us to the next important lesson embedded in Zechariah's vision.

The respective positions of church and state are determined only in relation to the golden lampstand. Remove the menorah— the cohering dynamic of Jesus Christ and His kingdom—and there is cultural chaos. In some societies, the church—or religious institution—jumps over and tries to become the state. This is the case in an Islamic nation like Iran, where the top mullah is also the supreme leader of the nation. To a lesser extent, there is role confusion between church and state when there is a state church. In Britain, the monarch is not only king or queen of the nation but also head of the Anglican Church. The result there is in some periods a sad parody, as in the brief time when Edward VIII was having an affair with Wallis Simpson, a married woman. Prince Charles, now in line for the throne and the headship of the state church, was also engaged in a notorious affair and even at times seemed uncertain about the distinctiveness of biblical faith![8]

In other nations, when the lampstand is absent or ignored, the state tries to become the church. This happened in Nazi Germany, when the regime attempted to create its own church, centering on Aryanism and Nazi doctrine. North Korea is another example, as the cult of Kim has become the state religion.

What we learn from all this can be summed up as follows:

- Christ and His kingdom must be at the center of culture.
- All the institutions of a society will be positioned with respect to one another in relation to Christ and His kingdom.
- As both Joshua and Zerubbabel had roles to play in the covenant nation, so each key cultural institution in a society has a distinctive kingdom mission.
- Although each sphere has its own role to play, the spheres are interdependent, and the overarching goal uniting their respective assignments is alignment with Jesus Christ and His kingdom.

When Christ and His kingdom are removed, the solar system no longer exists. What is left is a chaotic mass of crashing spheres, like a band of wild asteroids rather than worlds in carefully balanced orbits established by a larger dynamic. Institutional leaders recognize the danger of fragmented societies and try to figure out how to get social cohesion. This is the crisis now faced by the United States and other Western nations as they blast themselves away from their historic reliance on the biblical worldview. They try to unite the spheres institutionally, but this produces only heightened competitiveness for cultural dominance and conflict.

The real unity between the spheres comes through people and their relationships, not laws, regulations, contracts, and charters. Any given individual will lead and function in each of the spheres. Horizontal flow occurs as people who have embraced Jesus Christ and His kingdom participate in the church, carry its values into their families, instill kingdom principles in the educational process, reflect their biblical worldview in the voting booth and political office, and build businesses on the underpinnings of Christian ethics, as Alex Preston observed above.

There are, then, six spheres where we all function. *The way to apply the principles of the unshakeable kingdom to make our world safe, sane, and stable is to implant the kingdom in each of these spheres.* We must bring God's world into our worlds.

As the horizontal flow moves from one sphere to another, the kingdom of God begins to impact the whole society and its culture. This leads to genuine transformations rather than mere revolutions, which are a dime a dozen in the swiftly changing Globequake world. A revolution that doesn't mature into a true transformational movement sputters and fades. Jesus has often been described as a revolutionary. In fact He was and is a transformer. His message and ministry were revolutionary, but as they gave birth to the church and then began to penetrate the spheres of human endeavor, they became a transformational catalyst, and are still affecting the world.

So, before we study our worlds and how they can be made safe, sane, and stable in a world gone wild, we need to zoom in on the differences between *revolution* and *transformation*.

1. Revolution aims at the top, but transformation is bottom up.

Jesus offended and disappointed some who initially got excited about His message and ministry. They hoped He would ignite a revolutionary force heading straight for the Roman governor's palace to topple Rome's dominance of their nation. Instead, Jesus assembled a mishmash of bottom feeders. He seemed disinterested in the people at the top, but He spent much of His time with needy crowds in villages and in the countryside. Jesus' critics were after mere revolution, but His passion was transformation. Revolutions replace regimes, but transformations change the people who can topple the powers at the top.

2. Revolution is forced from outside in, while transformation is embraced and flows inside out.

The establishments of the period of Jesus' incarnation were fussy about the outside of the cup, but His concern was the inside. He knew that you can polish a vessel until your image is reflected, paint a creaky old house until it looks new, and wrap a corpse in a fancy purple robe but that until you deal with the death, decay, and grime inside, nothing is really changed. Eighteenth-century political theorist Edmund Burke said that people are qualified for liberty in proportion to their willingness "to put moral chains upon their own appetites." Revolution imposes chains on the exterior, but transformation occurs when people embrace truth and freely live under its guidance and restraints.

3. Revolution is short-term, lasting only as long as its instigators have the muscle, but transformation is enduring.

Jesus could see well beyond Herod and Pilate and all the other pompous figures sitting at the top of the regimes. He knew they were ultimately all in the hands of His Father, and as Daniel saw,

> *It is He who changes the times and the epochs;*
> *He removes kings and establishes kings.*
> (Dan. 2:21)

The revolutions that come in "the times and the epochs" are nothing but short-lived seasons of agony unless their new ideas become systemic and embraced by majorities of populations. Had the American Revolution, for example, not been embraced by a substantial number of the colonists, it would have died on forests of gallows. Instead, because the revolutionary ideas were embedded in a constitutional system affirmed by the new states, revolution itself was transformed into an enduring edifice of freedom and opportunity.

4. Revolution relies on raw power, but transformation is based on true authority.

The revolutionary Christ brought a stunning new way of living to the world. Had He remained only a wonder-working, mind-stretching revolutionary, His ideas would have left the world when He did. He would have gone down as just another footnote in history books. The enduring strength of Jesus' message and ministry is in the fact that they were based on genuine authority. Matthew's gospel tells us, "The crowds were amazed at His teaching; for He was teaching them as one having authority, and not as their scribes" (Matt. 7:28–29). The scribes and Pharisees relied on raw power to try to force people into compliance with their interpretations of the Torah. Jesus spoke with an authority that made people want to follow Him and that inspired many to such commitment that they were willing to die for Him. The shaking up of Jesus' followers through His authority and power changed them from shrinking cowards to men and women of valor.

The Globequake brings revolutionary furor everywhere it strikes. The answer to destructive revolution is positive transformation. There is much travail and panic as people look at the devastation the turbulence has brought to individuals, churches, homes, schools, governing agencies, and businesses. But men and women who have a biblically based worldview know there is immense opportunity for transforming all these spheres by reestablishing them on the rock-solid truths and principles of the kingdom of God.

That means we must get God's world into our worlds. We will now explore how we can penetrate our spheres with the transforming catalyst of God's kingdom.

PART 2

STABILIZING THE SPHERES

*We will not boast beyond our measure, but within the measure
of the sphere which God apportioned to us as a measure.*
—2 Corinthians 10:13

RENEWAL, REINVENTION, AND TRANSFORMATION

Early in the twentieth century, a Globequake in the form of the
combustion engine and automobile hit businesses manufacturing
wooden wheels and horse-drawn wagons. Many of the old companies went under. There was a secret shared by all that survived:
*they were able to expand their vision to understand that they were not in
the buggy or carriage wheel business, but the transportation business.* That
renewal of vision led to reinvention that transformed the enterprises and helped them thrive while others fell.

All the spheres we will discuss in part 2 must have *renewal, reinvention*, and *transformation*. So, before we explore the six spheres in
detail, we need to dig into the meaning of *transformation*.

The best source for understanding what transformational
change is and how it happens is the ultimate authority—the Bible.
Its overarching theme is transformation—the restoration of fallen,

flawed human beings and their world to God's glory, represented in His pristine character.

To understand what transformation really is, it's helpful to examine the Greek words the Holy Spirit implanted in the New Testament. When we do, our comprehension of change and transformation—including organizational transformation—becomes clear.

Change appears in several biblical passages. One Greek word is *metathesis*, referring to a change of position.[1] Another is *metamorphoomai*, indicating a change of form. *Metamorphosis* derives directly from this Greek word. When we link the two Greek terms, we get a full picture of what transformation is—a change in form and position.

A caterpillar undergoes metamorphosis and emerges from its cocoon as a graceful flying creature rather than a multilegged bug. And because it now has wings, the former caterpillar can move to a higher and different position on the same tree that holds its now empty cocoon.

Ironically, the answer to the dizzying alterations forced on us by the Globequake is metamorphic *change*—the kind of metamorphosis that transforms a bug into a butterfly. Renewal, reinvention, and transformation must begin with us personally to impact the spheres of our daily endeavors.

THE SPHERE OF PERSON

CHAPTER 6

STABLE PEOPLE IN AN UNSTABLE WORLD

Seven anchors that will hold you steady

"We're expecting ninety-mile-an-hour winds through here tonight," our driver told us as we drove through downtown Halifax, Nova Scotia.

Irene and I, eager to see the glory of autumn in New England and eastern Canada, were on a fall cruise. We sailed from New York to Quebec, then back down the Canadian coast. From Halifax we were to cruise to Bar Harbor, Maine, stop for a visit, then travel on to New York and the end of the voyage. As our host told us about the weather about to blast Halifax, I was grateful that in less than two hours we would sail away, heading for Bar Harbor before the front hit. As we slipped out of Halifax, I stood on the ship's deck and watched the pretty skyline fade in the distance. *Poor people . . . ninety-mile-an-hour winds*, I thought.

The "poor people" turned out to be us. The gales socked into our ship about midnight. Irene and I watched the TV screen attached high in a corner of our cabin as it showed the present weather conditions. We were amazed as it told us we were in a Force 11 and then a Force 12 wind. At Force 11 the gales were howling at sixty miles an hour, and at Force 12 our ship was blasted with hurricane fury, the winds exceeding seventy miles per hour. The vessel rose on seas cresting at more than thirty feet. At one point we lost our televised weather report because the TV set was jerked loose from the wall and flew across the cabin. We could hear glass cracking all over the ship.

A day later the monster weather system was still throwing its might at us. Periodically Irene reminded me I had insisted on taking her to the *Titanic* museum in Halifax before we sailed into the maelstrom off America's East Coast.

"Ladies and gentlemen, the port of Bar Harbor has been closed due to the winds, and we regret we will not be able to dock there," the captain announced. "We will proceed to New York and expect to arrive the day after tomorrow."

On the "day after tomorrow" we again heard the captain's voice on the ship's speaker system: "Ladies and gentlemen, we have been informed that immigration and customs officials are not ready to receive us, and we are uncertain when we will be able to return to New York."

The feeling was eerie over the next two days. The perfect storm refused to yield. The winds shrieked, the seas peaked at mountainous levels, and we hung on for dear life. *What a strange, terrifying experience to have no port, no place to drop anchor*, I thought.

SEARCHING FOR STABILITY

Such is the anxiousness stirred in the human psyche by the turbulence of the Globequake. Millions of people search desperately for a point of stability, for hefty anchors to hook into stable anchorages for themselves and their families. On Sunday many go to churches that have unanchored from biblical doctrine and look to culture as their authority. They have Sunday lunch with children who have been yanked loose from values the parents were taught from childhood. On Monday they send their kids to schools shaping students' minds with faddish nonsense, go to companies scrambling frantically to survive the marketplace upheavals, and read about politicians and governing policies that have lost their constitutional moorings.

Young Daniel would have understood the anxiety of a world in turmoil. Snatched from Jerusalem and the temple that had been the solid anchorage of his nation and his own life, Daniel was carried off to alien Babylon. Because he was the cream of the crop, Daniel was taken to the royal palace, where he would be groomed to serve fierce Nebuchadnezzar. First Daniel would be molded into conformity to Babylon's culture. He would be taught by the Chaldeans, the keepers of Babylonian political correctness. Daniel would dine at the king's table, eating the same diet as Nebuchadnezzar. However, in doing so, Daniel would violate the Scriptures and lose his integrity. Therefore Daniel determined in his heart, the core of his being, that he would not defile himself with the king's food and wine. (See Dan. 1:8.)

That verse and the worldview it reveals should be concreted into our souls in the age of the Globequake! Daniel's attitude must be ours. We need strong anchors sunk in unyielding anchorages. We must determine in the core of our lives not to be moved from the core of truth.

TIDES OF TIME AND CIRCUMSTANCE

There's something sublime about the sea bottom. Snorkel off the coast of the little Hawaiian island of Lanai and you will get my point. Manele Bay, just outside Lanai City, is a wonderful place to ride the swells tracking in from the Pacific. The water is clear enough you can see the bottom, thirty or forty feet below, as you skim the surface.

The richly colored sea plants do a gentle ballet under the rhythms of the waves, but down where they are anchored into the bottom, they refuse to be uprooted. Schools of multihued fish add their steps to the dance, with seemingly thousands moving as one under the cadence set by the swells up top.

But below, the bottom is immovable.

It's a wonderful symbol of the Word of God. The tides of time and circumstance sweep over our lives, sometimes driven by destructive Force 12 gales, sometimes caressed along by gentle trade winds. We relish the good times and hold on with all our might in the terrifying storms, but through it all, the bottom, the place of our anchorage, is there, undisturbed, bothered by none of the tempests above.

How can we anchor into the solid bottom in the midst of worldwide disorder? Unstable people cannot bring stability to their churches, homes, schools, institutions of government, or workplaces. Before we can consider how to make the spheres of our daily engagement and responsibility safe, sane, and stable, we must focus on how we can discover personal strength.

As I began to think seriously about the Globequake, I thought about the unshifting anchorage of God's whole Word. I listed the anchors I have learned to sink deep into its stable mooring. These are attitudes arising from the Bible in its entirety. My anchors are made of the stuff of this immovable foundation and are rooted into its substance. Here are the seven anchors that, by God's grace and goodness, have moored my life during the tsunamis ignited by the Globequake:

1. I will anchor my mind, its speculations, reasonings, and worldview, to God and God alone, as revealed in the Bible and disclosed in Jesus Christ and His kingdom.

Ages ago, through the Holy Spirit, the prophet Isaiah penned these words:

You will keep him in perfect peace,
Whose mind is stayed on You,
Because he trusts in You.
(Isa. 26:3 NKJV)

Speculation is the sawdust of the information age. Commentators, opinion makers, media talking heads, academics, and hosts of others run the hard news of current events through their grinders and cover us with the grit that spews out.

Our own minds take over, creating scenarios and fantasies. As a young man during the Cold War, I reasoned that there was no future for the world, that I would never live to sire and raise a family. Nuclear war was inevitable on a planet where big nations had enough warheads to wipe out global populations many times over.

The Bible calls these "vain imaginations" (Rom. 1:21 KJV) and "lofty" things (2 Cor. 10:5) raised up in the place of God's sound truth. The "Gentiles"—the nonbelieving pagans—walk "in the futility of their mind," said Paul (Eph. 4:17). Thus, wrote Paul, we must be firmly anchored in Christ, His Word, His kingdom, and sound doctrine, lest we be "tossed here and there by waves and carried about by every wind of doctrine" (Eph. 4:14).

I had to learn to anchor my mind somewhere other than in current events and the circumstances and experiences of a particular season of my life. Now, in the midst of the Globequake, I have found it vital to sink my mental and emotional anchors deeper than ever in the bedrock of God and His Word.

2. I will refuse anxiety and lay it all on the Lord and His sufficiency.

The mind manufactures its speculations and scenarios and then transmits them to the emotions, which go crazy with fear and trepidation. The anxiety is like a vulture circling us, waiting for us to die. Our moments of happiness are soon suffocated in the tight chamber of worry.

Sitting in the dankness of his Roman cell, facing the chopping block, Paul had remarkable stability amid his personal Globequake. In those worrisome days he wrote his letter to the Philippian church, a message some have called the "Epistle of Joy."

The secrets of stability are embedded throughout the letter and rise to their peak in Philippians 4. There Paul wrote,

> Rejoice in the Lord always; again I will say, rejoice! Let your gentle spirit be known to all men. The Lord is near. Be anxious for nothing, but in everything by prayer and supplication with thanksgiving let your requests be made known to God. And the peace of God, which surpasses all comprehension, will guard your hearts and your minds in Christ Jesus. (vv. 4–7)

The comprehension of God's complete sufficiency for every situation and condition we face is vital for standing firm amid the Globequake.

A few years ago I decided to build a four-bay garage on our ranch. I would do it myself, with help from my son, son-in-law, grandson, and a few friends. I bought a set of plans, and soon we were embedding huge wooden posts in the ground for the twenty-four-by-forty-foot structure.

Within months, I was in way over my head. I explained some of my construction problems and confessed my mistakes to Carpenter Jack, a professional builder and friend at our church. He came out, took a look, and shook his head.

"Jack, why do you think I thought I could do this by myself?" I asked. Never a man to mince words, Jack replied, "Wallace, you were delusional."

How right he was!

Jack took over the project. Saturday after Saturday we worked on the big structure. What had been such a burden when I was trying to carry it now became a delightful, relaxing activity. I did what Jack told me, watched as he straightened out my mistakes, and rested in his sufficiency for the task.

We will be anchored while the Globequake shakes all around us if we learn to release our fears and anxieties to God.

3. I will concentrate and focus my mind on the honorable, right, pure, lovely, things of good report, of excellence and praiseworthiness.

Thousands of times every day we are bombarded with data and demands for decisions. In a supermarket line, we stare at near pornographic magazine covers. One day while buying groceries, I mused at the irony. An impulse-buy display advertised an evening of "relaxing entertainment." The movie suggested was *Texas Chainsaw Massacre*.

I enjoy the old movies with carefully developed plots and characters with depth, films that did not rely on flashy special effects, thirty-second scenes, gore, graphic sex, bathroom scenes, and sewer language. "Honey, do you know they make movies in color now?" my wife kidded me awhile back.

I admit my tastes are shaped by my age. But we all should be concerned that so many feast on a mental and emotional diet that only adds to anger, moral confusion, and anxiety.

So, in that mountaintop chapter, Philippians 4, Paul urged, "Whatever is true, whatever is honorable, whatever is right, whatever is pure, whatever is lovely, whatever is of good repute, if there is any excellence and if anything worthy of praise, dwell on these things" (v. 8).

My son-in-law had to travel sometimes in war-torn places. His company provided security and housed him in walled, guarded compounds that established solid boundaries that enemies could not penetrate.

Boundaries establish the safe zones when turmoil surrounds us. We need the strongly walled mental garrisons in the midst of the Globequake. The criteria for the focus of our minds revealed by the Holy Spirit through Paul constitute the strong boundaries that assure our sanity when our world is falling apart!

4. I will keep my eyes on Jesus rather than the turbulence around me.

Peter learned the need for this anchor the night when, with a mix of genuine passion and a flash of bravado, he went out walking on the stormy water to meet Jesus. "But seeing the wind, he became frightened, and beginning to sink, he cried out, 'Lord, save me!'" (Matt. 14:30). Peter's eyes shifted from Jesus to the wind-whipped waves, and he lost courage.

So the Holy Spirit, through the book of Hebrews, reminds us to be constantly "fixing our eyes on Jesus, the author and perfecter of faith, who for the joy set before Him endured the cross, despising the shame, and has sat down at the right hand of the throne of God" (Heb. 12:2).

There's a principle I discovered many years ago on the icy slope of a German alp as I tried skiing for the first time: *you go in the direction of your gaze.* I was having a hard time mastering turns, with bloody results. Finally someone showed me if I would slightly turn my focus in the desired direction, my weight would shift automatically, and I would execute the turn.

In the Globequake we have to fix our gaze on Jesus. His steadiness will become ours when the seas are raging around us.

5. I will be a champion for my family and all the spheres with which I engage and for the people for whom I have watchcare and stewardship, and I will hold the ground of truth even when others are giving up.

A *champion*, in Old Testament Hebrew, is the person who stands between his own people and the enemy out to destroy them. The destiny of a family, a nation, a business rides on the victory or defeat of its champion. David wins, Goliath loses, Israel celebrates victory, and the Philistines head for the hills.

Every sphere with which we engage needs a champion. There

must be people who won't surrender truth and core values when everyone else panics, gets angry, or runs away in defeat.

Most of us have heard arguments like these:

- "Those old ideas from twenty or more centuries ago just won't work anymore. We need new values, new ethics."
- "Dad, everybody is doing it! Why can't I?"
- "We have to bend the facts just a little to generate positive response to our product and its brand."
- "The Constitution is a living document, and we can't continue to govern the nation by the worldview of eighteenth-century farmers!"

Against all this, the champion remembers the warning of Proverbs 22:28:

> Do not move the ancient boundary
> Which your fathers have set.

The champion won't negotiate the absolutes, won't change the boundaries, won't surrender the ground, no matter how hard the Globequake shakes or how intense the pressure to cave in.

6. I will walk by faith, not by sight.

This principle is given in 2 Corinthians 5:7. Globequake upheavals require lifestyles guided by faith, not the dangers and portents looming in the trembling world.

In 1965, Irene and I, with our first child (now a mom with her own daughters), sailed the Atlantic for the first time, on a ten-day passage from Boston to Rotterdam aboard a Dutch freighter. We were moving to Europe and found it would be cheaper to sail with our worldly goods than to fly. The crossing was in December, not the best season for hauling out across the fierce Atlantic. The heaving sea was gray, the clouds were gray, and it seemed we were being hurled around in a realm where there was no separation between ocean and sky. I wondered, *How can we find our way into the English Channel and through the needle-thin approach into Rotterdam harbor?*

One night this landlubber found the answer. I had crawled up onto a little platform above the ship's bridge. I looked down at a pedestal, just outside and immediately in front of the helmsman, who steered the ship. A green glow tinged the darkness, rising from a glass globe atop the pedestal. When I looked closer, I saw a huge and complex compass housed within the transparent globe, lit by greenish light that could distinguish it in the night's gloom. The man at the ship's wheel could see no landmarks and no mileposts, but as long as he held to the compass bearings, we were on course to Rotterdam.

So it is with faith. The Globequake topples our signposts; its tremors try to hurl us off course. We can spot no markers. But if we steer by faith in God, we will safely arrive at our *telos*, our purpose and destination, even if the turbulence and fog rip out our landmarks and obscure our visual capacities.

7. I will hold on to the reality that God is sovereign and is working all things according to His plan, for His glory and our good.

"We *know*," said Paul, "that God causes all things to work together for good to those who love God, to those who are called according to His purpose" (Rom. 8:28, italics added).

Sometimes in the Globequake's tempest, things don't seem to make a lot of sense. I remember horrific nights when my alcoholic dad tried to break into our house by shattering glass in the windows or front door, and I huddled in terror with my mother, sister, and aunt. *Where is God? Where is our Protector?* my childish mind asked. Years later, I saw He was there all along, implementing the promise of Romans 8:28.

From the perspective of several decades later, I have understood and wept over the torment in which my dad lived and from which he was finally set free by Jesus Christ. My torment was healed as I forgave him and grew to love his memory, though he died in 1966.

More than anything else I have come to understand that everything that happens in the lives of people who love God and are called into relationship with Him fits into a master plan. Aging is like climbing a mountain. The higher you go, the more you can see where you've been and how it all fits into the plan that gets you to your destiny.

So one day I awoke to my calling as a pastor. I was dealing with people who needed a sensitive ear and an understanding heart. I grasped the wonderful truth that wounds heal wounds. My ability to serve others in pain was related to my own pain and the way God used it in my life to give sensitivity and compassion to a stony-hearted guy. All along God had seen that and was using the tremors in my childhood to equip me for the work of my adulthood.

The same God who has done this in the past of your life and mine is the One at work right now in the midst of the shaking we experience. We cannot be ripped from His hands or from His plans. *He is in charge.*

In the seven decades I have been alive, I have not known more global instability than in the present. Yet I know the anchors that have secured me for a half century, and the ground in which they are embedded, are sturdy enough for whatever comes!

CHAPTER 7

SAFE AND SECURE IN YOUR "AMNESS"

Secrets of the well-secured life

William Ernest Henley—not a relative I claim, at least—was an atheist and humanist who had no hope beyond himself. He suffered physical, mental, and emotional pain throughout his life. He had to hang all that grief, disappointment, and hurt on his human soul. From that stark determination in 1875 came his poem "Invictus":

> *Out of the night that covers me,*
> *Black as the pit from pole to pole,*
> *I thank whatever gods may be*
> *For my unconquerable soul.*
>
> *In the fell clutch of circumstance*
> *I have not winced nor cried aloud.*
> *Under the bludgeonings of chance*
> *My head is bloody, but unbowed.*

Beyond this place of wrath and tears
Looms but the Horror of the shade,
And yet the menace of the years
Finds, and shall find me unafraid.

It matters not how strait the gate,
How charged with punishments the scroll,
I am the master of my fate:
I am the captain of my soul.[1]

Henley might have been appalled to know that Timothy McVeigh, who slaughtered more than 150 people, including children, in the Oklahoma City bombing, lived by the "Invictus" philosophy and died with Henley's poem on his lips.

Does the stability lie in ourselves alone, as Henley thought? Where can we find solid places to cast down our anchors? How do we secure ourselves to these anchors? How do we stabilize our personal lives amid the turbulence of the Globequake?

We will pose these questions regarding each of the spheres in the chapters to come. In each we will begin the answer by considering God's biblically revealed strategic plan for the specific sphere. As we will see in following chapters, there are four elements in a solid strategic plan:

1. *Vision*—the ultimate purpose or destiny of a person, institution, or other corporate structure
2. *Values*—the treasured truths and principles revealed in the vision that hold the person, institution, or other corporate structure on track toward its purpose
3. *Mission*—the overarching action that will lead toward fulfilling the purpose and attaining the destiny
4. *Goals*—the specific major accomplishments that will help achieve the mission[2]

Let's look at each of these with respect to our personal lives and how these elements can help us be stable people though we might dwell right at the epicenter of the Globequake.

STABILIZE THE STRATEGIC PLAN

Each of us will have a distinctive strategic plan based on God's specific purpose and calling. However, there is a strategic plan for humanity in general, of which our special plan will be a part. Here is my understanding of God's strategic plan for all His image bearers, as revealed in the Bible:

Vision for the Sphere of Person
To be God's image bearer in the created domain as His child and spread the dominion of God's kingdom into all the earth as His colaborer.

Values for the Sphere of Person[3]
1. God as Creator and Owner of all, and Father of humanity
2. Intimate fellowship with God
3. God's plan for the world
4. All human beings as God's image bearers
5. The self as valued greatly by God
6. The world as created and greatly loved by Him
7. The specific purpose revealed in the individuals, gifts, talents, skills, and calling

The Kingdom Mission for the Sphere of Person
To be an ambassador of Jesus Christ and His kingdom in all the spheres to which we are sent, advancing His kingdom of righteousness, peace, and joy in the Holy Spirit, and representing its interests wherever we function.

RECOGNIZE, EMBRACE, AND CELEBRATE WHO YOU ARE

Few things destabilize people as much as confusion about their identity. If we are going to be anchored firmly amid the Globequake upheavals, it's vital we have a strong, confident understanding of who we really are. The most important factor leading us to an accurate view of self is how God sees us. Looking in the mirror doesn't reveal the real person. Peering into God's revelation reflects the truth.

"I-amness" vs. "I-wasness"

Many of us miss our true identity because we see ourselves strictly in terms of the past. Past mistakes haunt us. Past successes taunt us. On the one hand, we live with accusing guilt that robs us of self-respect and hope. On the other hand, our past achievements suggest that we have peaked and that it's all downhill from here.

The Scripture is clear about our status: *if anyone is in Christ, he or she is a new creature; the old things passed away; behold, new things have come* (2 Cor. 5:17, paraphrase). To be "in Christ" is to be in "amness," not "wasness." That is, through Christ it is not your past actions for good or bad, for success or failure, that define you, but the timeless state of your being in Christ right now and eternally.

A man in his forties came to see me. "I understand you are an adult child of an alcoholic—an ACOA—and I am too," he told me. "ACOA research says we will manifest certain behavioral and mental patterns," he added.

"No, I am not bound to those," I replied, to his surprise. "I *was* the adult son of an alcoholic, and I *did* display some of those styles of thinking and acting, but my identity is not defined as being a son of an alcoholic."

His eyes grew big. "But you said your dad was an alcoholic!"

"True," I replied, "but I am now a new creation in Christ Jesus, and the impact of my father's drinking in my past does not control or determine who I am. I refuse to allow ACOA to define my identity. Only Christ does that!"

To be stable, live in your amness in Christ, not in your wasness.

Gender

Kathy Witterick and David Stocker, a Toronto couple, revealed they are attempting to raise a "genderless child."[4] They want to protect their baby from the expectations that people place on gender as the child grows up. "Experts, however, question whether the odd experiment will work or be good for the baby, and note that gender identity is a complex, mysterious force that has at least as much to do with biological factors present at birth as the person's social interactions," reported the *Montreal Gazette* about the case.

Gender is an important facet of our identity. God has given vital and distinctive roles to male and female. Consider a significant and controversial Bible topic—submission. Ephesians 5:22–25 (NLT) instructs wives to "submit" to their husbands, and husbands to "love" their wives as Christ loves His church. However, as comembers of Christ's body, the church, they are to be submissive to one another (Eph. 5:28–33). Submission without mutuality is suppression.

Without the distinctive elements provided by gender, there is no mutuality in the absolute sense. When a man submits to a man, he is placing himself under conditions with which he feels a measure of comfort, since they are the same that he himself would likely impose. But when a male is submitted to a female and a female to a male, each is brought into the disciplines that establish stability common to the respective genders. Mutual submission recognizes there are important elements a woman brings to the spheres with which she engages, precisely because she is a woman. Likewise, males contribute distinctively to the spheres in their role as men. Without the gender distinctions, balance is lost, and cosmos deteriorates into chaos.

Gender, therefore, is of great importance in God's plan, and affirming our gender is crucial in affirming our identity.

Gifts

What did God know about you, and when did He know it? Here's what the Father told Jeremiah:

> *Before I formed you in the womb I knew you,*
> *And before you were born I consecrated you;*
> *I have appointed you a prophet to the nations.*
> (Jer. 1:5)

Did such foreknowledge apply only to Jeremiah and the other major characters in the Bible? Did God know and set *you* apart for His service before you were even conceived?

Absolutely!

Think of it this way: you're the chief designer of the Large Hadron Collider (LHC), the world's biggest, strongest particle accelerator. Your mission is to design a vast machine in a tunnel with a seventeen-mile circumference circling underneath Swiss soil. The purpose of the LHC is to uncover the deepest secrets of physics and the universe. As a highly trained physicist, you know the reactions that must take place, the speed that particles will have to travel, and their trajectory through the long tunnel.

As the designer you know every component that will generate the energy that will hurl the subatomic particles around the seventeen-mile circular tunnel—down to the last screw, *before* they are manufactured. The nuts and bolts holding the machinery together are formed for the specific task assigned them and the loads they will have to carry. They are in your mind as the designer before they are manufactured. And that goes for the big components of the LHC as well. Everything has to carry out its function if the goal is to be reached.

When God designed His universe, He had a grand purpose in mind. The Creator also knew the plan that would achieve the purpose. He knew every element that would fit the plan and realize the purpose. You and I are strategic components in that plan. We have purpose related to it. That's why God saw Jeremiah—and each one of us—even before we were made.

How do you know your part in God's big plan? *Your spiritual gifts reveal where you fit.* You have been formed spiritually as well as physically to fit into God's big picture. Your grace gifts enable you to carry out His purpose for creating you.

Spiritual gifts reveal much more than what you can do. They reveal who you are in His kingdom.

Personality

In 1992, Windsor Castle burned. It upset not only upset Queen Elizabeth II, but Irene and me too. We had walked through the castle several times, going all the way back to 1971. One of my favorite rooms was the big hall housing armor worn by kings and nobles through the centuries. I would always chuckle when I saw the metal suit into which King Henry VIII squeezed his bulk. A classic portrait showed the oft-married monarch with a considerable girth. Where I grew up we had a name for such a stomach, but in polite company we simply say he loved his beer. The armor flared out at the level of the king's midsection, perfectly molded for it.

Personality and spiritual gifts are like that. Think of your personality as the tailor-made outward covering of your complex of spiritual gifts. Your personality is shaped perfectly to display and manifest your gifts. Prophetically gifted people, for example, will often have a blunt personality style. They see and want to straighten every picture on your wall and do it with a flourish. Folks with the gift of discernment will warn you the picture is crooked. Those with the helps gift will quietly take the frame off the wall and adjust the hanger. They won't leave a calling card because they need no recognition. Exhorters will brag on your taste in art and note how much better it will look once it's straight. Men and women with the shepherding gift will be concerned there might have been a big family fight and that somebody threw a shoe that struck the tilted picture. Individuals with the giving gift will buy you a bigger, prettier picture with the fanciest, costliest frame they can afford.

In short, relish your personality. It is shaped for those wonderful gifts God has given you, and it reveals your identity. This produces stability in who you are as an individual fitting precisely in God's design.

Bent

Louis Capet loved tinkering with locks. He could spend hours probing their innards. His wife, Marie, would try to get his attention, but Louis's mind would be noodling over the mechanisms that made a lock work. He delighted in designing new ones. Louis would have been the happiest creature on the planet if he could have been a locksmith. Unfortunately, however, he was destined to be king of France—Louis XVI. In that identity he was a failure and was hauled off by a mob and guillotined. Had Louis been free to follow his bent, he would have doubtless opened a little shop, fixing the locks of the nobility he wearied of as king and the peasants who chopped off his head.

Our bent is a huge clue to our identity. Our parents are to recognize it before we are old enough to figure it out: "Train up a child in the way he should go [and in keeping with his individual gift or bent], and when he is old he will not depart from it" (Prov. 22:6 AMPLIFIED BIBLE).

Society agrees there is a broad set of knowledge we must all have, so when we go to college, we must first study the general curriculum. A student who yearns to write classic poetry has to study algebra and slice up a frog in biology lab. Another pupil who can't wait to design oil pipelines has to spend hours analyzing and memorizing Chaucer. But then comes the glorious period when they can go their own ways by declaring a major. Their bent becomes evident for all to see. Now it's time for the young men and women to recognize what their parents saw first.

Paul encouraged us to "work out [our] salvation with fear and trembling" (Phil. 2:12). We are to allow our gifts, talents, and skills to come out into the open for the glory of God and the good of other people and ourselves. We are to do God's unique will for our personal lives. And we know that will by understanding what we "will" as persons under the lordship of Jesus Christ. "For it is God who is at work in you, both to will and to work for His good pleasure," continued the apostle (Phil. 2:13).

Our identity becomes clear when we place ourselves under the lordship of Jesus Christ and then follow our bents or inclinations!

Calling

All these elements of stable, unshakeable identity come together in our calling. "Walk worthy of the vocation wherewith ye are called," we read in Ephesians 4:1 (KJV). *Klesis*, the Greek word for "calling" in the New Testament, refers to an invitation to enter a relationship and an assignment to a specific task.[5] First, we are called to a relationship with God through Jesus Christ. Then, we are called to our mission in God's kingdom. It's not just full-time pastors, vocational missionaries, and church staff who are called, but everyone who has embraced Christ and His salvation.

To deny your calling is to deny your identity. You and I may try to resist our callings and may even refuse to carry them out, but they will never let us go. We will always have the sense that we missed our destiny and failed to live in our true identities. I know because I tried for seven years to flee my core calling.

I entered a relationship with Christ when I was fourteen. At fifteen I felt an undeniable urge within me to preach and build up the church. At sixteen I asked my church to license me to ministry, and it did. I attended a church-related college and, on graduation, went straight to seminary.

Then things got confused. I turned away from my core vocational calling that centered on the church and wandered for seven years. During that time I had brief careers in journalism and politics. Through a series of events too involved to detail here, I became a presidential aide at the White House. One day I was standing in the outer office of one of the president's top counselors. The man's administrative assistant and I were chatting. "Aren't you an ordained minister?" she asked. I laughed. "I will *never* do that!" I quickly replied.

Two years later, as the Watergate scandal closed in on Washington, I returned to the newspaper where I had worked in Birmingham, my hometown. I was increasingly unstable emotionally and in my career. The anxiety over running from my calling intensified. I couldn't go to church without trembling with frustration that sometimes brought me to tears.

Then one late spring day in 1973, I was driving to a meeting where I was to make a speech about my White House experiences. I yanked a pen from my pocket to make notes. As I glanced at it, my whole life suddenly came together. It was the fine writing instrument that, a decade before, friends had given me as I left for seminary to encourage me to take good notes. As I looked at the silvery elegant pen, I thought of the joy I had known preaching, teaching, and building up churches.

I realized that though I had ridden through Washington's streets in a White House limousine and been inside the Oval Office, and though my byline had appeared on front-page banner stories in our newspaper, circulated statewide, nothing gave me the fulfillment and satisfaction of helping people understand God's Word and edifying His church. In that moment, I heard the Holy Spirit clearly calling me to my original mission. Later that day I told my wife, and within three months I was pastor of a small church.

During the years of my "desert wanderings," my family experienced instability as I changed vocations frequently in the search for my destiny. But when I embraced my calling, I functioned in my identity. Everything came together—my amness (as well as the formative influences of my wasness), maleness, gifts, personality, bent—when I began functioning in my calling.

That doesn't mean it's easy. There have been times when I've joked that working in the Watergate-scandalized White House was ice cream and cake compared to the mental, emotional, and physical rigors of being a pastor and helping people deal with life-changing, life-threatening crises week after week. Yet there are joy and fulfillment way down deep that the typhoons up top don't disturb.

When I am doing what God called and equipped me to do, I function in my true identity. Our *doing* arises from our *being*, not vice versa. But to resist the *doing* our *being* calls for is to miss our true self and to fail to bring forth the fruit of our real nature. When identity and action align, we are as stable as the giant pecan trees deeply rooted in our Texas soil. They nourish us on the product that comes from their identity, and they do it generation after generation!

Goals

Know the spheres into which God sends you and your purpose for being there, and embrace them.

"I have found what I'm going to do the rest of my life!" Brad Hays almost danced as he made that declaration to me one day years ago. Brad had been executive vice president of one of America's largest companies, CEO of his own company, and a marketing consultant with clients like the *San Francisco Chronicle*. Then came the Globequake for Brad personally. Divorce. The death of a son. In the weeks and months following the death of his child, Brad groped for the future. The emotional devastation had knocked down his markers.

One day in the depths of his pain, Brad went to see his pastor. A long summer stretched before him. More months to weep and hurt. "What should I do with myself?" Brad asked.

The minister had come to know Brad and his passion to help businesses function with excellence. "Spend the summer going through the book of Proverbs, looking for all the business principles you find there," replied Brad's pastor. "Then at the end of the summer, bring me back a report on your discoveries about what Proverbs has to say about business."

At the conclusion of the summer, Brad had confirmed more than ever that business was his vocational sphere. Brad knew he had found his future and purpose. He founded Bible in the boardroom and became a leader in Convene, a national organization that helps CEOs build and lead their businesses with biblical principles. The intensity of upheaval that struck Brad was enough to destroy a person. Instead, because he sought stability in God, he found himself and his destiny, along with personal steadfastness.

Brad and many others like him are personal examples of a principle revealed in Isaiah 37:31, which says, "The surviving remnant of the house of Judah will again take root downward and bear fruit upward." The "remnant" in every age and every sphere is comprised of people who remain faithful to God and His kingdom no matter where they are and no matter how great the challenges.

Such people are well anchored and have a solid life-vision, strong values, a thrilling mission and purpose for living, and inspiring goals. They have received and embraced the person God has made them to be. All who know them enjoy the fruit and reap the rewards of the work of God's remnant people.

THE SPHERE OF CHURCH

CHAPTER 8

THE ROCK-SOLID CHURCH
Foundations that cannot be destroyed

The strength and stability of a society are related directly to the strength and stability of the authentic, biblically based church.

Russell Kirk, a brilliant political theorist and author, said of America and the West, "Fundamentally, our society's affliction is the decay of religious belief. If a culture is to survive and flourish, it must not be severed from the religious vision out of which it arose. The high necessity of reflective men and women, then, is to labor for the restoration of religious teachings as a credible body of doctrine."[1]

Every culture has some form of "church." As Kirk suggested, all civilizations rest on a belief system, the worldview that arises from it, and the values emerging from the beliefs. For the ancient Jews, the church was the temple, the synagogue, and the Torah they taught and preserved. In a Communist society the church is the political party that protects and spreads Marxist doctrine. The church may be the mosque in an Islamic nation, a Hindu or Buddhist temple in Oriental cultures dominated by those religions, the shrines of scientism that revere and guard Darwinism in the secular West, or even great urban towers where altars of materialism are worshipped throughout the world.[2]

The quality of the beliefs enshrined in those churches will shape the quality of the society itself. Philip Jenkins, an Anglican academic who has written extensively about the nature of global Christianity, said, "The twenty-first century will almost certainly be regarded by future historians as a century in which religion replaced ideology as the prime animating and destructive force in human affairs."[3]

In the early nineteenth century, Alexis de Tocqueville traveled from one end of America to the other. He came to the United States from his native France to try to understand the character of American democracy. What Tocqueville discovered was the importance of the belief system that constituted the foundation of the nation. He wrote,

> Because Roman civilization perished through barbarian invasions, we are perhaps too much inclined to think that that is the only way a civilization can die. . . . If the lights that guide us ever go out, they will fade little by little, as if of their own accord. . . . We therefore should not console ourselves by thinking that the barbarians are still a long way off. Some peoples may let the torch be snatched from their hands, but others stamp it out themselves.[4]

Jesus told His followers they were the "light of the world." The Holy Spirit would awaken Paul to the same reality, and he would write, "You were formerly darkness, but now you are Light in the Lord; walk as children of Light" (Eph. 5:8). The authentic church is a great lighthouse, and its Spirit-soaked people radiate the light that guides whole societies. But lighthouses are anchored to stony escarpments rising from the sea that batters them relentlessly. If the lighthouse is not embedded in the rock, it will collapse.

The sad truth about the great Western civilization that arose around the biblical belief system is that it is pulverizing the foundations on which it stands. It's not the Muslims, the media, or bad politicians; it's millions of people in the West who have abandoned and even tried to chop up the roots that gave their societies life and vitality. These biblical foundations are conserved by the true, Bible-believing church. As the Globequake intensifies, it's vital the real church remain immovable and rock solid.

JESUS BUILDS THE ROCK-SOLID CHURCH

As He spoke to His disciples at Caesarea Philippi, Jesus knew His followers would soon experience a quake that would shatter the spiritual, emotional, and mental ground on which they stood. Jerusalem and the cross loomed in their future, and they did not know it. They would have to be solid as stone to keep standing when the cataclysm burst upon them.

For that stability, Jesus' team needed unshakeable confidence in His true nature and their identity in Him. So the Lord asked them, "Who do people say that the Son of Man is?"

"John the Baptist," replied one of Jesus' followers.

"Elijah," answered another.

"Jeremiah or one of the prophets," piped up yet another.

"Who do *you* say I am?"

Simon stepped right up and said, "You are the Christ—the Messiah—the Son of the living God!"

The Bible doesn't report it, but you can sense the smile on Jesus' face as He responded to Simon's confession:

Blessed are you, Simon Barjona, because flesh and blood did not reveal this to you, but My Father who is in heaven. I also say to you that you are Peter, and upon this rock I will build My church; and the gates of Hades will not overpower it. I will give you the keys of the kingdom of heaven; and whatever you bind on earth shall have been bound in heaven, and whatever you loose on earth shall have been loosed in heaven. (Matt. 16:17–19)

Jesus was Gibraltar, and Simon a hefty chunk of the Rock. Simon needed to know that about Jesus as well as himself to be stable for the turbulence ahead.

Further, Jesus had said, His real church would be rock solid because it would rest on the sturdy stone of the reality behind Simon's confession: *Jesus is the Messiah, the Anointed One, the only begotten Son of the living God!* Simon Peter's future, and that of Christ's church, would be thrust from one tumultuous situation to another. But Simon, despite early stumblings, would keep standing, and so would the rock-solid church firmly established in Jesus Christ. The real church would be so strong that not even the "gates of Hades" would overpower it!

History would prove it again and again. Tyrants would craze themselves trying to shatter the church. The blood of the martyrs would prove to be seed, and the chips of the rock would become new stones that grew to mountains the enemies of the church couldn't bring down.

John Lennon, on March 4, 1966, thought he was prophesying the disintegration of the church. The singer said his music group, the Beatles, was "more popular than Jesus now." When a furor erupted over Lennon's statement, he answered that he was actually lamenting the state of culture. However, the *London Evening Standard* recorded all John Lennon's words that day: "Christianity will go. It will vanish and shrink. I needn't argue with that; I'm right and I will be proved right. We're more popular than Jesus now; I don't know which will go first—rock 'n' roll or Christianity. Jesus was all right but his disciples were thick and ordinary. It's them twisting it that ruins it for me."

Actually what went was the Beatles. Many observers have noted the decline and disintegration of the group in the years following Lennon's statement. But the rock-solid church and the message it preaches do not pass away. What dies is the flimsy faux church that becomes the shrine of its own culture, whose doctrine is shaped by the most recent declarations of the high priests of the elitist establishments that shape the consensus of the moment, and whose vision extends no further than the current social trend. The rock-solid church keeps standing no matter how intense the shaking!

WHAT THE REAL CHURCH LOOKS LIKE

The real church is the *ekklesia*, the community of people "called out" from the rest of the world to walk in intimate relationship with God, through His Son, and in the power of His Holy Spirit. In this relationship, the church radiates blessing to the rest of its society. It is the remnant community that blesses its society and world. Whole cultures feast off the verdant tree that is the real church, relishing truth, love, grace, justice, freedom, and all the other fruits it yields.

When Solomon built the awe-inspiring temple in Jerusalem, God told him,

> If I shut up the heavens so that there is no rain, or if I command the locust to devour the land, or if I send pestilence among My people, and My people who are called by My name humble themselves and pray and seek My face and turn from their wicked ways, then I will hear from heaven, will forgive their sin and will heal their land. Now My eyes will be open and My ears attentive to the prayer offered in this place. For now I have chosen and consecrated this house that My name may be there forever, and My eyes and My heart will be there perpetually. (2 Chron. 7:13–16)

A striking revelation leaps out here: *what happens at God's house determines the quality of life in the society at large.*

Centuries later, when Israel's religious establishment rejected their Messiah, Jesus told them, "The kingdom of God will be taken away from you and given to a people, producing the fruit of it" (Matt. 21:43). The baton is passed to the real church. The continuation of God's promise to Solomon regarding the temple is through the authentic church.

In the Revelation visions John saw the impact of the real church on the world's history and events. Among the things John observed at the throne of God were "golden bowls full of incense, which are the prayers of the saints" (Rev. 5:8). As the vision unfolded, John watched as an

> angel came and stood at the altar, holding a golden censer; and much incense was given to him, so that he might add it to the prayers of all the saints on the golden altar which was before the throne. And the smoke of the incense, with the prayers of the saints, went up before God out of the angel's hand. Then the angel took the censer and filled it with the fire of the altar, and threw it to the earth; and there followed peals of thunder and sounds and flashes of lightning and an earthquake. (Rev. 8:3–5)

What the genuine church prays for in intercession is what is poured back on earth!

This is why the Scriptures describe the community of Christ's followers as a priesthood. Peter wrote, "Coming to Him as to a living stone which has been rejected by men, but is choice and precious in the sight of God, you also, as living stones, are being built up as a spiritual house for a holy priesthood, to offer up spiritual sacrifices acceptable to God through Jesus Christ" (1 Peter 2:4–5).

A classical definition of *priest* refers to a person who represents God before people and people before God. The real church, in a sense, is the House of Representatives for humanity before God's throne, as well as God's "ambassadors," as Paul put it, within the world.

As a young aide at the White House, I came to the conclusion that the authentic church is the most important agency in the whole world. Governments can wield power but not true authority, unless it's granted by God. Political leaders and movements can spark revolution, but not enduring transformation. Regimes will change, administrations will come and go, but the foundation of a nation that is a blessing to its people is the genuine, constant church.

FOUR CHARACTERISTICS OF THE REAL DEAL

How do we recognize it? In more than forty years of studying the doctrine and history of the church, working with congregations in more than twenty nations, and seeking to build biblical churches as a pastor, I have observed four qualities manifested by a true church, no matter what the culture. I have seen these features in bustling American urban churches, as well as in congregations in Asia, Africa, Latin America, and Europe. It mattered not whether the language was Mandarin or German, Hindi or Spanish, French or Farsi, the style contemporary or traditional, the church large or small, denominational or nonaligned. The real church in today's world looks like this:

1. The authentic church is Jesus centered.

The genuine church is passionate in its love, devotion, and commitment to Jesus Christ. He is its head and its heart, the center of her focus. It is dedicated to continuing His incarnational ministry as His body. It thrives on His intimacy as His bride.

2. The real church is Spirit energized.

Through a consistent ministry of worship and prayer, the genuine church engages with the Holy Spirit. It is linked to the pentecost moment when the Spirit ignited the church, and it functions in the "anointing [that] remains" (1 John 2:27 NIV). Its people serve Christ through their spiritual gifts, resulting in a fruitful harvest.

3. The true church is Word anchored.

Neither cultural trends nor philosophical fads shape the belief and practice of the true church. The Bible is its only ultimate authority, and the real church is confident it is the very Word of God.

4. The genuine church is kingdom focused.

The real church pulsates with the adventure of its kingdom mission. It knows history is the arena for the advance of the kingdom of God. The authentic church agrees with Abraham Kuyper's statement we saw earlier, that Christ is Lord over "the whole domain of our human existence."

Irene and I once stumbled on a group of Christ's followers who believed every "square inch" of Kuyper's homeland was under Christ—even raunchy Amsterdam. It was not our intention, but we had arrived in the Dutch city on Queen's Day, when the monarch's birthday had become an excuse for all the lurid sensuality of the red-light district to come out onto the main streets. As we walked the mile or so from the train station to our hotel, we tried to ignore the bacchanal around us.

About halfway, we heard voices worshipping God in song. We turned left toward the refreshing sound. A band from an Indonesian immigrant church had set up in the midst of hell. To Irene and me, their radiance and their worship in the core of that darkness shone out like pure gold!

CHAPTER 9

WHEN THE GLOBEQUAKE PUTS THE LIGHTS OUT

A golden age for the church

Earthquakes put out the lights. "The whole city is in darkness, you have thousands of people sitting in the streets with nowhere to go," reported a newspaper after a 7.0 quake shattered Port-au-Prince, Haiti.[1] But down deep in the gullet of that darkness could be heard the sound of people singing worship songs, just like those faithful Indonesian believers in Amsterdam.

They joined a chorus of millions across history who have declared their faith when the lights went out in their lives and lands. This is among the reasons the Globequake era is a golden age for the authentic church. Isaiah declared,

> *The people who walk in darkness*
> *Will see a great light;*
> *Those who live in a dark land,*
> *The light will shine on them.*
> (Isa. 9:2)

Because of the Globequake it's getting dark enough in the nations to see the light. Malcolm Muggeridge, who had spent much of his life in spiritual darkness before "rediscovering Jesus," as he described in a book of that title, said,

[I]t is precisely when every earthly hope has been explored and found wanting, when every possibility of help from earthly sources has been sought and is not forthcoming, when every recourse this world offers, moral as well as material, has been explored to no effect, when in the shivering cold the last stick has been thrown on the fire and in the gathering darkness every glimmer of light has finally flickered out, it's then that Christ's hand reaches out sure and firm. Then Christ's words bring their inexpressible comfort, then his light shines brightest, abolishing the darkness forever.[2]

"It is true that sometimes an enveloping darkness aids one to clearer vision," observed early twentieth-century French writer Pierre Loti.

Unquestionably we are living through one of history's truly dark hours. We are once again at a critical point of time when the very survival of free civilization is at stake. As I reflected on this, I was reminded of a speech given by Winston Churchill on October 16, 1938. He was broadcasting to isolationist America, as well as to an audience in London. The speech had another title, but history would remember it mainly for Churchill's opening lines: "*The lights are going out* [on freedom and civilization]."

As you read the following excerpt from Churchill's speech, rather than think *Nazi*, substitute *global terrorism* or any other of the dark threats of our time. Churchill said,

We are confronted with another theme. It is not a new theme; it leaps out upon us from the Dark Ages—racial persecution, religious intolerance, deprivation of free speech, the conception of the citizen as a mere soulless fraction of the State. To this has been added the cult of war. Children are to be taught in their earliest schooling the delights and profits of conquest and aggression. A whole mighty community has been drawn painfully, by severe privations, into a warlike frame.[3]

We could not better or more accurately describe the world in our times.

Sociologist Robert Nisbet believed America was in its "twilight" years, as he wrote in the last quarter of the twentieth century. The declining years of the United States looked strikingly like ancient Rome to Nisbet. The explosion of the occult, antirational spiritualism, a warped emphasis on the subjective and therapeutic, the pursuit of pleasure as the highest aim of life, and many other factors led Nisbet to his conclusions.[4] Bread and circuses were the constant preoccupation of the Roman masses, and this is certainly true of our times. Rampant sexual preoccupation and indulgence, along with violence and the quest for the easy life, characterized Rome and now are the mark of contemporary culture.

The "mushy middle" is disappearing from American culture, says Tim Keller, author and founding pastor of New York's Redeemer Presbyterian Church. Secularism and "devout religion" are "growing together."[5] One result is deeper commitment because people will no longer go to church merely because it's the cultural expectation. While this leads to polarization in society, it reflects the Roman world where the early followers of Jesus established their churches. They planted the church from their belief in and commitment to Jesus Christ, not because of a desire to mesh with Roman society or meet its expectations. In fact, living together in the community of faith in Christ collided with Roman culture. Against that backdrop, as Jesus' followers dug in with their message and Christ-reflecting lifestyle, their witness was enhanced!

This is why we should be excited now: the ancient church flourished in that society to the point that within three centuries it had spread throughout the empire. Through "many tribulations," churches are purified, get more intensely focused, and become increasingly effective. The increasing purity and radiance of the church occur at the same time darkness deepens over the nations.

The golden age of the real church dawns in the grim night of the Globequake. *And the deeper the darkness, the brighter the light.*

HOW CHURCHES BECOME ROCK SOLID

To the Roman world, the real church was an upsetting presence. When the gospel of the kingdom penetrated Thessalonica, Christ's opponents became hysterical. They searched frantically for Paul and Silas, but couldn't find them. They grabbed Jason, one of the Christ followers, as they shouted, "These who have turned the world upside down have come here too" (Acts 17:6 NKJV).

Under contemporary Globequake conditions, however, the world is turning many churches upside down. Author and theologian David Wells wrote, "Every aspect of Western society, every nook and cranny, is now awash with change," which "has in the profoundest sense been *spiritual*."[6] Rogue waves of nonbiblical, even idolatrous spirituality have swamped and capsized many a church and denomination. It's vital to understand how to make churches so stable and strong that not even the worst tsunamis, tremors, and jolts of the present can upset them. Following are important principles for making a church Globequake-proof.

STABILIZE THE STRATEGIC PLAN

Vision for the Sphere of Church

Christ's vision for His church was that it be the extension and continuation of His incarnational ministry in the world (John 14:12), an impregnable, unshakeable sanctuary where people could find hope and salvation in a world in upheaval (Matt. 16:18), and the living model of the new humanity that constitutes the citizenship of God's kingdom (Eph. 3:10).

Values for the Sphere of Church

Here are some of the values revealed in Christ's vision for His church, which can keep the contemporary church rock solid:

1. Jesus Christ as the world's Savior and the head of the church
2. The ministry of Jesus Christ within the nations as the world's ultimate hope
3. The authority of the Bible and sound doctrine as the means of giving the church stability and constancy
4. The kingdom of God as the expression within the world of Christ's reign of love, grace, peace, and justice
5. The responsibility of those who comprise Christ's church to be ambassadors of Christ's kingdom and His servants within creation
6. The believer's duty to care for needy people everywhere who need Christ and His salvation

The Kingdom Mission for the Sphere of Church

"Go therefore and make disciples of all the nations, baptizing them in the name of the Father and the Son and the Holy Spirit, teaching them to observe all that I commanded you; and lo, I am with you always, even to the end of the age" (Matt. 28:19–20).

To be rock solid, churches must reconnect with the strategic plan given by Christ Himself. They must recommit to following its mandates and reestablish themselves on its enduring foundations!

ANCHOR INTO SOUND DOCTRINE

David Wells has written of the dilemma of mainline American churches that have imploded under the Globequake. Their problem was their attempt to maintain relevancy in an increasingly secularized, materialistic culture. Said Wells: "Caught between a traditional

111

Christian worldview and the emerging secular consensus within a modernized culture, these churches were unable to put together a faith that was both modern and Christian. The more modern they felt themselves compelled to be, the less Christian were they able to remain."[7]

On the other extreme were churches that bowed at the altar of style. Like those of the mainline churches, their motives initially were laced with purity: they wanted to communicate the gospel to people. But after a while, rather than theology governing style, style determined theology. Such churches became entertainment centers. They were focused on presenting events rather than developing the ministry infrastructures that would help them raise up mature followers of Christ and give them the structural stability to resist the Globequake's pounding.

Somewhere in between were the political churches, those whose doctrinal anchorage was in the flinty pebbles of a particular political order or philosophy rather than the deep rock of the biblical theology of the kingdom. In the early twentieth century, the political churches tended to be on the left, promoting socialist causes their leaders were convinced would bring in the kingdom. By the late twentieth and early twenty-first centuries, the political churches grouped around the right wing. They had confused the mission of conserving biblically revealed absolute and eternal values, which are foundations for all free and prospering societies, with conserving the particular society itself, as if its momentary cultural expressions were greater than the eternal foundations on which it had once rested.

Many of these churches were evangelical. Strangely, as they deepened in civil religion, they became more like nationalistic churches whose aim was the preservation of a national way of life rather than the advance of the kingdom that spans all cultures and national groups.

I learned these lessons the hard way. In the turbulent 1960s, as a religion reporter for a daily newspaper, I observed and wrote about change in the church. I interviewed spiritual explorers like Episcopal Bishop James Pike, who resigned after being censured by his fellow bishops in 1966. I talked with and wrote about theological edge-runners like Thomas Altizer, a primary theologian of the God-is-dead movement, and New Age gurus frolicking happily through the age of Aquarius.

Later, as a pastor, I became an active participant in many movements that lost sight of sound theology in the pursuit of the trendy, the political, the stylistically relevant, and the spiritually adventuresome. I know firsthand what it means to be taken "captive through philosophy and empty deception, according to the tradition of men, according to the elementary principles of the world, rather than according to Christ" (Col. 2:8).

Therefore, for the church to be safe, sane, and stable amid the furious tremors, it must cut loose from the frail rope of the trendy and chain itself to anchors set firm in the deep rock of sound doctrine. This is not a new concern. Paul's words to the church at Ephesus are as true today as twenty centuries ago:

> He gave some as apostles, and some as prophets, and some as evangelists, and some as pastors and teachers, for the equipping of the saints for the work of service, to the building up of the body of Christ; until we all attain to the unity of the faith, and of the knowledge of the Son of God, to a mature man, to the measure of the stature which belongs to the fullness of Christ. As a result, we are no longer to be children, tossed here and there by waves and carried about by every wind of doctrine, by the trickery of men, by craftiness in deceitful scheming; but speaking the truth in love, we are to grow up in all aspects into Him who is the head, even Christ, from whom the whole body, being fitted and held together by what every joint supplies, according to the proper working of each

individual part, causes the growth of the body for the building up of itself in love. (Eph. 4:11–16)

SAFEGUARD TRANSCENDENT VALUES

The real church will be both liberal and conservative. It is liberal in the ministry of the gospel of grace. The genuine church is seen in the makeup of the first-century Corinthian congregation—former fornicators, idolaters, adulterers, effeminate persons, homosexuals, thieves, coveters, drunkards, revilers, and swindlers (1 Cor. 6:9–10). The liberality of grace is inclusive: all who repent of former lifestyles and turn to Christ are received with open arms, even if they are in the midst of the journey of transformation.

The authentic church will also be liberal regarding race, gender, and socioeconomic status. This is the new humanity made one in Christ that is revealed to angelic principalities and powers in the heavens, through the genuine church (Eph. 3:10). So the true biblical church recognizes and embraces the truth of Galatians 3:28: "There is neither Jew nor Greek, there is neither slave nor free man, there is neither male nor female; for you are all one in Christ Jesus."

The biblical church, however, is also conservative. It is the conservatory of transcendent beliefs and values revealed in the Scriptures and demonstrated in the life and ministry of Jesus of Nazareth. As we saw earlier, a church distorts its mission when its aim is to conserve a particular society rather than the absolute principles on which all nations and cultures are to be built. Therefore, the real church will conserve biblical authority and truth amid the Globequake turbulence that threatens to sever people, their institutions, and society from the firm foundations of the Bible's principles.

As the conservator of biblical authority and truth within a nation and culture, the real church takes seriously Jude's admonition to "contend earnestly for the faith which was once for all handed down to the saints" (Jude. 3). This is the call for the church to conserve and preserve apostolic doctrine within society at large. Theologians refer to this as the *kerygma*, a Greek term signifying the content of the "message preached." Peter's pentecost proclamation and teachings of other apostles recorded in the book of Acts are often viewed as providing the broad outlines of the *kerygma* that the genuine church is to conserve and preserve even as the Globequake shakes apart everything else.

TIGHTEN THE LINKAGE BETWEEN ORTHODOXY AND ORTHOPRAXY

Prior to World War II, Germany could be described as a theological society. Famous schools attracted top scholars. The impact in the early and mid-twentieth century was such that major seminaries in the United States stipulated that graduate students in theology had to have a working knowledge of German.

So how could a nation so steeped in theology embrace Hitler, Nazism, and the occultic spirituality and warped mysticism on which it based its ideas? Why was so much of the German church shaken to its foundations by the quakes ignited in the society by Hitler and the Nazis?

Perhaps a major cause was the introduction by Friedrich Schleiermacher in the early nineteenth century of "theology as science."[8] The result was the study of theology for theology's sake. Theologian Edward Farley, of the Vanderbilt Divinity School, believes this approach has led to "the fundamental flaw in clergy education today . . . the fragmentation of theological studies."[9]

Farley and Robert W. Ferris, professor emeritus at Columbia Bible Seminary and School of Ministry, and others believe what is needed is a focus on "theology as message" (which focuses on making biblical truth understandable) and "theology as engagement" (the application of biblical truth in practical ministry).

The bottom line is that theology that does not lead to action is incomplete. Anything incomplete is weak, and it's no wonder the Globequake has been so disturbing to some theologians and their theologies. Few phenomena illustrate this better than process theology. This field of study promotes the idea that God Himself is changing. Process theologians observe the redefinitions occurring in the world and assume God is riding along the tectonic plates as well, Himself in a state of change and redefinition. Their mistake is the same one noted of others earlier—allowing phenomena and culture to be authoritative in understanding God rather than defining phenomena and culture against the absoluteness of God.

Orthodoxy is "right belief." Theology is important to help us lock on to pure biblical doctrine. *Orthopraxy* is "right practice." When the two are in balance, there is alignment between belief and action. The genuine church stands on those two sturdy legs and cannot be brought down by the Globequake.

STAND SOLID, BUT DO NOT STAND STILL

In fact, in the world's darkness, the real church is running fast and far on those two sturdy legs.

As we have seen, Jesus links the "end" directly to the global progress of the gospel: "This gospel of the kingdom shall be preached in the whole world as a testimony to all the nations, and then the end will come" (Matt. 24:14).

Author Tim Stafford wrote in *Christianity Today* that "the most important development for the church in the 20th and 21st centuries has not been in the West at all, but in the astonishing shift of Christianity's center of gravity from the Western industrialized nations to Asia, Africa, and Latin America. *In a short time, Christianity has been transformed from a European religion to a global one.*"[10] The glo-balization of the gospel of the kingdom is possible for the first time in history because of jet travel and electronic media. Two hundred years ago, when missionaries like Hudson Taylor sailed for China and other fields, it would take them months to get there. Now the gospel can be shot across the world in mere seconds.

The Joshua Project, which tracks the progress of global evange-lization, reports that Christian radio broadcasts are available in 91 percent of the world's languages, at this writing. As of September 2011, there had been 6.5 billion viewings of the *Jesus* film, which is accessible to populations speaking more than 1,100 languages, 95 per-cent of the world's people groups. Huge advances in communicating Christ's message are being made through the use of Internet-based social media. Based on Joshua Project data, about 70 percent of the earth's inhabitants have heard the gospel in some measure.[11]

Mission Frontiers sees so much progress that it leads one of its reports with the assertion that "the world is blind, deaf, and dumb to what God is doing!"[12] At the dawn of the twenty-first century, *Mission Frontiers* noted examples like the following:

- As the new century dawned, there were 23,000 new Christians in China daily.
- In Africa, there were 16,000 new Christians daily on a continent that was 6 percent Christian in 1900, but 40 percent Christian in 2000.
- In Latin America, the Christian population was growing three times faster than the general population. Three million followers of Christ participated in a March for Jesus in Sao Paolo, Brazil, on June 15, 2006, making it the largest in the world at that time.
- The world population in AD 100 was 181 million, of which about a half million were followers of Christ. That meant there were 360 nonbelievers for each Christian. However, by

1900, the ratio of nonbelievers to believers had been reduced to 27 to 1. By 2000, advance of the gospel in the nations had reduced the ratio to only 7 nonbelievers for each Christian.[13]

"God has entrusted to us the continuation and consummation" of world evangelization, wrote the late New Testament scholar George Eldon Ladd. "We have come far closer to the finishing of this mission than any previous generation. We have done more in the last century and a half in worldwide evangelization than all the preceding centuries since the apostolic age."[14]

There is no room for triumphalism here because the advance of the gospel often comes with a huge and bloody price. Nor should the church assume that the work is going so well it can pull back from its missions task. At least 30 percent of the world has had no opportunity to hear about Christ and respond to the invitation to follow Him.

Rather than see this mission as a wearying burden, the church must see it as an opportunity to be seized. Instead of mourning the immensity of the task, Jesus' followers should open their eyes to the vast opportunities of this golden age. Nations are in such trouble that people are searching for solutions and hope. They know that they need transformation and that something good needs to happen at the front door of their homes!

THE SPHERE OF FAMILY

INDESTRUCTIBLE FAMILIES
Building solid homes

Brooke Hyde walked over to the ruddy log a worker had skinned and shaped 162 years earlier, and she kissed it. None of the people watching her had to ask why. She and her husband, Luke, with their twenty-two-month-old son, Dirk, had survived one of the worst tornadoes in history inside the sturdy walls of their pre–Civil War house in Harvest, Alabama.

After the two-hundred-mile-an-hour winds galloped on to pound other areas, the Hydes ventured outside. A church roof was in their front yard. Someone was calling for chainsaws to free a couple trapped in a storm shelter. Then Brooke and Luke looked back at their home, built in the 1850s. "Our house is the only one that's still livable on this side," Luke would later tell a reporter as his eyes scanned the devastation on Autumn Lane.[1]

The storms that raged over Alabama on April 27, 2011, couldn't destroy the Hyde family because they were sheltered in a home that had been built to survive the worst nature could hurl at it. Three decades before the Hydes occupied the house, Victor Lyle had discovered the old structure in Tennessee and moved it to Alabama. In the ensuing years Lyle and another owner had updated and expanded the old log building, but the original core remained.

It was there, at the historic heart of the antique home, that the Hydes found security, sheltered by the aged logs. That's why Brooke Hyde kissed one of the thick beams that formed the room that was their sanctuary amid the tempest. Inside there, on that horrible night, the Hyde family was indestructible.

The "forever house" was the tag that Brooke and Luke Hyde had given the log building when they moved in. "It's the one thing that's going to stand the test of time," said Brooke after the tornado. "It stood the test of that storm."

Brooke and Luke Hyde lived through the deadly Alabama tornadoes because of the strength of their house. In an even deeper sense, that's the way we can secure our families today from the battering trends amplified by the Globequake. The Hydes lived in a sturdy house made of massive wooden logs. We discover the style of structure that makes families indestructible through a close look at a Greek word that appears in Acts 10:1–2: "Now there was a man at Caesarea named Cornelius, a centurion of what was called the Italian cohort, a devout man and one who feared God with all his household, and gave many alms to the Jewish people and prayed to God continually."

"Household" is a translation of *oikos*. Other meanings include "house" and "family." *Oikos* is also a root term from which English speakers get words like *economics* and *economy*. To get those words, *oikos* is linked to another Greek term, *nomos*, meaning "law" or "custom." *Oikonomea* is thus "economics." The core idea is the management or administration of a household.

Cornelius, the exceptional Roman soldier, "feared God with all his household." The *oikos* was a unit of cohesion and togetherness. In fact in some languages, *oikos* carries the idea of "those who have the same fence" (this being a reference to a group of huts surrounded by a fence and thus constituting a single "family unit").[2] In the broadest sense, *oikos* signifies a shelter, a place with boundaries, even a sanctuary.

THE *OIKOS* OF FAMILY

The family is to be the successor to the garden of Eden in the fallen, Globequake-pounded world. *Garden*, in the Hebrew of the Old Testament, refers to a "hedged-in" place, a zone set apart by distinct boundaries. *Oikos*, as we saw earlier, shares many of these meanings. In God's original and intentional design of the cosmos, there was to be no disruption between the paradise of the natural world and the paradise of the kingdom of heaven. Humanity's fall into sin broke the continuum of heaven and earth. Because of their choice of sin, Adam and Eve were driven from the garden. They no longer had Eden, but they had *oikos*—family, a "household."

Order and Protection in a Fallen World

Chaos wars against cosmos. "And there was war in heaven," wrote John (Rev. 12:7). Michael, a leader of the holy angels who are the emissaries of God in the world of space, time, and matter, battled the "dragon"—Satan—and his forces for the destiny of the created realm. Centuries before John saw his visions of the heavenly dimension, Daniel also had seen the conflict in the heavenly realms. The prophet had cried out to God for understanding of the staggering images he had observed, but heaven seemed silent. Then an angel appeared to Daniel and explained that

> from the first day that you set your heart on understanding this and on humbling yourself before your God, your words were heard, and I have come in response to your words. But the prince of the kingdom of Persia was withstanding me for twenty-one days; then behold, Michael, one of the chief princes, came to help me, for I had been left there with the kings of Persia. Now I have come to give you an understanding of what will happen to your people in the latter days, for the vision pertains to the days yet future. (Dan. 10:12–14)

The conflict in the heavenly dimension spills over into the earth like the World War I battles between European empires spilled over into other nations. The nature of the war in the heavens and its impact on earth is revealed in the meaning of cosmos and chaos.

The root Greek term, *kosmos*, refers to an "orderly arrangement" or "decoration."[3] The Globequake upsets the orderly arrangements in every sphere, throwing everything into chaos. *Kaos* refers to the "confused mass of elements" and "the unformed mass of primeval matter described by the sacred historian in Genesis 1:2."[4] It's no surprise the Antichrist is the "man of lawlessness," whose intent is spiritual and moral chaos throughout God's beautiful cosmos.

Every family knows the turbulence of chaos at some point. Newlyweds relish the delights of sparkling romance. Young parents begin with dreamy thoughts of their children always being cuddly creatures who bring them pleasure. But somewhere on the journey from youthful romance to mature relationship almost every husband and wife will experience upheaval in their marriage. Cute kids become excessively adventurous adolescents, who throw whole families into an uproar. On top of all that, as conservative columnist Rebecca Hagelin wrote, America's families are "suffering from a home invasion that is robbing our children of their youth and futures." The "home invasion" is through "cultural terrorists" who enter homes "under the guise of entertainment and education" and who are allowed "to destroy our sensibilities, personal values, and the innocence of our children," she said.[5]

The family, however, is to be the sphere where individuals can find harmonious order in the heaving worlds beyond its walls. Chaos, with its violence and destruction, is the primary threat against which people need protection in the Globequake-battered world. God Himself is the covering of His people, as the psalmist makes clear:

> *He who dwells in the shelter of the Most High*
> *Will abide in the shadow of the Almighty.*

I will say to the LORD, "My refuge and my fortress,
My God, in whom I trust!"
(Psalm 91:1–2)

The *oikos* is a major component of God's protective "wings." For example, when the last plague was about to descend on Egypt because of Pharaoh's refusal to allow the Hebrew slaves to depart, the Jews were told to take action to protect themselves and their families. God would pass over all Egypt "to smite the Egyptians," Moses told the Hebrews. He ordered them to smear the blood of a sacrificial lamb on the doorposts of their homes, and "the LORD will pass over the door and will not allow the destroyer to come in to your houses to smite you" (Ex. 12:23).

Though the circumstances have changed, the principle has not. When those who occupy offices of authority in the home enter covenant with God through Jesus Christ, the "blood" is on the doorposts. God's desire is to establish His order and extend His protection primarily through the family. Social order can be imposed by might, whether a dictatorship or system of oppressive law, or it can arise from healthy, loving relationships. The order established through strong families nurtures respect and personal responsibility. This is the order that establishes cosmos and resists chaos. And it starts at home!

Structure in a Fallen World

The Greek root word *kosmos* also includes the concept of structure, and stable families are basic in the structural strength of societies. When families break down, nations and civilizations fall apart.

Chaos is an assault on cohesion. God puts things together; the powers of darkness seek to take them apart. God creates, but Satan's aim is de-creation. God's creative work is progressive, as revealed in the six days of creation (Gen. 1). De-creation, therefore, is regressive, as shown in Romans 8, which reveals that because of the fall, and its departure from God's glory, the whole creation is enslaved to corruption. Death, decay, and disintegration are the steps that reverse creation.

Structural coherence sustains creation. Structure can be cold and impersonal, or it can be dynamic and caring. The structure of relationship is the bond that provides togetherness. Nowhere is this seen more than in families who find themselves like Abraham and his household centuries ago living in Sodom. There Abraham's family was under intense assault by chaos and division. God's design and desire were for the patriarch's household to stand unified in the midst of Sodom's spiritual, moral, and violent siege. As Lot would discover, there is no safety in Sodom outside the *oikos*. (See Gen. 19:1–7.)

The crisis of the de-creation of the family and the loss of its reassuring and strengthening unity have reached such proportions as I write that there is hunger for the recovery of structural cohesion that only the family can provide. A *USA Today* survey found that 76 percent of twelve hundred teens interviewed desire more time spent with their parents. One in four reported they had *never* had a meaningful conversation with their fathers. Andree Aelion Brooks, lecturer and former *New York Times* columnist, authored a book titled *Children of Fast-Track Parents*. In it she wrote, "If there was one theme that constantly emerged from my conversations with the children [of parents who have it all] it was a surprising undercurrent of aloneness—feelings of isolation from peers as well as parents despite their busy lives."[6]

People yearn for solid structure in the chaotic Globequake age, and they should be able to find it in the family.

Boundaries in a Fallen World

"Do not move the ancient boundary / Which your fathers have set," states the writer of Proverbs (22:28). Many forces in modern culture try to set the boundaries: law enforcement agencies and their officers, schoolteachers, religious authorities, and even the anarchists who say they respect no boundaries—but just try to steal one of their wallets!

When young Daniel was in his early days in Babylon, the Chaldeans determined to box him in, as we saw in an earlier chapter. The Chaldeans were the dominant class in Nebuchadnezzar's empire. The king had seen the potential in Daniel and his friends, and he assigned the Chaldeans, who were also the keepers of Babylon's political correctness, to thoroughly propagandize the Hebrew captives.

Nebuchadnezzar went too far, however, when he messed with Daniel's boundaries. Daniel made up his mind he wouldn't eat the king's food; instead, he would stay with a diet consistent with his beliefs and practice. Daniel's friends—Shadrach, Meshach, and Abednego—also had firm lines they wouldn't cross, as when there was an attempt to make them worship a golden image. They preferred facing the fiery furnace to crossing sacred frontiers and worshipping an idol. Darius the Persian took Babylon and okayed a decree outlawing prayer to any deity but him. Once again a ruler had bumped into one of Daniel's boundaries. He refused to cross over into idolatry and soon felt the hot breath of lions—though they couldn't get a tooth into his hide. (See Dan. 6:16–24.)

Daniel and his friends were a long way from home. Parents and wise teachers and priests were no longer part of their daily lives. But the boundaries laid deep in the good soil of their hearts couldn't be moved.

Boundaries are set best in the context of families, as the proverb says. Parents are the best boundary builders because when cold institutions and their bureaucrats try to establish a boundary, all they can do is write a law that then becomes the responsibility of a police officer or some other magistrate to enforce.

In the absence of love and relationship, laws have a way of deteriorating quickly to raw force and tyranny. Yet without law the world would be overwhelmed with anarchy. Chaos would blast through every institution and every life. In God's kingdom design, therefore, the family is to be the realm where boundaries are established in the context of relationship and administered in and through love—sometimes tough love. Proverbs 13:24 has a bite to it, but its admonition is right on the money:

> He who withholds his rod hates his son,
> But he who loves him disciplines him diligently.

Spanking has become a major social issue. Parents are intimidated, reported, and sometimes hauled off by the authorities for striking a child. Those who do so abusively *should* be restrained by law and public opinion. However, the "rod" mentioned in Proverbs is not only for hitting but also refers to a shepherd's staff. In that sense, the rod is not for beating but for guiding. Sometimes the shepherd uses the staff to prod the sheep, but never to thrash them. Thus, discipline should be administered firmly but positively to keep a child from straying.

Such positive discipline is crucial in a culture that often regards discipline as the means of squelching the pleasure that has become its top objective. The Hebrew word in Proverbs helps us understand what positive discipline looks like. The term carries the meanings of warning and instruction as well as chastisement. *Warning* means the parent is not to strike a child impulsively, driven by frustration and anger, but to let the youngster know he or she is on a path that could lead to discipline. *Instruction* signifies that a mom and dad should engage with the child in a learning environment, helping the boy or girl understand a wrong behavior in its larger context.

The aim of discipline is always the internalization of principles and the restraint they provide. For example, I jog with my two dogs most mornings on an off-road dirt track. When they were pups, I kept them tightly leashed and taught them essential commands. Now all three of us are older. I no longer have to keep the leash always around their necks. They have internalized the leash. All I have to do (usually) is to give the command. This is the outcome of positive disciplining. It may be easier with puppies, but the value for providing your children with positive discipline is much greater. Someday they will be running through the world without your leash around their necks, but if you've been successful, there will be self-restraint on their hearts!

One pleasure of aging is getting to see your kids raise their kids. I know of a dad who used to tell his teenager, "You're going to get yours someday!" The good news was the father, in disciplining his own child, was seeding the kid's life with the foundational principles that, later in life, the dad would see the son apply with his own teenage children.

Without knowing it, the dad had laid the foundations in the heart of his son for building a home that would span generations—a forever house.

CHAPTER 11

DESIGNING THE FOREVER HOUSE
Stormproofing the family

The Globequake disorders the world through its destructive romps. It rips down all the structures where people seek safety, sanity, and stability, and knocks down the boundary posts that have stood for generations. "What can the righteous do?" To borrow Brook Hyde's words, how do we build a "forever house"? How can we strengthen the family and make it safe, sane, and stable in a world gone wild?

STABILIZE THE STRATEGIC PLAN

Vision for the Sphere of Family

God's vision for the human family is that its members enjoy and manifest the love-bonded oneness of the diverse persons of the Trinity within the created world.

Genesis 1:27 reveals two facts. First, God created human beings in His own image. Second, God made humans male and female. The ability to reproduce, and to do so through healthy sexuality, is a wonderful blessing, but it is not the primary reason we are made as man and woman. Humans are created as male and female so we might enter into and enjoy the rich fellowship and communion of the Trinity—Father, Son, and Holy Spirit. Man alone does not carry the full image of God, but male and female together are able to know the oneness within diversity that is characteristic of the triune God. "For this reason," says Genesis 2:24, "a man shall leave his father and his mother, and be joined to his wife."

The Trinity is the foundational model and source of all healthy relationships. The family is the human sphere where the relational style of Father, Son, and Holy Spirit is carried out at the greatest levels of intimacy.

Jesus' great desire is that His bride—the church and the people in fellowship with Him who comprise it—enter into the oneness of the Trinity (John 17:22–26). The family, with a dynamic marriage between male and female right at its core, and God, at the core of the core, bring the wonderful love, fellowship, and communion of Father, Son, and Holy Spirit into actualization in the world. The sexual relationship is the means by which a man and a woman become "one flesh." This is the human means by which two people know the intimacy and oneness in God. A healthy sex life between one man and one woman within a marriage is therefore sacred. Sexual intimacy between a husband and a wife is to be the affirmation of the union of whole persons, the joining of spirit and soul as well as body.

Values for the Sphere of Family

An analysis of the vision for the family reveals the values that will sustain it according to God's design:

1. God in His wholeness, as Father, Son, and Holy Spirit, diverse persons dwelling together in perfect oneness
2. Gender and sexuality as essential for reflecting the unity-in-diversity of the Trinity
3. Respect for the distinctive roles of male and female
4. Marriage as the dynamic within a family where the human

expression of this communion is actualized through sexual intimacy

5. Other members of the family as beneficiaries of the fellowship of the relationship between husband and wife

Kingdom Mission for the Sphere of Family

The kingdom mission for the human family is to teach, transfer, and transmit the principles of the kingdom of God across the generations.

The family is the sphere that shapes history. "The hand that rocks the cradle is the hand that rules the world," wrote nineteenth-century poet William Ross Wallace. The Bible reveals the critical role of the father also in molding history. God's generational mission for the family is highlighted in Psalm 78:

> Listen, O my people, to my instruction;
> Incline your ears to the words of my mouth.
> I will open my mouth in a parable;
> I will utter dark sayings of old,
> Which we have heard and known,
> And our fathers have told us.
> We will not conceal them from their children,
> But tell to the generation to come the praises of the LORD,
> And His strength and His wondrous works that He has done.
>
> For He established a testimony in Jacob
> And appointed a law in Israel,
> Which He commanded our fathers
> That they should teach them to their children,
> That the generation to come might know,
> even the children yet to be born,
> That they may arise and tell them to their children,
> That they should put their confidence in God

And not forget the works of God,
But keep His commandments,
And not be like their fathers,
A stubborn and rebellious generation,
A generation that did not prepare its heart
And whose spirit was not faithful to God.
(vv. 1–8)

STABILIZE THE GATES

When Nehemiah saw the wreckage of the walls and gates of Jerusalem, he "sat down and wept" (Neh. 1:4). There is much reason now to weep over the battered walls and gates that should surround and give protection to the contemporary family. For moms and dads there is no greater responsibility than defending the gates of their homes and maintaining the walls of values and biblical beliefs that protect their families.

The gates of ancient towns and villages were made extremely strong. Even today, the old gates surrounding Jerusalem are thick and heavy. Gates were open during the day (unless there was a threat) and closed at night. The gate sections were large enough that people could gather there to hear the teachings and judgments of the city elders, conduct business, and stroll through markets. They were heavily defended; watchmen stood guard day and night atop high towers positioned beside the gates. In fact, the gate sections were so large they often represented the glory of a city. Just as today a nation is designated a superpower based on the strength of its nuclear arsenal, in ancient times, a city was respected because of the size and strength of its gates.

Everything the Bible shows about ancient city gates has meaning for us today. Defending the people began at the gates of ancient cities, and protecting our families today begins at the gates.

Our situation is like that of Lot in Sodom, when two angels came to visit. Lot, Abraham's nephew, was sitting in the city gates (Gen. 19:1). To his credit, Lot recognized the nature of the visitors and opened the gates to them. Then he did more than that. Lot opened the doors of his home to these spectacular beings. Sex-crazed men had seen Lot's visitors and "surrounded the house . . . from every quarter" (Gen. 19:4). They pounded on his doors, demanding that Lot bring out the handsome angels "that we may have relations with them" (v. 5).

This is a picture of contemporary culture. Homes are under siege from forces demanding that those inside whom they want to exploit be delivered to them. Lot was foolish enough to think he could negotiate with the frenzied crowd at the gates of his home. In the Globequake age we must learn from Lot—*there can be no negotiation with the cultural marauders who lay siege against the gates of our families.*

This means every home needs a champion. As we saw in previous chapters, the rich Hebrew word behind the English term refers to the open ground between two opposing armies. The *champion* is the person who stands in that ground on behalf of his comrades to battle for them. The destiny of the champion's army rests with his victory or defeat. The champion holds the ground, as David did against Goliath. Lot needed to be the champion in the gates of his home, and so must we. The champion does not negotiate or compromise with the turbulent forces and their powerful representatives who seek to surge through our gates.

"But they said, 'Stand aside'" (v. 9). In our time, politicians, courts, and legislatures all shout to parents, "Stand aside!" School systems and their boards demand, "Stand aside!" Social engineers pound on the gates of the home, crying, "Stand aside!" Media ram the doors, hollering, "Stand aside!"

The crowd at Lot's house "pressed hard" and "came near to break the door" (v. 9). This tells us there was no perimeter, no safety zone around Lot's house. It's vital in the Globequake age for parents to set extensive boundaries that protect the door of the home. This means not lowering spiritual and moral standards to the point that the exploitive forces can come to the very doors of our homes.

Billy Ray Cyrus learned the principle the hard way. He watched his famous daughter, Miley, known to millions as Hannah Montana, as she was exploited by entertainment moguls. Miley Cyrus went from being a beautiful, innocent child to an eighteen-year-old who, in the words of one report, had gone "a bit publicly wild."[1] Billy Ray's indulgence of Miley's career "instead of fulfilling his responsibilities is the way he explains how it all went wrong."[2] Fulfilling responsibility means protecting the gates of the family.

In ancient times—and even today—Jerusalem had many gates. The same is true for the city that is your family. The most effective gatekeeping focuses on the gates of the personalities sheltered in the household. Paul was talking about the protection of our personal gates in 1 Thessalonians 5:23: "Now may the God of peace Himself sanctify you entirely; and may your spirit and soul and body be preserved complete, without blame at the coming of our Lord Jesus Christ."

To sanctify something is to set it apart as God's exclusive property. The human spirit, soul, and body of your household and each person in it are to be "preserved complete." "Preserved" comes from a Greek word meaning to guard and surround with protection. This is the essence of gatekeeping. "Entirely" and "completely" are the whole of the spirit, soul, and body.

Guard the Spiritual Gates of the Family

Is there opportunity for all in the household to know God and grow in His truth? Years ago, as a newspaper reporter, I worked for a city editor who was an atheist. "One of my greatest regrets is that I have never given my children an opportunity to know about God and make their own choice," he told me. He had opened the spiritual gates of his home to everything but God and was experiencing the consequences.

Protect the Soul of the Family

Rebecca Hagelin wrote perceptively about the invasion of our homes by media and culture.[3] Effective gatekeeping means keeping out the things that warp the mind, confuse the emotions, and weaken the will of the family and its members. Good gatekeepers know what to let in that will inform and renew the mind, stimulate the emotions positively, and strengthen the will to make wise, godly choices.

Keep Out Things That Weaken the Health of the Family

Gatekeeping involves the body. It also encompasses the way time is allotted. Gatekeeping actions related to the body cover family recreation and togetherness experiences, diet, physical fitness, and good health practices.

STABILIZE THE ROLES

Parents share the role of authority in the family, with the father in the primary place of accountability. Working together according to God's design, a dad and a mom bring a crucial balance that stabilizes a household and all its members despite the rigorous shakings of the Globequake. Healthy people can stay relatively stable and calm when the world around them flies apart. Such strong, confident people are built in homes where positive parental roles maintain a steady equilibrium between immanence—approachability and nearness—and transcendence—authority and accountability Children who are nurtured, loved, and accepted, on the one hand, and, on the other, have a clear understanding of authority, grow up to be solid people who keep their bearings when the Globequake rips out the markers and blurs the horizon.

The principle is found in Ephesians 6:4 (KJV), which says children are to be brought up in the "nurture" and "admonition of the

Lord." "Nurture" is the ministry of immanence, the environment in which a child feels parents to be welcoming and "close," and "admonition," that of authority. This verse is addressed to "fathers," and thus, the ideal administration of the balance of nurture and admonition is to be under the leadership of the godly dad. When such a man is not present in a home, the oversight devolves to the godly mother.[4]

Fathers *and* mothers in healthy families are engaged in immanence and transcendence, but each has distinctive responsibilities regarding these dynamics. The father, in God's design, has the primary role of transcendence, while the mother has chief responsibility for immanence. When the father attempts to fill the nurturer role at the level of the mother, he often becomes a wimp. When the mother tries to assume the admonition responsibility of the father, the temptation is for her to become a nag. A family with a wimp as a father and a nag as a mother is unstable and will be battered down by the Globequake.

The fundamental tactical objective of the powers of darkness is to do all possible to de-create God's good creation by hurling everything back into a state of chaos. Godly governance resists the pull into chaos, and this applies to the home as well as the state and the nation. Paul wrote, "Understand that Christ is the head of every man, and the man is the head of a woman, and God is the head of Christ" (1 Cor. 11:3). If the man decides to operate out from under the headship of Christ, he loses his authority as surely as a general who refuses to submit to his supreme commander. A woman who attempts to seize the power and control of a family from a godly husband is also out of order. If mom and dad stand together under the design God has given, they will present a unified front that will stabilize the family when everything around them falls apart.

Transcendence means there is a final authority in the home, someone who sets the ultimate limits and boundaries. Billy Ray Cyrus, in the interview just cited, unwittingly reflected on his abdication of the transcendence role. He described the problem many dads face because of role confusion. He told a reporter:

> How many interviews did I give and say, "You know what's important between me and Miley is I try to be a friend to my kids"? I said it a lot. And sometimes I would even read other parents who might say, "You don't need to be a friend, you need to be a parent." Well, I'm the first guy to say to them right now: You were right. I should have been a better parent. I should have said, "Enough is enough—it's getting dangerous and somebody's going to get hurt." I should have, but I didn't.[5]

When both father and mother exert authority at the same level, with little emphasis on immanence, the atmosphere of the home will be authoritarian. When mom and dad vie with each other for the role of immanence, with minimal establishment of authority, the atmosphere will be that of indulgence. Fathers must be approachable and affectionate without surrendering their authoritative role, and mothers must be strong in authority without sacrificing their responsibility for nurturing a warm, accepting environment.

Parental role confusion has been one of the most devastating effects of the Globequake, as a Heritage Foundation study showed. The study found the following:

- Over the past thirty years, the rise in violent crime parallels the rise in families abandoned by fathers.
- High-crime neighborhoods are characterized by high concentrations of families abandoned by fathers.
- State-by-state analysis by Heritage scholars indicates that a 10 percent increase in the percentage of children living in single-parent homes leads typically to a 17 percent increase in juvenile crime.

- The rate of violent teenage crime corresponds with the number of families abandoned by fathers.
- The type of aggression and hostility demonstrated by a future criminal often is foreshadowed in unusual aggressiveness as early as age five or six.
- The future criminal tends to be an individual rejected by other children as early as the first grade who goes on to form his own group of friends, often the future delinquent gang.

On the other hand, the study found this information:

- Neighborhoods with a high degree of religious practice are not high-crime neighborhoods.
- Even in high-crime inner-city neighborhoods, well over 90 percent of children from safe, stable homes do not become delinquents. By contrast only 10 percent of children from unsafe, unstable homes in these neighborhoods avoid crime.
- Criminals capable of sustaining marriage gradually move away from a life of crime after they get married.
- The mother's strong affectionate attachment to her child is the child's best buffer against a life of crime.
- The father's authority and involvement in raising his children are also a great buffer against a life of crime.[6]

But what about the home not guided by God's intentional plan? What about the single-parent home? How can it be Globequake resistant? How can such a family be stabilized and enter into God's strong design? This is a crucial question, since multitudes of children are raised in single-parent homes.

My sister and I were brought up in such a family. Divorce ripped apart our home in 1951 when I was ten and my sister three. Our mother, however, instinctively knew the principles of building a strong family. God really did put eternity in her heart and write His laws on her heart. Because of that, my sister and I knew both transcendence and immanence. Our single mom's secret was in linking us to a strong church with a solid, healthy leadership structure. The shaking was intense at times, especially as Mother struggled to keep food on the table and clothes on our bodies. But through the worst of storms, our family held fast. Though our mom worked six days a week to support us, her arms were still open to us, and my sister and I experienced much love and nurture. And because of the strong leaders in our church's organizations for children, we had solid authority figures.

"Pure and undefiled religion before God and the Father is this: to visit orphans and widows in their trouble, and to keep oneself unspotted from the world," wrote James (James 1:27 NKJV). The church of our childhood practiced such a "religion." Because of that and our extended family on both sides, my sister and I were blessed with the balance of transcendence and immanence that kept us strong and healthy despite divorce.

More than sixty years later I still enjoy touring my old neighborhoods. Economic and social quakes have made them crime-ravaged areas, but to me it is all sacred ground. When I see the old, weary houses where I was raised, I can understand Brooke Hyde.

I want to kiss their timbers.

THE SPHERE OF EDUCATION

CHAPTER 12

SANE EDUCATION

Characteristics of solid, stable schools

"Everyone who went to Sunday school yesterday raise your hand so I can give you credit." I can still hear Miss Boozer, my second-grade public school teacher, asking our class that question every Monday morning.

The year was 1948, and the public school board in my hometown gave credit to students who attended Sunday school regularly. Most people still believed that the Ten Commandments framed on schoolhouse walls, prayer and daily Bible reading in the classroom, and other elements of biblical faith were not bad things.

But much has happened in the decades between 1948 and now. Ed Young, my friend, mentor, and pastor, in his book *Healing Broken America*, wrote about the Old America (from the nation's beginning to the 1960s) and the New America (from the 1960s to the present). We could also speak of Old Western Civilization and New Western Civilization. A massive fault line opened between these two cultures, and the sphere of education has been shattered.

To stabilize education amid the Globequake, there must be a recovery of understanding of God's vision for this vital sphere. He is the Author of all truth and the Creator of the human mind. To understand what God intends for education, we should look at the initial commands God gave Israel regarding the schooling of the covenant nation's children, especially in Deuteronomy 6.

CHARACTERISTICS OF SOLID, STABLE EDUCATION

Solid, stable education is God centered.

"Hear, O Israel! The LORD is our God, the LORD is one! You shall love the LORD your God with all your heart and with all your soul and with all your might" (Deut. 6:4–5). This declaration is known as the *Shema*, a Hebrew word meaning "hear" or "listen." The inference is that the truth of the Shema is the core principle people are to heed, listen to carefully, and meditate upon. It establishes the fact there is a focal point where all reality converges and from which it springs. The absolute God is the Center of all things.

Being centered on God does not limit but actually stimulates the inquiry that is essential for learning. Education centered on God does not fear truth because it knows that if something is true, it comes from the Author of all truth. No theories can unseat the Lord because if they are proved true, their truth came from Him. Further, education centered on God recognizes that truth is not fragmented, but whole. Scientific truth is not a separate piece from theological or artistic or economic or moral truth. They are all patches on the same quilt, not stacks of separate blankets. Science's greatest thinkers, like Michael Faraday, Lancelot Law Whyte, Albert Einstein, James Clerk Maxwell, and Sir Arthur Eddington, have sensed the oneness of all truth and searched for the unifying field. Mystics in many religions have emphasized this oneness. The center of all things, however, is found not in a scientific equation or a mystical chant, but in a Person: "Hear, O Israel! The Lord [Yahweh] is our God, the Lord [Yahweh] is one!"

Centeredness on God liberates students to explore and run wide in the intellectual fields of the Lord. They are free to examine every theory, every claim to truth. But when theories are centered on God, there is an established and trustworthy point of reference by which all information can be evaluated and determined as being true or untrue. Without the true north found in God and His revealed truth, all conclusions and theories will be regarded as equally valid, no matter how contradictory to one another and alien to fact they may be. This lack of centeredness on the absolute God explains the strange and diverting curricula that waste the resources and energy of so much education today in schools gone wild.

When education lacks its vital center on the Absolute, academic institutions and curricula are tossed by the surging winds into the alien landscapes of *apostasy* and *equivalency*. *Apostasy* is a falling away from truth. *Equivalency* is the judging of all things as equally good (or bad) and equally true (or false). Under these Globequake-stirred conditions, confusion enters the schoolroom. In the assumption that all things are equally true and right, uncentered education loses sight of what is *really* true and right. Instability is the result. Therefore, solid, stable education is centered on God.

Solid, stable education is parent directed, with specialists as needed.

In God's educational design parents sit in the office of authority when it comes to their children—not politicians, experts, or professional educators.

When George W. Bush became president, I was working for John Culberson, a Texas congressman who was a member of the House Committee on Education. Bush's first piece of legislation submitted to Congress was the No Child Left Behind bill, which sought educational reforms and expanded the federal government's involvement in America's schools. I was present the first day the House committee began considering the bill. The room in the US Capitol complex was packed with people from all sorts of special interest groups. As I watched the process, I realized how many individuals, pressure groups, and philosophical and methodological advocates were trying to wield authority over the nation's public education systems. It seemed everyone was represented officially except parents!

The Bible is clear about the educational leadership of both fathers and mothers. Fathers are history teachers, according to Psalm 44:1:

> *God, we have heard with our ears,*
> *Our fathers have told us*
> *The work that You did in their days,*
> *In the days of old.*

Further,

> *[God] established a testimony in Jacob*
> *And appointed a law in Israel,*
> *Which He commanded our fathers*
> *That they should teach them to their children.*
> (Ps. 78:5)

Proverbs 4:1 admonishes sons to listen to "the instruction of a father." Proverbs 6:20 shows it's not just dads who are to instruct their sons and daughters, but mothers as well. The verse states,

> *My son, observe the commandment of your father*
> *And do not forsake the teaching of your mother.*

The Proverbs 31 woman is one who "opens her mouth in wisdom, / And the teaching of kindness is on her tongue" (v. 26).

Parents are not experts in all fields of knowledge and sometimes must entrust their children to specialists and scholars. Some do this through homeschool consortiums, some place their children in private schools, and others look to public schools. Children in Old Testament Jewish homes were placed in apprenticeships where they learned trades. The rabbis (teachers) in synagogue schools taught young pupils the Torah and the culture and history surrounding it. But always there were tight coordination with the home and recognition that the parents were ultimately responsible for their children's education.

In modern times, the Globequake's social agitations have intensified efforts to unseat parents as the authority over the education of their children. Many fathers and mothers have abdicated leadership, and power groups have moved into the vacuum.

Power is the fundamental temptation. When spheres of church and family crumble, and their authority devolves to the public school, it quickly deteriorates to the exercise of arrogance backed by raw compulsory power. This weakens the entire educational process, making schools vulnerable to the Globequake's intellectual and academic devastations.

Strong and stable education, however, is God centered and overseen by responsible, godly parents.

Solid, stable education is aligned with absolute truth, not cultural necessity.

The church is weakened when it shifts from the foundation of *Sola Scriptura* (the Bible as authority) to *Sola Cultura* (the culture as authority). Education is hammered by the Globequake when cultural necessity becomes more important than alignment with absolute truth.

Deuteronomy 6 warns of the dangers coming from the compromise that puts culture in the driver's seat of education:

Then it shall come about when the LORD your God brings you into the land which He swore to your fathers, Abraham, Isaac and Jacob, to give you, great and splendid cities which you did not build, and houses full of all good things which you did not fill, and hewn cisterns which you did not dig, vineyards and olive trees which you did not plant, and you eat and are satisfied, then watch yourself, that you do not forget the LORD who brought you from the land of Egypt, out of the house of slavery. You shall fear only the LORD your God; and you shall worship Him and swear by His name. *You shall not follow other gods, any of the gods of the peoples who surround you,* for the LORD your God in the midst of you is a jealous God; otherwise the anger of the LORD your God will be kindled against you, and He will wipe you off the face of the earth. (vv. 10–15, italics added)

Like the Israelites, we all come into "great and splendid cities" we "did not build." These "cities" and the "houses full of all good things," along with all the resources we did not plant and cultivate, constitute the civilization of which we become a part by birth or immigration. We are intensely tempted to embrace the "gods of the peoples who surround" us—their presuppositions, belief systems, and worldviews. As we mature and as we learn more about God's kingdom, we awaken to the fact that the foundations of the culture we enjoy have been altered and weakened by the Globequake.

When culture becomes the authority for education, we are building the whole academic edifice on what is new, not in the sense of the inventive and creative but in the sense of the novel, which is as changing as the sand on a wind-swept beach.

Educational arrogance results when cultural necessity drives academics. When contemporary sexual preferences, politically correct tastes regarding the interpretation of history, novel views about gender, and hosts of other rapidly emerging and vaporizing beliefs and behaviors become the heart of education rather than absolute, proved, established truth being its core, the academic edifice is weakened and trembles under the Globequake's shaking.

Contemporary cultural issues must be addressed, but they must not become the authority for what is taught as truth. When educators do that, they are following the "gods" of the people who surround them and who happen to be walking across history at that moment. Malcolm Muggeridge described the culture that produced deconstructionist ideas that focus on the stripping of meaning as "nihilistic in purpose, ethically and spiritually vacuous, and Gadarene in destination."[1] "Gadara," the haunt of a demonized man Jesus encountered and healed, is hardly a destination for the future of the social order and authority of education.

To stabilize education, we must determine to align cultural phenomena and ideas with absolute truth. This will be the task of the spheres of church and family primarily since public school systems are unlikely to present clear biblical values as the counterbalance.

Solid, stable education produces constructive outcomes and does not intensify the destabilization and destruction of the other spheres.

As I write this book I think of Jane Sivley and Sam Mitchell. These two teachers recognized a bent in me for writing and nurtured it. Any failures to organize my thoughts and write well are my own and not a reflection on those two teachers. They built me up. Sometimes to do so, they had to tear down flawed understandings, styles, and methods before they could do the work of construction. There is a deconstructive element in the educational process, akin to the assignment given Jeremiah:

> *Behold, I have put My words in your mouth.*
> *See, I have appointed you this day over the nations and over the kingdoms,*
> *To pluck up and to break down,*
> *To destroy and to overthrow,*
> *To build and to plant.*
> (Jer. 1:9–10)

Educators fail students when *deconstruction* does not have *construction* as its objective. False ideas must be shown to be wrong; misconceptions must be cleared up; barriers to learning must be removed. However, if teachers "pluck up . . . break down . . . destroy . . . overthrow" without the goal "to build and to plant," they weaken students and the future.

Solid, stable education helps students establish a worldview that conforms to actuality and aligns with truth.

"You shall not follow other gods, any of the gods of the peoples who surround you," said Moses (Deut. 6:14). The Holy Spirit, through Moses, was preparing God's covenant people for what they would encounter in Canaan. It would be stark, shocking, in-your-face paganism. "Our god is just as good as your God . . . even better" would be the claim.

Presuppositions are the bricks of a worldview, basic assumptions about the way the world looks and how it operates, built into us from early childhood. The Globequake does two things to our presuppositions—often, sadly, with education as its tool. First, the Globequake tears down the right presuppositions. Second, it infuses us with the wrong presuppositions. When that happens, the building of the worldview is crooked and weak. The only way to stabilize students and education is through what the Bible refers to as the "renewing of the mind." Paul wrote,

> I urge you, brethren, by the mercies of God, to present your bodies a living and holy sacrifice, acceptable to God, which is your spiritual service of worship. And do not be conformed to this world, but be transformed by the renewing of your mind, so that you may prove what the will of God is, that which is good and acceptable and perfect. (Rom. 12:1–2)

This passage speaks directly to the Globequake's devastating impact on education. *To renew*, in the Greek of this text, means "to cause something to become new and different, with the implication of becoming superior."[2] The renewal of the mind through Jesus

Christ and His absolute truth results in transformation—literally, a metamorphosis, or change in form, as we noted in the introduction to part 2. Further, one is freed from conformity to this "world." The Greek word translated "world" is *aion*, which signifies an age, historical period, or culture.

Students must be helped to discover a new worldview, a new way of interpreting the world. *This means learning to think biblically.* In 1963, Harry Blamires, a British educator and Anglican theologian, was concerned because "there was no integrated approach to the increasingly secular culture arising around the church."[3] Blamires was alarmed that the popular worldviews of culture were infiltrating churches with hardly a notice. To voice this issue, Blamires wrote a classic, *The Christian Mind*. There Blamires wrote,

> A prime mark of the Christian mind is that it cultivates the eternal perspective. That is to say, it looks beyond this life to another one. It is supernaturally orientated, and brings to bear upon earthly considerations the fact of Heaven and the fact of Hell. . . . The Christian mind sees human life and human history held in the hands of God. It sees the whole universe sustained by his power and his love. It sees the natural order as dependent upon the supernatural order. . . . It sees this life as an inconclusive experience, preparing us for another; this world as a temporary place of refuge, not our true and final home. . . . Modern secular thought ignores the reality beyond this world. It treats this world as The Thing. Secularism is, by its very nature, rooted in this world. . . . Secularism puts its trust in this life and makes earthly happiness and well-being its primary concern.[4]

The person stabilized by biblical truth, therefore, sees the full scope of reality. He or she looks at the world with two healthy eyes. One sees the immanent and the other the transcendent. One eye can glance back at the past, and the other can peer into the future. When the sight from both eyes is brought together, there is insight about the present. Put out the eye that sees the immanent, and there is only dreamy romanticism and idealism. Blind the eye that looks on the transcendent, and all that's left is secularism, naturalism, and humanism. Darken the eye that sees the future, and there are only the haunting past and the empty present. Close the eye that sees the future, and hope is lost, along with the inspiring tug forward and upward.

The worldview provided by the lens of biblical truth sees it all and gives clarity in the present. The person whose life is guided by such a worldview sees reality as it *really* is.

Solid, stable education teaches the value of revealed values.

Are values revealed or self-developed? Are there absolute values everyone intrinsically recognizes and embraces, or are values formed by a person's preferences and opinions?

These questions constitute a dividing line between education in the Old America and educational philosophies in the New America. Old America worked under a consensus that there were certain values given by the Creator. No one had to develop them. They were not contingent on people's tastes. Educational philosophy in the New America—in public schools, anyway—veers away from the notion of absolute values.

Old America said values are quite clear. New America says values need clarification. The values clarification movement was birthed from the womb of moral relativism, sired by a string of philosophers and psychological theorists who became the gurus of the New America.

The background for this philosophy and its system is moral relativism and situational ethics. Moral relativism is built on the presupposition that there are no absolute values. Situational ethics is the logical outcome of the presupposition that there are no absolutes; it is the notion that ethical and moral behavior is determined by the situation an individual faces.

Social disaster ensued. Writing in 1995, historian Gertrude Himmelfarb said, "It was not until this century that morality became so thoroughly revitalized that virtues ceased to be 'virtues' and became 'values.' "[5] Virtues were long viewed as absolute and universal, but the new concept of values "brought with it the assumptions that all moral ideas are subjective and relative, that they are mere customs and conventions, that they have a purely instrumental, utilitarian purpose, and that they are peculiar to specific individuals and societies."[6] Nothing expresses the dilemma of moral relativism and situational ethics as accurately as Judges 17:6, which describes a period when "every man did what was right in his own eyes."

The problem for education and society comes when subjective values collide with objective, absolute values. Whose values are you going to teach? That's like asking a building contractor, "Whose measuring tape are you going to use, Bill's, for whom an inch is the length of his little finger, or Sam's, whose inch is the length of his thumb?"

Finding the answer is not that hard. At the root of the educational system in Old America was a consensus around a certain set of values. Some early American leaders were deists; others, evangelicals. There were Unitarians and Catholics, Puritans and Jews. However, even skeptics like Thomas Paine embraced the consensus, as revealed in a speech he delivered in Paris in 1797. Paine had supported the French Revolution, and maybe he'd had his fill of its godless chaos. In his speech to the Society of Theophilanthropists, Paine said,

> It has been the error of the schools to teach astronomy, and all the other sciences and subjects of natural philosophy, as accomplishments only; whereas they should be taught theologically, or with reference to the Being who is the author of them: for all the principles of science are of Divine origin. Man cannot

make, or invent, or contrive principles. He can only discover them; and he ought to look through the discovery to the Author.[7]

When we value God's kingdom as our first priority, "all these things will be added to [us]" (Matt. 6:33). Everything essential for high-quality life results from having the right values in the right place in our lives. Education that teaches students such truths stabilizes them in the present and contributes to a solid future for their society.

Solid, stable education teaches students how to connect the dots of history.

Remember those drawing aids you played with in first grade? The canvas or sheet of paper had nothing but dots. I can still recall the thrill every time I connected the dots and the whole picture emerged. It wasn't just a random sprinkling of dots on a hugely boring stretch of paper, but what came into focus meant something. It was a real picture!

Empty humanism doesn't believe there are any purposefully placed dots on the canvas of history. There are only random, unrelated events that sometimes tangle accidentally with one another, producing evil and good capriciously. Because there are no dots to connect, there is no big picture. This is the philosophy underlying much of the history taught in public schools and colleges. No wonder many students would agree with Henry Ford, when he said, "History is bunk."

Teachers who make the study of history boring ought to be made to stay after school and write ten thousand times, "I will not make history boring." History is the arena of God's engagement with His creation. History is full of His presence, loaded with His purpose. And the canvas is covered with dots. It's thrilling to study history from the Bible's perspective, to connect all those dots, and then stand in amazement when all the linkages produce a coherent, beautiful picture.

In the United States and other Western nations, the study of history has been ripped, pummeled, distorted, and falsified. Fragmentation of society has been the result. The sense of shared roots and common identity has been lost. For example, an academic study of American history books published in the 1970s and 1980s found that "the central processes that integrated American society are trivialized."[8]

The disconnect between people and their history, and between historic events and history's meaning, begins in educational philosophies and institutions that trivialize historic experience. Stable and solid education, on the other hand, strengthens students by helping them understand, appreciate, and see the purpose and plan of which their historic moment is a part, the way in which the present was shaped by the past, and the future implications of contemporary thought and action.

The only problem with most of what I've written in this chapter is that it can't be done in the majority of school systems. How, then, do we stabilize education? We explore this question in the next chapter.

CHAPTER 13

REBUILDING THE EDUCATIONAL RUBBLE WORLD

Taming academics gone wild

In May 2010, thousands of spectators amassed on the Fockeberg, a five-hundred-foot hill near Leipzig, Germany, to watch daredevils compete in a soapbox derby. A newspaper reported the mound was "created entirely from rubble leftover after the bombing of Leipzig during World War II."[1] The drivers in their colorful and crazy contraptions would race "on the ruins of Hitler's Third Reich."[2]

The physical debris from the conflict, however, was nothing compared to the wreckage of Germany's institutions. The scrap from the spiritual, personal, family, educational, political, and commercial devastation of the nation would have comprised not a hill but a mountain range equivalent to the Himalayas!

Germany desperately needed reform in every sphere. The Allied commission charged with postwar reconstruction designed a strategy around what they termed the "4D" policies: *denazification*, *demilitarization*, *decartelization*, and *democratization*.

The reform of the sphere of education was essential, especially as it related to denazification and democratization. Germany entered the twentieth century with one of the finest educational systems in the world, but German curricula developed a creeping disease. Quack theories of eugenics seeped into the schoolroom.[3] The Nazi worldview fed the fictions and fantasies. When postwar reformers began looking at schools and curricula, they found "an acute problem of textbooks, since even in relatively unideological [sic] subjects like mathematics existing textbooks from the Hitler era were heavily impregnated with Nazi propaganda."[4]

The challenges of denazification seem remote and irrelevant to contemporary needs in education. However, there is an eerie similarity. As there was a dividing line between education in pre-Nazi Germany and the schools in the Hitler era, so, as we have seen, there is a dividing line between education in Old America—Old Western Civilization—and schools in New America—New Western Civilization. The dividing line is actually a fault line, opened up by the Globequake.

THE PRESENT WRECKAGE

Spiritually, morally, and ethically, we live in a rubble world already, and the Globequake seems only to intensify the wreckage. Syndicated columnist Mona Charen contemplated her son's entry into college. "We scrape together our hard-earned income (lots of it) to deposit our cherished offspring at schools that are determined to teach them to despise everything we revere—even learning," she wrote.[5] She cited a National Association of Scholars study showing that in 1964 fifty leading colleges it surveyed required a course in Western civilization. By 2010, however, none of them required Western civilization courses. "American students are graduating with scads of courses on zombies and queer theory—which is why we're importing an ever-larger number of our Ph.D.s," Charen added.

The Allies had to *denazify* Germany's institutions, especially their schools. We must *detoxify* contemporary education by bringing it back to its original foundations. This seems an impossibility, however. In a society abandoning its historic roots and core values, it's difficult to stabilize public education. Therefore *the primary objective must be to stabilize the students*. To do that, we must pull back, as we have in other chapters, and consider the big picture for education, the transcendent view, which comes through God's eyes only.

STABILIZE THE STRATEGIC PLAN

Vision for the Sphere of Education

God's vision for education is human beings—His image bearers—who are able to exercise their dominion over the created realm in a knowledgeable manner, through application of the principles of the kingdom of God.

"You're in charge!" Adam and Eve were wide-eyed with wonder when God gave them that assignment. The array of His colorful, fragrant, symphonic creation was all around them, and the Creator told them they were to have authority over it all. "Be fruitful and multiply; fill the earth and subdue it; have dominion over the fish of the sea, over the birds of the air, and over every living thing that moves on the earth," the Father told His image bearers (Gen. 1:28 NKJV).

Maybe it was like a dad who builds an insurance business. As a creative entrepreneur, he has had fun shaping the company that feeds his family. All along, he has his son and daughter and their future in mind. Through the years he forms them into his image. They think like him, dream his dreams, pursue his purposes. Then comes the day when he says to his now adult children: "I'm turning the company over to you. I will continue as owner, but you will run it all. Here are the keys to the store!"

His children don't have to ask what to do. They've walked and talked constantly with their father. When they were teens, they helped clean the building, file papers, and answer the phone. They watched what their dad did in running the business and were ready to take over on his behalf, leading it just like he would.

When God gave Adam and Eve their marching orders, sin hadn't yet robbed them of God's mind and heart. They thought like He did, purposed what He purposed, and couldn't wait to get started. Otherwise they might have asked—as they would later, many times: "How do we do this? How do we carry out this dominion-command?"

Evil made us all dunces. God doesn't take back His calling and the gifts He supplies us to carry it out (Rom. 11:29), but in our fallen state we implement the dominion-mission like a highly trained business professional with a master of business administration degree who has forgotten all he or she has learned.

God's vision for education is to bring us back up to speed, to infuse in us the knowledge of truth that was inherent in His image bearers before the fall. Think of how God "educates" His kids—us, the human race. He starts with the basic stuff—the Law, the fundamental principles of how the universe works. The process takes not eight or twelve years, but centuries in human time. Theologians call this educational process "progressive revelation."

When, in God's plan, the basic curriculum has been assimilated, He takes humanity to the PhD level. The Logos—the Truth about everything—comes into the world in the form of a human. He looks like us, talks like us, walks like us, thinks like us, emotes like us, but with a huge difference: He is sinless; therefore He hasn't been stripped of the omniscience—the all-knowing—of the Father. He is our Teacher—our Rabbi—as well as our Savior. He is our Lord, and the way we allow Him to master us will form the way we carry out our authority. *Whatever has dominion over a human being will determine how he or she exercises dominion.*

Education is about theory and ideas and heady concepts, but in the end it's about doing the stuff. God made for us a world that has in it everything we need for a high quality of life. The Father knows the delights of creativity, and He wants His children to have those "Wow!" moments when He looked at everything He had made and it was very good. He wants us to play with the crayons and handle the scissors and make something beautiful too. Sin twisted our fingers, warped our understanding, and took away truth, but God wants to develop us and equip us for quality living.

God has given us the gift of education to "train us to reign,"[6] to exercise dominion over creation properly. We need qualitative education; otherwise we will use our dominion-mission as an excuse for exploiting the planet. Qualitative education focuses us on God's transcendent authority and on what it means to be a human, created in His image and conformed to His character. But education is also to provide us quantitative knowledge, the intricate how-tos of the application of truth.

Above all, we are to be trained to know Him and behave like Him. That guarantees that the world will be safe under our dominion and, at the same time, provide us a high quality of physical and material life.

There can be no higher vision for the sphere of education!

Values for the Sphere of Education

1. God's kingdom as the order by which the world functions at its best and which provides the highest quality of life for His image bearers within the natural domain

2. Human beings as God's image bearers who have the privilege and high calling of implementing the principles of God's kingdom in the world for the good of the nations and their own lives within them

3. Knowledge, intellectual comprehension of truth, as essential for the mission given God's image bearers within creation

4. The application of knowledge, which is the uniting of orthodoxy with orthopraxy, recognizing that the educational process is not complete if intellectual comprehension does not lead to positive, productive action

The Kingdom Mission for the Sphere of Education

The kingdom mission for education is to equip individuals to exercise their God-given dominion over the created realm by training them in the principles of God's kingdom and their application in every discipline of learning.

Many years ago I worked the graveyard shift for a major airline. I was a ramp agent, one of the workers who climbed up into the belly-bin of huge aircraft and unloaded and loaded baggage, mail, and freight. One of my duties on the all-night stint was fueling the fuel truck for the aircraft.

I still remember the first night on that job. A massive DC-8 jet (the biggest I had ever seen by 1966) landed about midnight, and we had it airborne about forty minutes later. Then it was time to gas up the fuel truck. "It's time to go to school!" barked the shift supervisor. He took me to the big truck. First we walked around it. My boss showed me every valve and switch. He pointed out the grounding wire and showed me the metal post embedded at each gate where the wire would be attached so that sudden lightning or electrical buildup wouldn't ignite the fuel. Then we crawled up in the cab, and he continued my education.

In the wee hours of the next morning, it was time for me to go solo. I drove the hefty truck to the fuel farm, where highly flammable jet fuel was stored. I eased under the huge nozzle that would flood the truck's tank with gas. I got out and walked around the vehicle, going through all the principles and procedures I had been taught. Then I climbed atop the truck's tank, opened the port, inserted the nozzle, and pulled the lever, causing fuel to surge into the tank. At one point I realized I was standing on a small ocean of explosive power. I was grateful for my schooling because if I made a wrong move, I could blow up myself and a good part of the airport!

That's the danger humanity faces constantly. "God said, 'Behold, I have given you every plant yielding seed that is on the surface of all the earth, and every tree which has fruit yielding seed; it shall be food for you; and to every beast of the earth and to every bird of the sky and to every thing that moves on the earth which has life, *I have given* every green plant for food'; and it was so" (Gen. 1:29–30, italics added).

All we have in the world He has given us, every resource to meet every need. However, we must know how to use responsibly and ethically the powerful things God has given us lest we destroy ourselves and everything around us. He gave us the atom. How shall we use it? He gave us fire. How shall we use it? He gave us chemicals. How shall we use them? Education must help us answer these questions.

Dominion is not a license for waste and excess. It is not a green light for taking earth's resources for granted and depleting them in great gorges of consumption. Dominion under the Lord is a recognition that resources are *given*. We are to receive them with gratitude and humility. If we want a culture that cares for natural resources, education must train the generations in the worldview that leads to reverence, respect, and appreciation. Caring conservation will be the result. The more spiritually and kingdom-minded we are, the more we exercise responsible stewardship for material resources.

STABILIZE THE ROLES

Parents

Stability is the delicate equilibrium between counterbalancing forces. Think of the wings of an airplane holding it aloft, but also restraining its tendency to yaw wildly out of control.

As we saw in the last chapter, parents are to play the key authoritative role in their children's education. Again, power is the fundamental temptation. Parents in control can quickly become controlling parents who stifle the child's freedom and development. Thus, the Bible establishes the equilibrium that makes the relationship between parent and children positive and constructive.

On the one hand, there is the command, "Honor your father and your mother, that your days may be prolonged in the land which the LORD your God gives you" (Ex. 20:12). Paul noted that this is the "first commandment with a promise" (Eph. 6:2). The guarantee attached to the commandment is that people who honor their parents are enhanced in their life "in the land." There is a direct connection between honoring parents and enjoying the quality of life. On the other hand, parents, especially fathers, are commanded, "Do not provoke your children to anger, but bring them up in the discipline and instruction of the Lord" (Eph. 6:4).

Thus, while the parent is in the driver's seat with respect to the child's education, the parent is not to be a tyrant. As the child matures, she is to recognize the importance of honoring her parents, and the parents are to recognize her bent and support educational choices that will help the child grow in its direction.

In fact, research has shown that involvement of parents in their children's school education, "in almost any form, produces measurable gains in student achievement."[7] Most educators desire such engagement. Parental involvement is a force for stabilization in education. They are the stewards of their children's educational development, especially in elementary and junior high years. Parents have the highest degree of accountability regarding the academic progress of their children.

Educational Professionals

If parents are the stewards of a child's education, educational professionals are servants. Neither parents nor educators have ground for arrogance. If parental oversight in the kingdom of God means holding a stewardship for which a person is accountable, career teachers and administrators work for the parents in a cooperative arrangement. Such a relationship helps bring stability to the child's schooling, even if the school has gone wild.

Many educational professionals are in the school business

because they have a strong sense of calling and spiritual gifts that propel them into running schools or teaching in classrooms. They are God's ambassadors in the sphere of education, and they know it!

Linda Morris (not her real name) was principal of a school in a semirural community. Linda owned farmland and hired itinerant workers to help her tend and harvest crops. An itinerant family lived awhile in a small house on the property. When the principal met the family, she noted they had a small boy, who appeared to be about eight years old. Linda was amazed and concerned when she discovered the child was actually thirteen. He was spindly and filthy and had never been to school.

However, as Linda, the educational professional, began to work with the boy's parents, they agreed to enroll him at her school. Rather than move after the harvest, the farm-worker family settled down. Their child was able to spend several years in special education programs aimed at bringing him up to speed in reading and other essential skills. The proudest day in the young man's life dawned when he was able to write his own name.

The principal modeled Jesus' concept of leadership and authority when He said,

> You know that the rulers of the Gentiles lord it over them, and their great men exercise authority over them. It is not this way among you, but whoever wishes to become great among you shall be your servant, and whoever wishes to be first among you shall be your slave; just as the Son of Man did not come to be served, but to serve, and to give His life a ransom for many. (Matt. 20:25–28)

Students

Contrary to some educational theories, the student is not the master or mistress of his or her education. But neither is the child a pawn shoved around an educational chessboard by parents and teachers.

When it comes to the formation of the child, including his or her education, parents are to "train up a child" in the way *he* or *she* should go, not necessarily according to the expectations or demands of the parents. This is the obligation of parents to recognize the bent of the child, as we noted earlier.

There are three tiers in the educational process by which this training up is done, each identified by a particular question posed theoretically to the student:

1. What does God, who is absolute, transcendent reality, want you to know?

    Even secularized, humanized, relativized public education acknowledges absolute, transcendent reality. Mess with answers on an exam testing your knowledge of the laws of physics or principles of geometry, and you will find out in a hurry your teacher won't let you relativize those facts. You can create your own clever answers, preferred responses, and opinion-based elaborations. They can be witty, entertaining, and inventive, but the F on your paper means there are absolutes that transcend your notions and theories!

2. What do we educators want you to know?

    Educators and the curricula they teach must help the student understand the world in which he or she lives and the times and culture through which that child walks. Good education recognizes the importance of equipping students to know the past to live in the present to provide for the future.

    Most students recognize there are times when what their teachers want them to know may not jibe with what they've been taught at home or think personally. "I'm just learning this stuff so I can get it right on the test, but it's not what I think," a pupil might say. Nevertheless there's an agenda set by educational professionals centered on what they want students to know, true or untrue. Students must be open to be stretched by the educational agenda and know to throw out the bad and keep the good.

3. What do *you* want to know?

At last the student's role becomes that of manager of his or own academic program. To place this responsibility on kindergarten or elementary children is too heavy a load. But after going through the first two tiers, a student is now able to call the shots. Majors are declared, skills for development are chosen, and grades even go up because the student is in his or her zone of highest interest.

I watched our children and grandchildren go through these three tiers. One told me she wanted to be "the female C. S. Lewis." She struggled with math and science grades but was eager to dive into her English major. Finally the day came, and she made a declaration that would have sent the average student into a daze: "Paw Paw, I get to read *Beowulf* again!" She had reached the third tier, and not only did her grades zoom up, but she was selected for a summer of graduate studies at Cambridge University.

STABILIZE STUDENTS

Teach true north.

True north is based on the actual geographical location of the North Pole and is a constant. Magnetic north shifts because it is centered on the earth's magnetic field, arising from its metallic core, which is molten, seething with heat and its effects. There can be as much as a five-hundred-mile difference between true north and magnetic north. Maps are aligned with true north, but compasses rely on magnetic north. Declination tables have to be worked out so that travelers don't miss their destinations.

Hardly anything better illustrates the challenge and confusion faced by students in public education. If they have godly parents, they are being taught true north values and ethics. But when they get to school, magnetic north is the only directional focus. Since public education separates itself from the authority of the Bible, there is no declination because, as far as secular educational philosophy is concerned, there is no true north that is absolute and constant.

Larry Elliott, economics editor for the *Guardian*, a British newspaper, may not put it in the terms we've used here, but he believes people need to discover true north. "America in 2011 is Rome in 200 AD, or Britain on the eve of the first world war," Elliott wrote. America, he said, is "an empire at the zenith of its power but with cracks beginning to show." Rome's and Britain's historic experience "suggests that it's hard to stop the rot once it has set in." Elliott's recommendation for America is that the nation "*must rediscover the qualities that originally made it great.*" He added, "That will not be easy."[8]

The declination has been great. For America to find its true north will be difficult. Education has a major role to play in helping the nation get back on track.

What, then, is the true north that must set the course of education? It is this: *the fear of the Lord is the beginning of wisdom.* The "fear of the Lord" refers to revering the Lord. It means to stand in awe of someone. What we revere, we respect. Sadly, reverence today is reserved primarily for people and ideas on the horizontal or immanent level. When we lose reverence for the transcendent, absolute God, we no longer respect what He has made, beginning with human life and the wonders of knowledge and truth.

Students who know true north aren't fooled when the compass spins with the shifts of magnetic north. They know that when someone says, "But everybody's doing it," this is a misleading declination from true north. Solid, stable students trained to set their compasses also understand that bandwagons always follow magnetic north, and they have the good sense not to hop on.

The Globequake may set the tectonic plates in a spin and the compass in a whirl, but young men and women who learn that the fear of the Lord is the beginning of wisdom always know the right direction!

ORTHODOXY TO ORTHOPRAXY: IMPLEMENTING THE PLAN

"This is totally unrealistic, unworkable, and idealistic." That's the response some might give to the suggestions I've made here for stabilizing education.

The critics would be absolutely right if they are thinking only of the public education system. We may have limited ability to implement such changes *inside* public schools, so we must focus on what we can do *outside* to help students who must go inside. It may not be possible to stabilize schools, but we can stabilize children's educational experiences. If we do that, the recommendations in this chapter are workable and effective.

Are the recommendations too idealistic? To answer this, we must think about the difference between ideals and idealism. Idealism is living in denial, trying to construct solid reality on the basis of wished-for fantasies and phantom-like dreams. Idealism is utopian and leads institutions and cultures into the illusion of progress and security. The Globequake knocks down the empires of idealism with the ease of a wrecking ball toppling a matchstick house.

Ideals, however, are essential for living in a world of spiritual and moral gravity and entropy. In a fallen world, the default drag is always downward. Take away the ideals of sound law and see how quickly things descend from a high ethical state to a lower. The speed of descent accelerates; and entropy, the slide into disorder, dissipates the energy of societies, cultures, and their institutions. Decay, deterioration, and death ensue. In a reverse alchemy, the golden age of civilizations turns into lead and finally disappears beneath the mounds of historic refuse, like Leipzig's Fockeberg.

Ideals are the booster rockets that enable cultures to resist orbital decay. Ideals provide lift. In our fallen world it's urgent that there be people who call their societies to higher levels. This is an important function of biblically based, kingdom-minded people working in education and all the spheres.

There are several ways the ideals of God-fearing, God-centered education can be advanced. Some parents opt for homeschooling. Homeschool parents sometimes create or participate in cooperative ventures where children are taught specialty topics, like foreign languages, or participate in competitive sports with other homeschoolers. Many dads and moms choose a public school educational process for their children but combine it with special teaching times at home to answer questions and provide a biblical counterbalance to what their children have been taught in a public school. There are partnerships between parents and their churches, in which a local church offers special courses on history, science, culture, and other topics taught from the perspective of the biblical worldview.

Much contemporary education, under the guise of being open and tolerant, is actually producing narrow people, locked into the tight boxes of political correctness. Education as God would have it encourages students to examine all the claimants to truth and sort out the genuine from the false through application of true north, absolute, unchanging, ultimate Reality.

No matter how hard the Globequake shakes, such well-grounded students don't cave in or lose the way!

THE SPHERE
OF GOVERNMENT

CHAPTER 14

THE CRACKED DOME

Making government trustworthy

The United States Capitol building was bombed on March 1, 1971. I was on temporary assignment at the Department of Justice. My boss, the assistant attorney general for internal security, summoned a group of us to his office. His normally stoic face was taut with worry.

For weeks word had been circulating that the most massive antigovernment demonstrations in history would take place that coming May. Was the March bombing the launch of a coordinated effort to strike at Washington's institutions? Planners of the May Day demonstrations vowed they would shut down the government. Were they going to bring down the Capitol building—literally?

The domed edifice wasn't destroyed, and the government wasn't shut down, though the May Day demonstrations of 1971 were massive. But for a few worrisome hours in our office and many others in Washington on March 1, 1971, we were not sure what would happen.

Many on extreme left and right wings of the political spectrum might rejoice at the shattering of government. Actually, however, in a fallen world, government is essential to restrain chaos. Sadly, governments and their regimes often create more chaos than they restrain.

Government affects us in two ways. Years ago I traveled in unstable parts of the world. One trip was especially difficult. I remember stepping out at the top of the stairway of the huge jet that had carried me to the desperate nation and felt the very atmosphere atremble. Angry soldiers herded my fellow passengers and me into a stark room where passport agents glared at us as they studied our documents.

Out in the streets it seemed a riot could be ignited as quickly as dry prairie grass. Driving into the city, we passed my country's embassy. My nation's flag stood gallant in the wind. Soldiers from my country's services stood guard. My government's presence signaled there was a place of refuge and safety in the event things went crazy in the country I was visiting. I thanked God for the government I have often criticized.

I have also seen and felt the other way governments affect us. Georgi Vins, one of the most courageous Russian dissidents during the Communist era in that nation, stayed for a few days in our home just months after his release from prison. Vins had spent many years in the Soviet gulag, the unbelievably terrible prison system where people were held until they died or lost their minds.

Vins did neither. He kept speaking for Christ. He was even accused and put on trial for writing the twenty-third Psalm! He had made copies to pass to believers, and biblically illiterate KGB officers had concluded he was the author. Vins and his family knew what it was like for government agents to watch and listen to them. My government was there to protect me and guarantee my freedoms, but his government was there to silence, imprison, and, if necessary, kill him.

Government, in the sense of one human ruling over another, was not in God's ideal and intentional plan for His creation. He made His image bearers to live in such an intimate relationship with Him that they would need no law to set them right and keep them honest. Irene and I have been married more than fifty years. I honestly don't remember what I vowed that day at the altar in 1961. Our marriage is not a contract, enforced by law, but a covenant strong in the bond of love.

Love requires freedom. We have to be able to choose. So God put *two* trees in the garden of Eden. Some complain that things would have been a lot easier and history much smoother if there had been only one—that luscious, fragrant, blossoming Tree of Life. Why would God monkey with us by putting *two* appealing trees before our eyes and telling us we could eat from only one of them? If God is absolute, His love is absolute, and the choices He gives us must be absolute. Absolute good or absolute evil—there is no middle ground. That way when we choose Him it's because we choose the way of love.

When the serpent lured Adam and Eve to the wrong tree and they chomped on the wrong fruit, the world experienced its first Globequake. Something evil came that way, something wretched— anti-God, antilife, antilove. The world that had once hovered in the glorious continuum of the kingdom of heaven was suddenly brought down by spiritual gravitational forces. Evil accelerated, entropy took over, and the whole universe fell into "slavery to corruption," as Paul wrote (Rom. 8:21). If something didn't restrain the free fall soon, everything would thud into hell.

God looked at the scene and gave a detailed description of what would now happen because of their disastrous choice:

> To the woman He said,
> "I will greatly multiply
> Your pain in childbirth,
> In pain you will bring forth children;
> Yet your desire will be for your husband,
> And he will rule over you."

Then to Adam He said, "Because you have listened to the

voice of your wife, and have eaten from the tree about which
I commanded you, saying, 'You shall not eat from it';

> Cursed is the ground because of you;
> In toil you will eat of it
> All the days of your life.
> Both thorns and thistles it shall grow for you;
> And you will eat the plants of the field;
> By the sweat of your face
> You will eat bread,
> Till you return to the ground,
> Because from it you were taken;
> For you are dust,
> And to dust you shall return."
> (Gen. 3:16–19)

One human being ruling over another was a new wrinkle in
what was once Paradise.

As the centuries passed, God revealed Himself progressively to
humanity. As He did, He showed the nations how to govern as He
governs, not with cruel power but with gracious authority. In fact,
He would give the gift of authority to those who will receive it:

> Every person is to be in subjection to the governing authorities.
> For there is no authority except from God, and those which exist
> are established by God. Therefore whoever resists authority has
> opposed the ordinance of God; and they who have opposed will
> receive condemnation upon themselves. For rulers are not a cause
> of fear for good behavior, but for evil. Do you want to have no
> fear of authority? Do what is good and you will have praise from
> the same; for it is a minister of God to you for good. But if you do
> what is evil, be afraid; for it does not bear the sword for nothing;
> for it is a minister of God, an avenger who brings wrath on the

one who practices evil. Therefore it is necessary to be in subjection, not only because of wrath, but also for conscience' sake. For because of this you also pay taxes, for rulers are servants of God, devoting themselves to this very thing. Render to all what is due them: tax to whom tax is due; custom to whom custom; fear to whom fear; honor to whom honor. (Rom. 13:1–7)

This passage reveals the nature of God's design for the sphere of government. It shows us characteristics of government that is stable, trustworthy, and a servant to society rather than an oppressor.

CHARACTERISTICS OF STABLE, TRUSTWORTHY GOVERNMENT

Stable, Trustworthy Government Functions Through God-given Authority, not Raw Power

As we have seen in previous chapters, there are glaring differences between real authority and raw power. Everyone who has charge of someone else, whether a parent in the home, a teacher or an administrator at school, a manager, a foreman or a boss at work, or a government magistrate, must know the distinctions and choose authority over power. Let's review major differences:

Real authority is granted from the higher to the lower, but raw power is seized. Jesus came into the world as the very embodiment of real authority. "All authority has been *given* Me," He said (Matt. 28:18 NASB). The most secure and trustworthy governments and regimes are those that recognize they are established and rule "under God."

Only people under real authority can be trusted with real authority, but anyone with enough muscle can wield the sword of raw power. A God-fearing Roman centurion asked Jesus to heal his servant. Jesus offered to go to the soldier's home, but the Roman officer replied, "Lord, I am not worthy for You to come under my roof, but just say the word, and my servant will be healed. For I also am a man under authority, with soldiers under me; and I say to this one, 'Go!' and he goes, and to another, 'Come!' and he comes, and to my slave, 'Do this!' and he does it" (Matt. 8:8–9).

The centurion understood how real authority works. Because he was under the authority of Rome, the military officer could command the resources of Rome. Therefore, he rightly concluded, if Jesus is under the authority of God, Jesus can command the resources of the kingdom of heaven, which includes healing power. No wonder Jesus complimented the Roman's perception and faith!

Real authority leads through respect and relationship, but raw power controls through force. Dudley Hall, a Bible teacher and author, lists four techniques by which raw power gets people to do what it wants: manipulation, intimidation, condemnation, and domination. People trying to control others by using raw power must trick them, threaten them, load them with guilt, and/or overwhelm them with sheer muscle power. Leaders with real authority let others see them modeling actions that need to be taken. They build relationships with their followers, as Jesus did. Such leaders don't have to cajole people into following because individuals have a desire to walk anywhere behind leaders with real authority.

Real authority resists the downward pull into authoritarianism, but raw power plunges eagerly and willingly into cold cruelty. An authoritarian compels obedience to his or her dictates, even though it restricts the freedom of others. People with real authority recognize their limitations and flaws and are alert to the danger of the subtle shift into authoritarianism. Those relying on raw power have no constraints and believe they have no flaws or limitations. They regard themselves as supreme and superior to all others.

Real authority is exercised through servanthood, but raw power exalts itself as the recipient of the servitude of others. The most authoritative person ever to walk the planet said, "The Son of man didn't come into the world to be served, but to serve and to lay down His life as a ransom for many" (Mark 10:45, paraphrase).

Stable, Trustworthy Government Instills
"Fear" in Those Who Do Evil

There is a direct correlation between what people revere and worship and the way they impact others. The fearless person in the worst sense of the term is a reckless individual. There are multitudes in every society who have no fear of God, and therefore, the sphere of government must lead them to fear the consequences of violating its just laws.

God's discipline of His covenant people is always corrective, aimed at their rehabilitation. Society attempts to base incarceration of criminals on rehabilitation. However, when the justice and penal systems sever themselves from God's authority, rehabilitative schemes become mere indulgence to be manipulated by savvy inmates.

"Two-thirds of inmates will be re-arrested within three years of their release," noted Mark Earley, president of Prison Fellowship. His organization, founded by Chuck Colson, introduced the InnerChange Freedom Initiative, a faith-based prerelease program that inmates enter a year before their sentences are completed. Among other things, the men and women learn biblical values, including the importance of reverence and respect. A University of Pennsylvania study showed that the recidivism rate for inmates completing the program was only 8 to 17 percent.[1]

Stable, Trustworthy Government Reassures and Gives
Security to Those Who Do What Is Good

Good, in the Greek of Romans 13:3, refers to contributing, benefiting, and providing profit to others. The sphere of government is to encourage the good that builds up the nation through high standards of civility and ethics. This means those who occupy elected and appointive offices in government are to be exemplary people who inspire others.

In 1776, George Washington sent a letter to his officers and said,

> The General is sorry to be informed that the foolish, and wicked practice, of profane cursing and swearing (a Vice heretofore

little known in an American Army) is growing into fashion; he hopes the officers will, by example, as well as influence, endeavour to check it, and that both they, and the men will reflect, that we can have little hopes of the blessing of Heaven on our Arms, if we insult it by our impiety, and folly; added to this, it is a vice so mean and low, without any temptation, that every man of sense, and character, detests and despises it.[2]

To understand how far the sphere of government has fallen in America from its biblical charge to encourage good and George Washington's ideal, consider modern history. Sadly, the decline is bipartisan. President Richard Nixon's voice, thanks to the Oval Office taping system, echoes across history encouraging his subordinates to lie with regard to the Watergate scandal in language straight out of hell. And don't forget Bill Clinton's abuse of the Oval Office through obscene behavior with Monica Lewinsky and who knows who else. When Vice President Joe Biden, standing near an open mike during President Obama's signing of the healthcare reform bill, described the moment with an expletive, no one who knew him was surprised. "Joe Biden's Potty Mouth: In Delaware, This Is Not News," declared one headline, referring to Biden's home state constituency.[3]

Stable, Trustworthy Government Serves as a Minister of God in Enforcing Law, Implementing Justice, and Avenging Evil

Frontier justice prevailed in the old American West before territories were fully incorporated into the United States. Judge Roy Bean was the law west of the Pecos. He and others wielded a tough and fast jurisprudence system long on hangings and short on due process. Many of the "lawyers" and "judges" read a smattering of law, declared themselves legal authorities, and hung out their shingles.

Centuries earlier, the Bible had a much higher view. The legal magistrate, charged with applying and enforcing the law, was actually a minister of God! The Greek word translated "minister" is *diakonos* (deacon). This means a government officer designated with enforcement of the law is to carry out his or her assignment with a sense of calling from God and the accountability that goes with it. This applies to police, judges, government attorneys, and all people in an official capacity related to enforcing the law.

Jim Squier, a friend of mine who spent more than two decades as a judge in family court, awoke to the fact he was a minister of God within the legal system. The most significant event in his life, for his clients as well as himself, was when Jim made a serious commitment to Christ. No longer did he see just a wearisome court docket, but he began to look at the cases coming before him in the role of designated servant of God in the courtroom. Jim's desire as God's minister was not to move the docket as rapidly as possible by granting quickie divorces. Rather, he wanted to help couples preserve their marriages, if possible. He prayed over the situations coming before him and sought biblical principles. Jim's commitment to Christ and His kingdom changed the way he did law. He was not merely a judge but a minister of God.

Citizens Are to Submit to Such Government and Honor It and Pay Taxes

With respect to taxes, Jesus said, "Render to Caesar the things that are Caesar's; and to God the things that are God's" (Matt. 22:21). Paul wrote, "Render to all what is due them: tax to whom tax is due; custom to whom custom; fear to whom fear; honor to whom honor" (Rom. 13:7).

That's the responsibility of the citizen. But the Bible, as always, presents a balanced worldview. When biblical principles form tax policy, government's revenue gathering is fair, just, nonmanipulative, and nonoppressive. Conversely, when policy makers ignore the Bible's truth, taxation is unfair, unjust, aimed at engineering society according to an agenda, and oppressive.

For example, in a report for the Claremont Institute, Edward J. Erler wrote,

The passage of the Sixteenth Amendment in 1913 was part of a larger decision by America's political and intellectual elites to make sweeping and fundamental changes in America. These changes were calculated to transform the limited constitutional government of the Framers into what is today called the welfare state. The principal goal of the welfare state is not the protection of the individual rights and liberties of citizens, but the promotion of "social justice" that is alien to the principles of the American founding. What is more, proponents of the welfare state believe that individual liberty (i.e., equal opportunity and property rights) is incompatible with social justice.[4]

If citizens must pay taxes according to biblical principles, government must construct tax policy aligned with the scriptural worldview. For example, hardly anything weakens a nation more than its debt. The Bible teaches no person should saddle his or her future through debt, and no government should tax its citizens' future through debt. This is the principle from Deuteronomy 15:1–6:

> At the end of every seventh year you must cancel the debt of everyone who owes you money. This is how it must be done. Everyone must cancel the loans they have made to their fellow Israelites. They must not demand payment from their neighbors or relatives, for the LORD's time of release has arrived. This release from debt, however, applies only to your fellow Israelites—not to the foreigners living among you.
>
> There should be no poor among you, for the LORD your God will greatly bless you in the land he is giving you as a special possession. You will receive this blessing if you are careful to obey all the commands of the LORD your God that I am giving you today. The LORD your God will bless you as he has promised. You will lend money to many nations but will never need to borrow. You will rule many nations, but they will not rule over you. (NLT)

The United States and many other nations are in a fiscal Globequake as I write. Much of the upheaval has happened because of burgeoning national debt. Those who think about it at all realize their children and grandchildren will be burdened with the current generation's debt, as well as that generated in their lifetimes. It will affect their future tax rates and the health of the economy they inherit. There seems no end to it!

But what if government budgets and the tax levels necessary to support them had to be formulated against a statute based on Deuteronomy 15? What if policy makers had to shape fiscal legislation against the backdrop of a law stipulating *all* debt had to be canceled every seven years, starting with the date on which an American president signed the bill into law?

The Globequake's impact on nations' financial and economic policies has greatly weakened them and the governments that administer national affairs. But there would be a return to strength and solvency if biblical principles were applied in fiscal policy, including taxation.

Stable, Trustworthy Government Knows Its Place

The smoke from the American Revolution had hardly cleared before another fire, which had been long simmering, erupted into a conflagration threatening the young nation's unity. The Federalists and anti-Federalists struggled to conform the country to their respective images. Their disagreements were intense and shattered partnerships and friendships that had held tight during the War for Independence.

The battle rages today. The Tea Party movement and others have risen to resist what they see as unleashed federalism. Many are alarmed as they see the central government forgetting its place and barging into the private sector as well as into matters constitutionally reserved for state government. The fracture is one of the many fault lines lacing through the contemporary United States and has contributed to national destabilization.

The answer lies in the ancient vision we saw in chapter 5 when we peered into the vision of Zechariah, recorded in Zechariah 4. The prophet had seen two olive trees, with a lampstand, or menorah, in the center. One tree, as we noted, signified Joshua, the high priest of that period, and the other, Zerubbabel, the civil ruler. This ancient vision tells us much about what the sphere of government ought to look like. To understand that, we will build on some of the principles listed in chapter 5.

Zechariah's vision is a God-given glimpse of how to order human society in a fallen world. God—the lampstand—is at the center. Church and state are ordered in their positions vis-à-vis each other in relation to God's centrality. Let's review what we learned in our previous look at Zechariah 4 that helps us understand how to secure the sphere of government now and guarantee its trustworthiness:

Both the spiritual leader and the civil ruler are ministers of God. We saw this amplified in Romans 13. The church and the state in a free society arise from the same roots, the biblical worldview that makes democracy, human dignity, human rights, a system of prosperity, and all the other privileges of a nation of liberty possible.

The church is not to cross over into the position of the state. "Sudan has no identity, no direction," without Islam, said Hassan al-Turabi as that nation in the 1990s nose-dived into a shattering civil war that wouldn't approach resolution until the twenty-first century.[5] For the Islamic Sudan, as well as for Iran and other Muslim nations, the religious institution in many ways has become the state.

The improper crossing over also occurred in Christianity after AD 843 and the division of Europe into territorial units, when "only the church, and in particular the papacy, survived as a symbol of the common universal culture of Europe, and, during the remainder of the Middle Ages, conflicting political impulses toward nationalism and internationalism found expression most often in the religious context of the struggles between popes and kings."[6]

The state is not to cross over into the position of the church. Dietrich

Bonhoeffer and the German Confessing Church resisted Hitler's efforts to impose the state as the ultimate authority with respect to spiritual values and belief.

Hitler told two German bishops, "Christianity will disappear from Germany just as it has from Russia. The German race existed without Christianity for thousands of years before Christ and will continue to exist after Christianity has disappeared."[7]

Hitler's dream of a one-thousand-year Reich was outpaced by Marxism's seventy-five-year reign over the Soviet empire. Marxism was even more successful than Hitler in attempting to position the state in the role of church. And it wasn't just in the Soviet Union. Mao Tse-tung, Communist ruler of China, said, "Today two big mountains lie like a dead weight on the Chinese people. One is imperialism, the other is feudalism. The Chinese Communist Party has long made up its mind to dig them up. We must persevere and work unceasingly, and we will touch god's heart. Our god is none other than the masses of the Chinese people."[8]

Mao's statement, of course, was typical Leninist misdirection. Mao tagged the people as "god," but the state suppressed and controlled the people. Therefore, the state was both deity and church.

The Globequake, by the standards we've seen here, has had a devastating impact on the sphere of government in the United States and virtually all the nations. It has upset the delicate balances between spheres, battered down gates, and brought an avalanche of corruption.

"What can the righteous do" to make government secure and trustworthy? We will explore answers to this question in the next chapter.

CHAPTER 15

STRATEGIC EQUILIBRIUM
Balancing government and governance

Tom Fox may have been among the most stabilizing influences in Lyndon Johnson's life during a grueling period in a tough presidency. If so, Fox is a prime example of how the sphere of government can be steadied, made dependable and secure.

Tom Fox was Johnson's barber.

When I first met Tom in the early 1970s, he had already been trimming the hair growing on the mighty heads of US senators for years as a Senate barber. Senator Lyndon Baines Johnson of Texas had sat often in Tom's chair in the Capitol complex. The two men had become good friends and swapped many a story.

Tom became a serious, committed follower of Jesus Christ. His personality was rigged for gab and good humor. Increasingly Tom was talking about Jesus Christ and the difference He was making in Tom's life. The political giants who were Tom's customers constituted a captive audience when they yielded themselves to his scissors, razors, and electric clippers. They didn't mind—everybody loved Tom.

In the toughest time of his presidency, Lyndon Johnson remembered Tom and reached out to him. The president was famous in Washington for his rugged demeanor and pungent talk. If you've ever toured the region where LBJ grew up along Texas's Pedernales River, you understand. Johnson was formed in the crusty world of cowboy lore. When he played, he played to win, no holds barred.

But in the late 1960s, as Vietnam's quicksand pulled him down to chin level and America's major cities burned, the cowboy slowly realized he was on a bronco that wouldn't be tamed. LBJ the unshakeable was in danger of being hurled off the bucking beast and maybe thrown under its wildly stomping hooves. The tough façade was sometimes creased with little streams of tears, like rare rainwater in a desert arroyo.

President Johnson was at the epicenter of a Globequake, and he reached out to his barber. Some weekends Tom would get a phone call from the White House. Lyndon Johnson would be on the line, telling Tom he wanted to go to church on Sunday. Tom would ride in the presidential limousine, sitting in the back with the president like a visiting potentate.

Sometimes Tom would see tears ebbing from LBJ's eyes as they sat in church. Tom and the president would pray together and talk about the Scriptures. It should not surprise us that Tom Fox was a key person in helping the president find stability. Tom was an ambassador of the kingdom of God, stationed in Washington, DC. In the order of that kingdom,

> God chose things the world considers foolish in order to shame those who think they are wise. And he chose things that are powerless to shame those who are powerful. God chose things despised by the world, things counted as nothing at all, and used them to bring to nothing what the world considers important. As a result, no one can ever boast in the presence of God. (1 Cor. 1:27–29 NLT)

God chose a barber to be a pastor and counselor to the president of the United States!

Power moves strong men and women off their foundations—even stubborn, resistant politicos like LBJ. It causes them to do chaotic and crazy things that harm the people in the nations they govern. The issue of stable government is that of dependability and security for the citizens and the societies they comprise.

"Can we count on our government?" many people ask in the turbulence of the Globequake times. "Can I trust the politicians who govern us?" "Can we rely on our government to protect us, to manage our resources and the tax money they take from us?" The deeper questions are these:

- Are those who lead us people of their word?
- Do the men and woman at the top have genuine integrity?
- What about the people behind the scenes, who create the policies, engineer the budgets, and write the speeches of the ruling elites? Are they individuals of trustworthy character, or are they pursuing self-generated agendas at the expense of the nation?
- Do our political leaders have the judgment and good sense to make sound decisions based on principle?

To return to a point made earlier: *whatever has dominion over the person determines how that person exercises dominion.* Those who occupy the offices of government must understand governance. *Government* refers to the institutions of governing and the regimes, or particular groups, that run them. *Governance* refers to the tasks of governing. Governance starts with one's personal behavior, his or her self-control.

Government without governance is a disaster. As I write, headlines are teasing people with juicy morsels concerning almost a dozen sex scandals involving government officials. As I read about them, my mind went back to a man whom Lyndon Johnson knew well and who irritated the Nixon White House like a pesky wasp.

Wilbur Mills was a member of Congress from a tiny Arkansas district, but he had the nation's purse strings wrapped around his clenched fingers. Mills wouldn't let even his own party forget the path to the pork barrel was through his office, and he seemed to take perverse delight in tormenting the opposition's fiscal policy. Wilbur Mills sat on top of the hill in Washington and could make presidents come to him as beggars.

Then one night Mills got toppled from the hill. It was neither his fellow Democrats whom Mills had angered nor Republicans he had tormented who brought Mills down. Wilbur Mills had no one to blame but himself. Mills reputedly enjoyed a drink or two—or more—and a good time. And he delighted in the company of a certain Washington showgirl. Late that evening a policeman pulled over Mills's car. The exotic dancer in the automobile with Mills hopped out and dived into the Potomac's tidal basin. Her behavior produced headlines the next morning. She may have had a merry swim, but her much-reported romp with Mills nearly drowned his political career.

When the mighty fall, it is often because, as Wilbur Mills and scores of other power figures across history show, they live in such delusion that they don't understand what the real world looks like. They become blind to their own lack of self-governance and the way it disqualifies them to sit in the seats of government. When they fall, whole nations are destabilized.

GOVERNMENTS AND DESTRUCTIVE BEHAVIORS

How do regimes within the sphere of government fall into destructive behaviors? There are at least six causes:

Governments are destabilized and become untrustworthy when they rely on power rather than authority.

Tyrants are always paranoid. They know when their muscles

shrivel and growls fade, the mobs surrounding the palace will shatter through. The Philippines were brutalized in World War II. Even before the war, however, the nation had suffered under foreign rulers, from the well-intentioned ones to the unrepentant exploiters. Following the war, however, Filipinos were able to elect their own leaders. Agnes Newton Keith, who lived in Southeast Asia, wrote *Bare Feet in the Palace* and described what it was like when the people at last were able to vote:

> There are fingerprints now on the palace walls, spoil marks on curtains. Rich carpets are growing thin. Souvenirs were taken, garden flowers were picked, and green grass is trampled on. For 200 years this palace has flourished while the people have grown thin. Today the people gather strength from the palace. Here they may come barefoot or well shod, ignorant or brilliant, poor or rich, bad or good, old or young. Now the palace grows slightly less polished and elegant while the people grow strong in the pride that this is their country, their government, their palace. Here they belong.[1]

Dictators and oppressive elites are always nervous because they know all those "barefoot" people are out there. The governments set up by tyrannical regimes are as unstable as the thugs who run them.

Governments are destabilized and become untrustworthy when their institutions are built on sand.

Jesus said a house built on sand wouldn't stand when the storms howled (Matt. 7:26–27). In 2008 it became shockingly clear that powerful American government institutions thought to be rock solid actually sat precariously on a bed of grit. Their collapse cracked the American economy, and the fractures extended across the world.

Some termed it the "subprime mortgage implosion." Financial experts who have analyzed the crisis trace it to government policy that itself rested on sand. The Federal Reserve drove interest rates into the basement in the belief that while "other financial assets might be prone to bubbles, housing was immune," as economist Mark Zandi wrote.[2]

The outcome was the destabilization of the whole financial landscape and the institutions of government that had laid it out.

Governments are destabilized and become untrustworthy when their DNA mutates.

DNA is the root of an organism. Alter it and the living thing changes. With change comes mutation, a radical departure from what rose from the core DNA, usually for the worse.

Jesus taught that if the roots wither, the fruit will wither and die as well. To make His point, Jesus caused a fruitless fig tree to wither away. The current American crisis is nothing less than the mutation of the nation. As the roots—the historic DNA—wither through neglect, disparagement, and complacency, the beautiful "lady of liberty" could change into an oppressive hag.

"Mutilate the roots of society and tradition," wrote Robert A. Nisbet, "and the result must inevitably be the isolation of a generation from its heritage, the isolation of individuals from their fellow men, and the creation of a sprawling, faceless mass."[3]

Governments are destabilized and become untrustworthy when they consistently push aside principle for pragmatism.

Rufus King, among the signers of the Constitution and one of the authors of the Bill of Rights, understood the importance of principled government when he said, "The law established by the Creator, which has existed from the beginning, extends over the whole globe, is everywhere and at all times binding upon mankind. . . . [This] is the law of God by which He makes His way known to man and is paramount to all human control."[4]

The judiciary especially shows the sweeping destabilization that comes when pragmatism overwhelms principle. When the judicial system loses the vision that "the law of God . . . is paramount to all human control," expediency and utility become "paramount."

Andrei Amalrik was a Soviet dissident during the Communist era. He knew firsthand the instability of the big government machine that tried to make itself look unbreakable. But Amalrik saw deep down into the rusting core of ethical philosophy. "Right" is what the state says it is, he observed in his book *Will the Soviet Union Survive Until 1984?* The only thing that mattered for the Marxists was the production and distribution of goods. Whatever worked to facilitate those ends was right and proper, including the imprisonment and execution of people who strayed from the "moral" path hacked out by raw pragmatism.

The Communists brought forth not a productive state, but one whose death was guaranteed by its abandonment to pragmatism over principle.

Governments are destabilized and become untrustworthy when they are controlled by hollow politicians and bureaucrats.

"We make men without chests and expect of them virtue and enterprise," wrote C. S. Lewis in his book *The Abolition of Man.* "Chestless" people are those without an "organ" that provides place and function for virtues and values. It's especially tragic when such people try to hold governments on their shoulders. "Chestless" people produce "heartless" institutions.

John F. Kennedy seemed as illusory as the Camelot imagery in which his administration floated. As the years added distance from his assassination in 1963, people started to take a closer look at Kennedy. One of them, Seymour M. Hersh of the *New York Times*, wrote a book titled *The Dark Side of Camelot.* The flyleaf reads, "Jack Kennedy had it all. And he used it all—his father's fortune, and his own beauty, wit, and power—with a heedless, reckless daring. There was no tomorrow, and there was no secret that money and charm could not hide."

Average Americans, under the Kennedy spell, didn't understand how shaky their government was. Kennedy's incessant—in some periods, daily—womanizing put himself and his country at risk. One of JFK's girlfriends apparently had connections to organized crime through affairs with other men. Kennedy's relationship with her, said Hersh, "exposed the president to blackmail by the mob and friends of the mob."[5]

Another woman resisted JFK's advances. Later she said she

asked him why he was doing it—why he was acting like his father, why he was avoiding real relationships, why he was taking a chance on getting caught in a scandal at the same time he was trying to make his political career take off. Finally he shrugged and said, "I don't know, really. I guess I can't help it." He had this sad expression on his face. He looked like a little boy about to cry.[6]

Richard Nixon, my boss, was highly intelligent, but history would reveal hollowness at his moral center. Nixon initiated Sunday worship services in the East Room, to the consternation of church-state separation purists. Once I accompanied a prominent preacher into the Oval Office. At the end of the meeting, the evangelist said he wanted to pray for Nixon and asked that the president pray for him. I listened to Nixon's prayer with hope and encouragement. Then a few years later I saw the same name with which Nixon ended his prayer used as an expletive in transcripts of the Oval Office tapes.

We learn from Proverbs 22:11 that

> He who loves purity of heart
> And whose speech is gracious, the king is his friend.

But hollow, chestless people have no place for the "heart," which is to be the repository of purity. And sometimes, it is the "king," who ought to be a friend of purity of heart, who is himself chestless.

Governments are destabilized and become untrustworthy when a majority of people in a society are complacent and uninformed.

Hollow people are placed in power by a hollow electorate. Hollowness is a lack not only of virtue and values but also of truth and information.

Josiah became king of Judah when he was eight years old. He came to power in a country empty of knowledge. His father, Amon, had continued a pattern of idolatry. The memory of the God who freed the Hebrews from Egyptian captivity and brought them into the land they now occupied was pushed deeper into a crevasse of forgetfulness. People no longer cared for such things. They didn't want to be bothered with historic facts.

The nation was in deep trouble.

Ten years after ascending the throne, Josiah woke up. He was old enough to understand how bad things were. Things had gone wrong at the core, and that's where Josiah would begin his reforms. He ordered Hilkiah, the high priest, to launch a restoration of the temple.

One day Hilkiah told Shaphan, a major court official, he had found the Torah, the Book of the Law, in the litter of the wrecked and neglected temple. Shaphan scampered to King Josiah, the Torah clutched in his hands, and Shaphan read the book to Josiah. The king was so powerfully struck by the words that he tore his clothes—a sign of immense grief and sorrow. Immediately Josiah connected the dots and wanted more. He commanded, "Go to the Temple and speak to the LORD for me and for the people and for all Judah. Inquire about the words written in this scroll that has been found. For the LORD's great anger is burning against us because our ancestors have not obeyed the words in this scroll. We have not been doing everything it says we must do" (2 Kings 22:13 NLT).

The facts jerked Josiah from his complacency. He knew he had to awaken the nation, so King Josiah summoned all the leaders of Judah and Jerusalem. And the king went up to the Temple of the LORD with all the people of Judah and Jerusalem, along with the priests and the prophets—all the people from the least to the greatest. There the king read to them the entire Book of the Covenant that had been found in the LORD's Temple. The king took his place of authority beside the pillar and renewed the covenant in the LORD's presence. He pledged to obey the Lord by keeping all his commands, laws, and decrees with all his heart and soul. In this way, he confirmed all the terms of the covenant that were written in the scroll, and all the people pledged themselves to the covenant. (2 Kings 23:1–3 NLT)

Nations today in the Globequake turmoil cannot survive amid complacency and ignorance. The discovery of the Torah in Josiah's time brought a recovery of truth. People now must dig deep in the ruins of history, rediscover truth, and pledge themselves to live in its light. We must put in office individuals who have been shaken from complacency and who don't fiddle—or golf—while their nation and world shake to pieces.

The sphere of government can do us much harm when its leaders panic amid Globequake blitzes. They try to anchor us with more and more laws and regulations. Some seem to believe the more buildings there are in Washington and other capitals, the more stable the landscape. They attempt to secure the present at the expense of the future by building more institutions of government. The people they govern lose freedoms and prosperity in the process.

But there's a better way to stabilize the sphere of government to withstand the Globequake's battering. We have seen the strategy in other chapters. Now let's apply it to the sphere of government.

STABILIZE THE STRATEGIC PLAN

Vision for the Sphere of Government

God's vision for the sphere of government is a world set in the good, peaceful, joyful order of His kingdom, despite the world's fallen state, by His image bearers within creation, living under the governance of His Son and empowerment of the Holy Spirit.

Values for the Sphere of Government

1. The Father's desire for the world's peace and well-being
2. Peace and well-being established, not by tyranny, but through the freedom given through God's kingdom
3. Jesus Christ, the Son of God, and His authority
4. The Holy Spirit and His empowerment of the human being
5. Human beings as God's image bearers in the world, and the ministers of His kingdom, under Christ, and through the empowerment of the Holy Spirit

The Kingdom Mission for the Sphere of Government

The biblically revealed kingdom mission for the sphere of government is that of encouraging good, enforcing justice, protecting the innocent, and defending the God-given rights of its people.

SET THE LIMITS ON GOVERNMENT INCURSION INTO OTHER SPHERES

Unstable governments try to control everything in their panic over the possibility of losing their power. They shove aside true authority in all the spheres. Look at what happens:

The Sphere of Person

Unstable regimes, trembling under the threats of the Globequake, try to become the supreme authority in a person's life. People in a nation ruled by tyrants lose their rights and liberties.

The Sphere of Church

Shaky regimes always target the church. The church represents higher authority, which means the power holders and their regimes are not supreme, and absolute truth, which puts glaring light on the lies of the regime's propaganda.

The Sphere of Family

Nervous rulers push parents aside and dictate how their families will be formed—even, in some cases, to the number of children allowed to be born. They know that reeducating parents and the older generation, as well as forming the minds and controlling the thoughts of children, are vital for perpetuating their illegitimate regimes.

The Sphere of Education

Tyrants and their forced systems must refashion a nation's history and reframe its worldview to create the illusion of legitimacy. Schools and their curricula must be redirected to the agenda of the regime rather than the pursuit of knowledge and objective truth.

The Sphere of Government

Regimes are illegitimate and without authority precisely because they seize control from the people. They will even label themselves "People's Republics" to foist the illusion that they are people based. The people are oppressed under such regimes and must be kept out of the palace or other halls of power.

The Sphere of Business-Marketplace

Regimes that depend only on power will attempt to grab proprietorship in the marketplace. They invariably nationalize the economies they dominate or significant portions of them. This brings serious instability to fiscal policy as well as to the whole landscape of commercial enterprise.

ENGAGE THE COVENANT COMMUNITY IN LEADING GOVERNMENT REFORM

Entire civilizations are nourished by the fruits when the covenant community, the church, digs in and deepens its roots. Freedom, proper restraints on rulers, systemic economic prosperity, just law, and all the other blessings taken for granted in the contemporary world are the fruits that grow on that well-rooted tree.

The church is not to try to step over and become the government, as we discussed earlier. But neither is it to be unengaged with the sphere of government. As we have seen, the spheres are not to be closed off from one another, but are to be strengthened through positive interactions and openness.

The church must therefore engage with the sphere of government in its unique identity as the covenant community, not as a political party or partisan movement. Every time the church has done that historically, it has lost its authority and had to settle for raw power. The church's only partisanship should be centered on the kingdom of God.

Those who comprise the covenant community must maintain their identity as people under the authority of the kingdom of God in the created world and as ambassadors of God's kingdom. They will lose their legitimacy if they come out from under the authority of Jesus Christ. Always, the church will serve the sphere of government and the others best by engaging according to its true identity.

The church is the body of Christ; therefore it should do what Christ did in His body. John wrote, "By this, love is perfected with us, so that we may have confidence in the day of judgment; because *as He is, so also are we in this world*" (1 John 4:17, italics added). All Christ's actions in the world fall in the threefold category of His functional being—Prophet, Priest, and King.

The Prophetic Community

The purview of the prophet is truth, the absolute reality of the kingdom of God. The church is present in the world as the purveyor of truth, without which life in the fallen domain is insufferable.

Two Old Testament prophets model how the prophetic community should operate. Amos is an example of the prophetic voice speaking from outside establishments of power. Nathan symbolizes prophets embedded inside establishments and speaking truth to them from within.

Amaziah, leader of Israel's religious establishment in Amos's day, heard that the prophet was speaking against the injustices of the king, Jeroboam, and the people in general. Amaziah commanded Amos not to prophesy in the "king's sanctuary," Beth-El (Amos 7:13 NLT). Amos would not be silenced, however, and began to prophecy against Amaziah as well.

Amaziah, the spiritual leader, operated from a myth still believed. *Beth-El*, literally, is "house of God," but Amaziah called it "a royal residence" (Amos 7:13). For Amaziah, all the spheres were absolutely separate. There were a place for the spiritual and a place for the material. In Amaziah's mind, they were closed off from each other, and the spiritual may not engage with the material. But Amos saw the king's throne as within the scope and boundary of the "house of God." Therefore he replied to Amaziah, "I am not a prophet, nor am I the son of a prophet; for I am a herdsman and a grower of sycamore figs. But the LORD took me from following the flock and the LORD said to me, 'Go prophesy to My people Israel'" (Amos 7:14–15). Amos was telling Amaziah that God's commands superseded those of the king and the high priest. Amos must speak because he served One greater than Jeroboam.

In our Globequake-rattled world there are many concerned with the sphere of government who tell the prophets from outside to stay inside the stained glass and leave the plain glass alone! But the prophetic community will continue to speak and do so in realms where popular opinion says, "Mind your own business."

Prophets inside and outside the power establishments see truth as their business, and God's truth applies everywhere. Amos spoke from outside, but Nathan sounded the prophetic voice from inside the power establishment. He reminds us we should not disdain Christ's followers called into the sphere of government as politicians, officials in the bureaucracies, activists, and aides to the power holders.

Amos was a herdsman with no easy access to the king. Nathan, however was able to operate within the palace and get a hearing with King David. So the day came when David's sin with Bathsheba came to light. There was no Twitter or Facebook to spread the scandal, but God Himself exposed it. Nathan went before the king and told him, "You are the guilty man" (2 Sam. 12:7, paraphrase).

The prophetic community must operate both outside and inside the system. Today it raises its voice through educational processes, exposing truth behind policies and practices of government. The prophetic community confronts the propaganda barrage of the world system and its power structures, providing people with a standard of truth by which all assertions are to be measured and with the truth to fight the propaganda. The prophetic community can train and send people inside the establishments, to bring light within. Sometimes the prophetic community will mobilize peaceful demonstrations so large numbers can speak with a common voice.

The Priestly Community

A prophet represents God to people, and a priest represents people to God. Jesus confronts the establishments with the biting truth of the kingdom of heaven, but he also intercedes for individuals at the throne of heaven as the Great High Priest.

There are two ways people in the covenant community can carry out the priestly role with respect to government. The first is *witness*. The church with a kingdom vision understands the full sweep of Christ's salvation. Not only does it save individuals from eternity in hell, but it also makes them kingdom citizens in the here and now.

Whole systems change when those who lead and control them

awaken to the reality of Christ and become His apprentices. When someone led physician Bernard Nathanson to Christ and he began to grasp kingdom truth, his worldview and world changed. He had performed sixty thousand abortions, but after his radical transformation by the Holy Spirit, Dr. Nathanson became an eloquent prophetic voice speaking against abortion.

The witness who combines the prophetic and the priestly demonstrates the equilibrium of justice and mercy embedded in the gospel of the kingdom.

The Kingly Community

Jesus is the only person in whom the three offices of Prophet, Priest, and King combine. The church, the covenant community, is the means by which He walks in the world now and into all the spheres. The church is to engage with the sphere of government in Jesus' kingly role as well as the prophetic and priestly ones.

The kingly role is carried out through leadership. Some in the covenant community are led by the Holy Spirit to run for political office. Frank Parsons was one of those, and God used him to stabilize the government of an entire city.

In 1979, Birmingham, Alabama, was at a crossroads. The city needed fresh leadership, and people who knew Frank encouraged him to run for mayor. Frank beat the incumbent and found himself in a runoff with Dr. Richard Arrington, the first African American to be a candidate for mayor of Birmingham. On the night of the runoff election, the vote margin was only about two thousand, a small percentage of the total votes cast. Many urged Frank to challenge the count. Frank and his pastor closeted themselves in a hotel room and prayed for God's guidance. As they did, Frank realized challenging the election might deny Dr. Arrington his victory and possibly reignite tensions that had ripped at the city in an earlier time.

Frank went before his supporters late that evening and conceded the election to Dr. Arrington. Frank's statement was so powerful that the incumbent mayor he had beaten called it the "classiest concession speech" he had ever heard. Frank's attitude and action set the tone and smoothed the way for Dr. Arrington to enter office. It was a historic moment for Birmingham since for the first time an African American became mayor of the city that was the cradle of the civil rights movement. Frank's leadership role was a vital part of that transition.

The kingly role does not give the institutional church the right to become a political party. However, the church, as the covenant community, nurtures individuals with the values of God's kingdom, and they take those principles into all the spheres with which they engage, including that of government.

STABILIZE THE ELECTORATE

Many assume it's the politicians, agents, and bureaucrats who occupy the seat of authority in the sphere of government. That may be true of a monarchy, a one-person dictatorship, or an oligarchy, but it's not the way of a biblically based democratic system. The Greek word *demos* is a dead giveaway, especially when coupled with another Greek term, *kratos*. *Demos* means "people," and *kratos* signifies the wielding and exertion of power. Therefore in a true democracy, the people are in the seat of power—especially the electorate.

The only problem is that people get what they elect. Old Testament Israel is an example. It was unique among the nations of the world. God was the direct Ruler of His covenant people. His ideal government is *governance*—every person in relationship with Him and choosing to govern his or her life by the standards of His purity.

However, as they scattered, the Hebrews took note of how other countries were governed. They had human kings all dressed up in splendorous attire that people could see and admire. These potentates were at the heart of pomp and ceremony that entertain and excite. "We want a king like everybody else," Israel murmured. The electorate had spoken. God is not a usurper; therefore, He heeded the will of the people.

The electorate got what it elected. Samuel tried to warn Israel about the consequences of having a human king. It wouldn't be the shining solution they thought it would be:

> "This is how a king will treat you," Samuel said. "The king will draft your sons into his army and make them run before his chariots. Some will be commanders of his troops, while others will be slave laborers. Some will be forced to plow in his fields and harvest his crops, while others will make his weapons and chariot equipment. The king will take your daughters from you and force them to cook and bake and make perfumes for him. He will take away the best of your fields and vineyards and olive groves and give them to his own servants. He will take a tenth of your harvest and distribute it among his officers and attendants. He will want your male and female slaves and demand the finest of your cattle and donkeys for his own use. He will demand a tenth of your flocks, and you will be his slaves. When that day comes, you will beg for relief from this king you are demanding, but the LORD will not help you." (1 Sam. 8:11–18 NLT)

"Give us a king anyway!" the electorate shouted. "We want to be like the nations around us. Our king will govern us and lead us into battle" (1 Sam. 8:20 NLT).

In many years of observation, study, and direct participation in politics, I have heard in every electoral cycle, whether Democrats or Republicans were in office, "Throw the bums out!" The simple assumption is, if we can change the person and regime in the mayor's office, governor's suite, or Oval Office, we will be returned to the garden of Eden. The solution is not in what is at the top because in a democracy it is the bottom that enthrones the top. Therefore to stabilize the sphere of government in the Globequake age, we must stabilize the electorate.

PRAYER AND DIPLOMACY

In the early 1970s I was part of a small delegation meeting with government leaders in a Latin American region. We assembled for breakfast one morning in the home of the president of one of the countries. After our meal it was time for remarks. Our host closed the session by talking about threats from a neighboring country, some of whose leaders were at the table. The president told us he was considering making preparations for war. It was a scary moment as the possibility of violent conflict in Latin America loomed so suddenly. The host president then sat down.

There was silence as all in the room considered the implications. Dr. Richard Halverson, chaplain of the US Senate, was seated at the end of the long table. In a quiet, steady voice Dick spoke: "Señor Presidente, let's pray about your problem."

Members of other governments represented at the table included both Catholic and evangelical Christians. Some of them began praying. By the time we finished, the atmosphere of the room had changed. Peace and hope had entered. The situation was stabilized.

And I thought, *What a strange and wonderful way to do diplomacy!* The moment showed the importance of maintaining another delicate equilibrium, that of the spiritual and civil realms. The balance is like that of pecan groves growing in Texas. To get a pecan, male and female trees must grow in proximity. They are separate trees, but their influence on each other makes an abundant crop.

When church and state are positioned properly, and recognize and respect the roles each plays in society, there is stability, and everyone benefits from the good fruit!

THE SPHERE OF
BUSINESS-MARKETPLACE

CHAPTER 16

BUSINESS IN UPHEAVAL
Six Globequake megatrends

"The Biggest Manufacturing Collapse in US History!" shouted a headline in a British paper on June 2, 2009.[1] General Motors had declared bankruptcy, sending shareholders, as well as business and government leaders throughout the world, into shock. It seemed the rapid tectonic movements detonated by the Globequake cracked the foundations of a corporation once a primary symbol of American prosperity.

General Motors' sudden fall made business-minded students of the Bible think about Revelation 18:16–17, where merchants cry out their shock over the collapse of the global economic system: "How terrible, how terrible for that great city! She was so beautiful—like a woman clothed in finest purple and scarlet linens, decked out with gold and precious stones and pearls! And in *one single moment* all the wealth of the city is gone!" (NLT, italics added). GM, the "great city," thundered down so suddenly it seemed only to take "one single moment." Observers everywhere were breathless as the hard facts of the huge corporation's implosion sank in. What would be next?

Already financial institutions were foundering under the

tsunami of the crisis in the housing market. The hull of the big banks' mortgage-based investments developed huge leaks. The sinking of such big companies created a vortex big enough to suck down global economies. In fact, as you are reading these lines, you may be wondering about the future of your own business and career.

"Virtually every job today is potentially temp work, and maybe half the careers as well," says pollster John Zogby. "Coworkers are for a season, not for life, or maybe they're not at all. Telecommuters know their colleagues mostly as names at the bottom of emails; their support staff is found at the all-night Kinko's, not down the hall."[2]

An executive we'll call Ann typifies what is happening to many in today's marketplace. Ann graduated from business school at the top of her class. Equipped with a shiny new MBA, she was courted by several major companies. Ann chose a burgeoning international corporation. Within a few years she was promoted to a director position, then two years later made vice president.

In 2006, fissures appeared in her company's foundations. Product lines were shifting so fast that research and development weren't keeping pace. Vendors were going bankrupt, and supply chains were breaking down. Credit lines of businesses in her corporation's distribution system were fading.

Then came a literal earthquake that devastated a country. Critical entities in Ann's supply chain based in the stricken nation were put out of business. Increasingly, she had to travel in the region, which kept her away from home weeks at a time. Suddenly Ann's success became a crisis. Her bosses regarded her as one of their best problem solvers. One day the executive vice president to whom she reported summoned Ann to his office. "You're going to have to move there," he told her. "We need you on-site."

That night Ann thought about the implications of being an expat. She was single and an only child. Her aging parents lived with her, and she couldn't bear to think about leaving them. Her only option would be to place them in a nursing home. That was unthinkable.

She went back to her boss. "Relocating is not possible for me right now," Ann told him. "I have family issues, and I can't go live in a foreign country. Maybe later."

"There may not be a later," the executive VP replied. "The company is facing a major reorganization. There will be many layoffs. If you're perceived as not being willing to make sacrifices when our business is in trouble, it will be hard for me to argue even for your present position."

Ann faced hard facts. She *had* to keep her job. Her parents' meager pension couldn't begin to cover their needs. She had no choice but to relocate overseas.

Executives like Ann and her boss are desperately questing for ways to stabilize their enterprises. In 2009, as the Globequake rocking intensified, a university's business school invited me to conduct a workshop for business leaders dealing with the Globequake's impact on business. My associates and I assembled a Globequake Business Brain Trust (GBBT). It consisted of men and women who led or worked with both multinational corporations and small to midsize companies. The GBBT included a former associate dean of the Harvard Business School, a former vice president of one of the world's largest oil companies, and representatives from many other business facets.

As they analyzed what was happening in their companies and others in their fields, they found businesses that were remaining stable despite the turmoil, and a few were actually thriving. In this chapter and the next, we will report on and discuss major findings of the GBBT.

It was important to pull together people from as broad a spectrum of the commercial world as possible. The sphere of business-marketplace includes products, services, and ideas. Manufacturing, retail and service enterprises, and those like media and computer technology companies that deal in ideas, information, and intellectual property belong in this sphere. Our GBBT research revealed six Globequake megatrends affecting all these areas. These movements are redefining companies and the way they do business. Here's a brief look at these unsettling developments.

INTERNATIONALIZATION

Internationalizing trends underlie and increase the Globequake's shift to increasing globalization. We have already seen some of the facts about globalization. Here we will note forces accelerating the trend toward increasing internationalization that leads to globalization.

Force 1: The cultural consensus in rising generations in the West is increasingly internationalist.

Nothing is more indicative of this than the fact that pollster John Zogby called the eighteen- to twenty-nine-year-old segment of the American population the "First Globals." This generation, he wrote, is "the first to be color-blind Americans and the first to bring a consistently global perspective to everything from foreign policy to environmental issues to the coffee they buy, the music they listen to, and the clothes they wear."[3]

This trend has begun to redefine the way businesses must market products, services, and ideas to the rising generation. "Ditch the Flags; Kids Don't Care Where You Come From," blared an *Advertising Age* headline in its June 4, 2007, issue. "They don't care about country of origin because of the way their world has been defined," said Ted Morris of Brand-Intel.[4]

Force 2: A new corporate consensus is emerging, brought about by focus on world markets.

In 1996, Ralph Nader wrote one hundred CEOs of top American companies, challenging them to open their board meetings with the Pledge of Allegiance to the American flag. Perhaps because Nader had often been a gadfly annoying many corporate leaders, half the companies never responded. Other corporations answered Nader with a firm no.

"As a multinational," replied Ford, "Ford is in its largest sense an Australian company in Australia, a British company in the United Kingdom, a German company in Germany." Nader's suggestion, wrote Aetna's leader, was "contrary to the principles on which our democracy was founded." The CEO for Kimberly-Clark found Nader's idea "a grim reminder of the loyalty oaths of the 1950s."[5]

Force 3: There is a political consensus that trade can redefine internal politics of nations.

In the late 1990s many conservatives were divided by the debate over whether to grant most favored nation (MFN) trade status to China. Doctrinaire conservatives were opposed, citing China's continuing violation of human rights. Many economic conservatives—like the leaders of the US Chamber of Commerce—backed MFN for China. They believed it would open vast new markets to American businesses and help reduce the nation's trade deficit. Politicians in both parties thought trade would further open China to the international community and force a liberalization of its internal human rights policies. "China's leaders today are committed to reform," said former US treasury secretary Henry Paulson, "at least as long as it improves the country's political and economic stability."[6]

Force 4: Due to technological advances, the planet is shrinking.

"The earth is flat," Thomas Friedman pointed out in his book of that title. The globally wired planet swaps information at dizzying rates. In mere hours, travelers zip over oceans that once required months to traverse. First Globals, wrote John Zogby, "expect to travel to exotic locales such as Cape Town and Dubai in their lifetimes. A quarter of them think they'll end up living for some significant period in a country other than America."[7] And it's not just First Globals jetting around the world, but people of all ages and cultures.

CENTRALIZATION

Even though globalization seems to disperse many business functions and interactions, there is also an accelerated move toward centralization. As dispersion occurs, there is a greater need to exert control to keep systems from flying apart, resulting in centralized planning and coordination even as globalization increases.

"Never before has change come so rapidly, on such a global scale, and with such global visibility," said the report of the UN-sanctioned Commission on Global Governance in 1995.[8] The commission's recommendations included acceptance of a set of global values on which all nations can agree and "a framework of rules and order for global competition," which would be developed through a Global Competition Office that would "provide oversight of national enforcement efforts and resolve inconsistencies between them."[9]

AUTOMATION

Globalization and centralization require broader automation to link widely dispersed internal business units, processes, vendors, and a host of other functions. "Information technology may tip the balance in favor of markets in the trade-off between using markets or hierarchies to coordinate economic decisions," wrote Jay Galbraith, an internationally known expert on organizational design. This may mean the reemergence of "cottage industries . . . coordinated by market forces rather than by superiors wielding authority."[10] Until that happens—if ever—technology will have increasing impact on organizational design and function. As hierarchical structures give way to a more lateral organizational flow, movement of information becomes even more important. Information must move freely, quickly, and with broad accessibility, necessitating highly developed technology systems.

SOCIALISM

Europe has long been moving in a highly socialized direction. With the rise of expectations for government aid and support in the United States, many Americans are giving at least some level of approval to the trend toward socialism. The impact on business is in the area of customer expectations, as well as government intervention. A highly socialized environment creates and thrives on an entitlement mentality, which socialism fosters.

REGULATION

Government's regulatory impact is not only on large multinational corporations but also on small businesses, which constitute 75 percent of the American marketplace. Small businesses are linked into these trends through their dependencies on vendors and other partners and also through the Globequake's impact on customer expectations.

SOCIAL NETWORKING

Facebook, Twitter, Cyworld, and other Internet-based electronic social networks are vital for businesses seeking to better understand and influence customer behavior, says Harvard business professor Sunil Gupta. For one thing, electronic networks can generate viral campaigns, in which advertising for a product is spread through social contacts at an infectious level. For example, on Valentine's Day, 2009, Honda "offered 750,000 Facebook members a heart-shaped virtual gift complete with the Honda logo that could be passed on to other members." This type of viral campaign "has the potential to be an enormous source of revenue," asserts Gupta.[11]

FIVE NECESSARY TRANSFORMATIONS

To meet the challenges brought on by these Globequake trends, companies must undergo radical transformation. Consider, then, the five transformations through which every leader needs to take his or her company if the enterprise is to thrive in the Globequake.

Transformation 1: From Terrain to Horizon

World War I was fought primarily in deep trenches. Soldiers hauled themselves and their weapons up the twelve- or fourteen-foot wall of a trench and fired quick bursts into a barren landscape, then hustled back down.

For days on end all they could see was mud and grime. They could never see the big picture. The doughboys in the ditches had no idea what the battlefield above looked like, who was winning, whether the enemy was advancing, or even if their volleys were on target. They desperately needed to get their eyes off the immediate terrain of the trench and up to the horizon so they could comprehend what they were doing and why they were risking their lives. Things look different in the deepest pit when you can see the horizon up above and out ahead.

Jesus shows us how this principle works. Matthew recorded that one day "Jesus began to tell his disciples plainly that he had to go to Jerusalem, and he told them what would happen to him there. He would suffer at the hands of the leaders and the leading priests and the teachers of religious law. He would be killed, and he would be raised on the third day" (Matt. 16:21 NLT).

Peter, one of Jesus' key team members, was upset. "Heaven forbid, Lord," he said. "This will never happen to you!" (Matt. 16:22 NLT). Jesus had to take Peter aside and straighten him out. Peter's problem was that he was focused only on the immediate terrain of suffering and death for Jesus at Jerusalem. Jesus, however, glanced at the terrain—Jerusalem—but kept His gaze on the horizon—the empty tomb. This enabled Jesus to stay on track to His purpose rather than cave in to the resistance of the shortsighted. The Holy Spirit, through the writer of Hebrews, gives a glimpse into the mind-set of Jesus as He faced the turbulence and terror of the cross:

> Let us also lay aside every encumbrance and the sin which so easily entangles us, and let us run with endurance the race that is set before us, fixing our eyes on Jesus, the author and perfecter of faith, who for the *joy set before Him* endured the cross, despising the shame, and has sat down at the right hand of the throne of God. (Heb. 12:1–2, italics added)

Every leader knows that at some point she must head herself and her enterprise to the hard place. She keeps a watch on the ground beneath her feet, but her focus and gaze are set out ahead, to the joy of success and victory.

Transformation 2: From Brontosaurus to Velociraptor

The Jurassic world was populated by a variety of beasts, some munching on vegetation, others furious predators feasting on their fellow dinosaurs. In sheer size, brontosaurus (apatosaurus) dominated, with an overall length of seventy-five to eighty feet and weighing as much as twenty-five tons. However, the bulk that made it so immense was also the big animal's downfall.

The brontosaurus was "thunder lizard," but the velociraptor was "swift seizer" (or plunderer). Velociraptor was only about seven feet long with a weight of approximately forty pounds. It was lean and mean, unintimidated by larger species. While the brontosaurus was no more nimble than an aircraft carrier, the velociraptor had the advantage of speed and flexibility. The brontosaurus was frightening in its immensity but theoretically could be brought down and eaten by the velociraptor.

Brontosaurus companies dominate the marketplace. But if the leaders of such companies fail to build in velociraptor characteristics, their huge enterprises won't have the capacity for change-response that enables survival through the Globequake and the ability to take advantage of the opportunities brought by the crises of tectonic change in the marketplace.

In referring to a velociraptor I don't mean to suggest companies should become vicious and predatory. Rather, we think of what Jesus said to His followers when He told them, "I send you out as sheep in the midst of wolves; so be shrewd as serpents and innocent as doves" (Matt. 10:16).

A brontosaurus is impressive, but a velociraptor wins the day.

Transformation 3: From Monument to Wheel

The Washington Monument has stood its ground since 1884. At 555 feet, it has towered over the nation's capital as a symbol of the nation's founding and its leader. It points to the past and, for those who think and reflect, points the way to the future if the principles of the founders can be recovered and applied.

But the Washington Monument is immovable. Monuments are intended to stay in place. That's their purpose. When the Hebrews crossed the Jordan to go into the promised land, God divided the river so they could cross on dry ground. After all had crossed over, the Lord commanded Joshua to have the leaders of the twelve tribes gather big stones from where the waters divided and then set them up where the people camped in the promised land the first night.

"In the future, your children will ask, 'What do these stones mean to you?'" Joshua told the leaders. "Then you can tell them, 'They remind us that the Jordan River stopped flowing when the Ark of the LORD's covenant went across.' These stones will stand as a permanent memorial among the people of Israel" (Josh. 4:6–7 NLT).

Monuments are important for linking people to their history. But a business must not see itself as a monument. When a monument mentality sets in, a company begins to lose its capacity for forward movement. This necessitates the "wheel" philosophy. A company with a "monumental" plan will have a strong start-up, but it is in danger of an ancient organizational pitfall: "We've never done it this way before." A wheel plan enables forward motion, turns, and on rare occasions, reverse movement.

Transformation 4: From Compliance to Commitment

Any enterprise hoping to survive a Globequake must have people who keep standing and advancing under the most difficult conditions.

Ken Lay was the leader of Enron, the huge energy company. Lay's leadership took the company to a high level of success, but Lay also watched the corporation collapse. Lay wanted to be a principled man, characterized by important values. Sadly, those values weren't embedded into Enron's culture.

As his world crumbled, Lay asked a pastor to meet with him. One evening the Christian leader met Lay in his executive suite, and the two discussed the company's crisis. The pastor reviewed Enron's vision and mission statements and found them exemplary in their high qualities. Yet Enron was coming apart because of unethical practices, amounting to delusion and deceit.

One of the problems, apparently, was that Lay spent much time on business travel, leaving the day-to-day operations to others who did not share Lay's principles and values. As noble as were Lay's vision for Enron and its mission, without a commitment to strong values up and down the organizational chain, Enron was doomed. Enron derailed because its vision and mission were not aligned with many of its practices. Values, as we've seen, are the ties that hold together an enterprise's essential being—its core nature and character—with its function. When there's little or no commitment to those values throughout the corporation, the tracks bend, twist, and separate under the pressures of daily business, and the enterprise wrecks—as did Enron.

Transformation 5: From Rigidity to Stability

Rigid things break under stress. The truly stable structure is one with the flexibility to yaw in the earthquake or tornadic winds without losing the connection to its foundations. Rigid companies crack under the tremors and upheavals of the Globequake.

For the entire three years of Jesus' public ministry, He and His team seemed to be on shaky ground. The threats were so great that Jesus would sometimes tell people who had been healed through His miracles not to reveal the miracles to anyone. It wasn't that the Lord was afraid of persecution, but that there was important timing to the execution of His mission. Thus, Jesus had to continually stabilize His team.

First, through it all, Jesus' followers saw His composure and peace. They experienced both at the beginning of their enterprise when Jesus and His team went to the synagogue at Nazareth, where He announced His mission. The crowd reacted and tried to throw Jesus off a cliff, but "passing through their midst, He went His way" (Luke 4:30).

Second, Jesus was visible and accessible to His followers. The only time He was away from them was in the early morning—sometimes predawn—when He would pull away to pray and fellowship with His Father. But the fundamental call Jesus gave His followers was to be "with Him" so they could watch Him, learn from Him, and be stabilized by His presence (Mark 3:14).

Third, Jesus' followers had the assurance of stability because, even though everything else around them seemed to change, Jesus' vision and values stayed in place. Not even His closest followers could divert Jesus from His passion to take the trail of destiny, even though it led through Jerusalem and its dangers. Pilate offered Jesus an easy way out. All He had to do was recant His claims of identification with God the Father, but Jesus wouldn't relent. By that time all the disciples had scampered away, but they watched and learned from afar.

Excellence characterized Jesus in all He did, and this continuation of quality under immense pressure is the fourth way He stabilized His followers. Jesus' services (ministries) to human need were extraordinary in their transformative impact. His product (the gospel) was so powerful it launched sweeping social and cultural as well as personal changes and continues today. The greatest stress did not pull Jesus away from the quality of His caring. One of the thieves dying beside Jesus acknowledged his need, and even in His personal agony, Jesus served the man with love, compassion, comfort, and assurance—the same things Jesus had done all His life.

Fifth, Jesus opened communication channels between human beings and God, and He went to great lengths to keep those channels open. He taught His followers about prayer and modeled it.

Sixth, Jesus was continually and intentionally moving among people who needed Him and His message. He even made Himself available to His enemies—the religious leaders—by going into the temple complex. Huge crowds gathered, and Jesus interacted with them, but He also took His team aside for special times of instruction and inspiration.

Seventh, Jesus understood how to handle conflict. When His disciples argued about who was greatest, Jesus quickly turned the situation into a teaching opportunity, defusing the edgy emotions.

Finally, Jesus prepared His team to deal with situations that could change rapidly. He sent out seventy of His followers to take

His message and ministry to the villages scattered across the region. He told them the conditions and responses they might encounter—from rejection to cautious interest—and how to deal with whatever might arise.

When everything crashed in at Jesus' crucifixion, His team was momentarily scattered and bewildered. But as its members began to recover from shock and remember their training under Jesus, they were able to recover. The fact that today hundreds of millions gather weekly to celebrate Christ's resurrection and learn His teachings is testimony to the success of Jesus' enterprise. Multitudes of these modern adherents of Jesus identify with Him and assemble in His name at great risk in nations where His followers are still harassed and persecuted, but they are still stabilized by His example and power, given by the Holy Spirit.

Leaders of companies aren't God incarnate, but they should do much to stabilize their businesses, employees, customers, investors, vendors, and others through applying the principles learned through a study of Jesus and His confrontations with the Globequake conditions He faced daily.

CHAPTER 17

GLOBEQUAKE-PROOF BUSINESS

Anchoring actions for companies in upheaval

Ed Lambert's company could have been demolished in the economic Globequake that began shaking the business landscape intensely in 2008. However, Lambert led his enterprise in renewal and reinvention, resulting in transformation and a corporation sturdy enough to withstand the Globequake's battering.

Lambert's Birmingham-based company, Hot Metal Coatings, focuses on manufacturing industrial coatings for the interior of underground pipes. Lambert, now in his sixties, started with the company in his youth in a minor job and rose to become its president. He has guided the enterprise through many tremors as Birmingham's industrial base crumbled and his national clients had to shift their own priorities.

"Think about a tomato grower," Lambert says. The savvy tomato farmer faces seasons not good for tomatoes. But the tomato grower knows there are farmers raising corn. Because of the decline in the tomato market, the tomato farmer has equipment for sowing and planting, so he hires himself out to help the farmer who raises corn. The industrious tomato grower knows how to maintain the balance of glancing at his terrain while gazing at the horizon. He spots an opportunity with the local water company and contracts to use his equipment to dig trenches for new pipelines. "The tomato farmer simply makes use of what he has available to expand into other services," says Lambert.

If the tomato grower has a brontosaurus mentality and its cumbersome inflexibility, he can't take advantage of the opportunities brought on by change and downturn in the tomato markets. If a tomato farmer is velociraptor minded, he can discern between what is fixed and what is flexible in his enterprise. His fields may be committed to tomato agriculture, but his equipment represents the velociraptor facet of his business.

When demand declined for the primary product of Lambert's Birmingham company, he implemented the "velociraptor" philosophy. Birmingham's steel industry uses five-foot-tall ladles to pour molten iron into blast furnaces. However, a thick residue builds up inside the ladles as the remnants of iron harden. The residue has to be hacked off daily with pneumatic hammers; otherwise the ladles will become so heavy they can't be lifted. Companies that knew Lambert's work in producing process coatings for the ductile iron pipe industry approached him about cleaning their ladles. Removing molten iron buildup from massive buckets hadn't been part of Lambert's strategic plan. However, when some of his equipment and employees' work demands were reduced by downturns in the economy brought on by the Globequake, Lambert realized he had the tools and workers to do the job. His Hot Metal Coatings company is more like a velociraptor than a brontosaurus because, under Lambert's philosophy, the business is flexible enough to take on projects not in the original plan.

Market upheavals necessitate renewal, reinvention, and transformation, which every business leader must know how to implement in the Globequake era. Critical actions bring the stabilizing truths into the day-to-day reality of a corporate environment.

Leaders able to take their companies through the transformational process know to read the times (*chronos*) and seize the moment (*kairos*). Back in chapter 2, we described the biblical view of time and the differences between *chronos* and *kairos*. *Chronos*, as you remember, refers primarily to chronological time indicating time's passage. *Kairos* signifies the events and opportunities that appear along the track of time's passage.

The concept is also present in ancient Hebrew. It appears, for example, in Daniel 2:21, where the prophet writes that God "changes the *times* and the *seasons*" (NKJV, italics added). Again, the *times* refers merely to the moment, but the *seasons* refers to the content of time, the special occasions and opportunities *chronos*-time brings. The Old Testament also speaks of the "sons of Issachar," one of the Hebrew tribes (1 Chron. 12:32). These leaders "understood the times" and had "knowledge of what Israel should do."

Jesus brought the concept of the two levels of time into sharp focus. "We must work the works of Him who sent Me as long as it is day; night is coming when no one can work," He told His team (John 9:4).

When we combine these concepts, some vital actions emerge for business leadership:

- Successful leaders seek to understand what's happening in a particular season by studying the culture in which they do business.
- Effective leaders watch for the opportunities that arise in the progression of time.
- Business leadership that not only remains standing but also succeeds in the Globequake knows opportunities will fade quickly.
- Successful leaders are ready to seize the opportunities while it is day.

Further, transformational business leaders work to reduce the fragility factors (FFs) that weaken a company or institution. The more FFs there are, the weaker the organization and the more vulnerable it is to collapse under Globequake conditions. Here are FFs that can bring you down:

- *Weak hubs.* As we noted earlier, an organization must see itself as a wheel. The hub is the core of strength. It consists of vision, values, mission, goals, leadership, and governance. If vision fades, values are abandoned, mission is forgotten, goals are ignored, leadership weakens, and governance deteriorates to raw power, the company is in peril of falling apart.

- *Fragmentation.* The spokes are the means by which a company does its business. They are manufacturing, marketing, sales, distribution, vendor relationships, customer service, financial and resource management, and all the other components that comprise an enterprise. When the spokes are not connected to the hub, the company falls apart.

- *Compliance rather than commitment.* Few things better reveal the actual (as opposed to the ideal) culture of a company than the way employees up and down the chain view their relationships to leaders and the company's other hub components. If employees aren't committed to the vision, values, mission, goals, leadership, and authority that hold the wheel together, the business will almost certainly collapse under Globequake conditions.

- *Conflict.* Conflict is inevitable in any human institution. Differing belief systems, interpretations of a situation, lifestyles, and hosts of other factors guarantee that people are going to collide. A company is fragile if it lacks an effective strategy for dealing with conflict. Such a strategy will not be based on maintaining peace at any price or wallpapering the real issues, but will face them honestly and build toward genuine resolution.

- *Communications breakdown.* When the information flow from the hub out to the rim is blocked, assumptions become rumors that become speculations that become delusions that lead to actions that will be misapplications, distortions, and even counters to the best interests of the company and its total enterprise. Leaders must focus on the art of communications and embed the business with a solid and specific strategy for keeping truth in the light.

STABILIZE THE STRATEGIC PLAN

Vision for the Sphere of Business-Marketplace

A biblically revealed vision for the sphere of business-marketplace is that of a society in which people's material and informational needs are met through a commercial system in which entrepreneurs are free to be cocreators with God and their enterprises are free to flourish to serve human need.

Values for the Sphere of Business-Marketplace
1. God as the Creator of entrepreneurship and enterprise
2. The material and informational well-being of society and its individuals
3. The freedom of entrepreneurs to be creative and enterprising
4. The freedom of businesses to flourish with a minimum of limitation and control

The Kingdom Mission for the Sphere of Business-Marketplace

To meet the physical and material needs of society in a fair and honest way, in line with the principles of God's kingdom.

BALANCE THE STABILITY EQUATION

$E = mc^2$ is hailed for its sublime description of the way the universe functions. Albert Einstein captured deep mysteries of the cosmos in the form of that equation.

Business leaders might wish such an all-encompassing, elegant equation existed that would capture the secrets of business success. Actually, such an equation does exist, and it looks like this:

$$CS + ES + CE \div 3 = SA$$

That is, customer satisfaction plus employee satisfaction plus cost effectiveness divided by three equals a company's stability average. Application of biblical principles in these three critical areas can contribute greatly to a company's stability amid the Globequake.

Customers

"We should know clearly who we serve and with what services," says Roger Wernette, leader of a large men's organization focusing on biblical values and leadership. Wernette sounds an important note: *there must be a clear balance between* who *and* what. Some corporations are so enamored with the *what* that they don't give sufficient focus to the *who*. They wind up spending precious resources to develop products irrelevant to the marketplace simply because they can.

Prior to Christ's coming, there was a stark devaluation of human life and hardly any concept of human dignity. There were as many slaves in the highly "refined" cultures of Greece and Rome as citizens. Unwanted children were abandoned, women abused, the unwary exploited, and cruelty dominated everyone. Jesus Christ launched a transformational movement, and the re-forming of the tectonic plates of entire cultures led directly to the ideas that produced Western democracies with their concepts of human worth, private property, and free markets.

Christ described principles that should be at the heart of a company's approach to its customers. He said, "Even I, the Son of Man, came here not to be served but to serve others, and to give my life as a ransom for many" (Mark 10:45 NLT). And again,

You know that in this world kings are tyrants, and officials lord it over the people beneath them. But among you it should be quite different. Whoever wants to be a leader among you must be your servant, and whoever wants to be first must become your slave. For even I, the Son of Man, came here not to be served but to serve others, and to give my life as a ransom for many. (Matt. 20:25–28 NLT)

Employees

The Bible provides important principles that will help a business establish best practices with regard to human capital and workplace issues. Remember, God's law-system was given to His original covenant people for their national and social well-being. God's laws lead to a high-quality lifestyle in society at large and the workplace. Here are six key principles to help mold employee policy:

1. *The Sharing Principle*: This truth is found in Leviticus 25:5–7: "Don't store away the crops that grow naturally or process the grapes that grow on your unpruned vines. The land is to have a year of total rest. But you, your male and female slaves, your hired servants, and any foreigners who live with you may eat the produce that grows naturally during the Sabbath year" (NLT). For a business the "crops that grow naturally" and "grapes that grow on your unpruned vines" are profits and dividends that accrue from past successes. Bonuses, profit sharing, and other incentives drawn from a company's historic performance should be shared with employees, based on their productivity and commitment to the company and its community of customers, management, and fellow workers.

2. *The Gleaning Principle*: This great practice is closely related to the sharing principle and is revealed in the beautiful story of a near destitute widow named Ruth:

> There was a wealthy and influential man in Bethlehem named Boaz, who was a relative of Naomi's husband, Elimelech. One day Ruth said to Naomi, "Let me go

out into the fields to gather leftover grain behind any-one who will let me do it." And Naomi said, "All right, my daughter, go ahead." So Ruth went out to gather grain behind the harvesters. And as it happened, she found herself working in a field that belonged to Boaz, the relative of her father-in-law, Elimelech. . . . When Ruth went back to work again, Boaz ordered his young men, "Let her gather grain right among the sheaves without stopping her. And pull out some heads of bar-ley from the bundles and drop them on purpose for her. Let her pick them up, and don't give her a hard time!" (Ruth 2:1-3, 15–16 NLT)

The gleaning principle was actually established in Leviticus 19:9–10, where we read, "When you harvest the crops of your land, do not harvest the grain along the edges of your fields, and do not pick up what the harvesters drop. . . . Leave [it] for the poor and the foreigners living among you. I am the LORD your God" (NLT).

The principle we bring forward for application in busi-ness today is that *workers should be able to glean when their companies enjoy an abundant harvest.* If there is the expectation that cutbacks, layoffs, and salary reductions may come with hard times, there should also be the anticipation of bonuses and other forms of gleaning—like extra vacation time and bonus days—when the company is enjoying success.

3. *The Stranger Principle:* Though the Jews constituted the origi-nal covenant nation, God's intention always was that all people would have opportunity to be in the same special relationship with Him (see for example Ex. 12:48). This is reflected as early as the Old Testament and its revelations about God's desire for inclusion of "strangers" in the bless-ings enjoyed by the covenant people.

For example,

> When a stranger resides with you in your land, you
> shall not do him wrong. The stranger who resides
> with you shall be to you as the native among you, and
> you shall love him as yourself, for you were aliens in
> the land of Egypt; I am the LORD your God. . . . You
> shall not wrong a stranger or oppress him, for you
> were strangers in the land of Egypt. (Lev. 19:33–34;
> Ex. 22:21)

It's easy for employees to feel alienated and estranged from the top echelons of a company's leadership. When workers feel like strangers, morale will be low, conflict frequent, and turnover high. All new workers enter as strangers, but *solid companies will have specific strategies for assimilating them into the corporate community.*

Further, executives, managers, supervisors, team leaders, and others with leadership responsibility should remember that they themselves were once in the lower ranks and *treat those who report to them as they wanted to be treated when in a lower position.*

4. *The Worthiness Principle*: "The workman deserves his support," says Jesus (Matt. 10:10 AMPLIFIED BIBLE). He was sending out His followers to take His ministry and message to people spread over the villages and towns of the region. Jesus told those who were undertaking the mission not to take provisions with them, but to receive what people would give them. The inference was that Jesus' followers were performing a service for the people who would hear and respond to the gospel, be healed, and set free from demonic oppression. Jesus' disciples would be performing a service and thus deserved compensation.

A modern company's compensation policies should be based on the understanding that employees are being paid for their services to the business and its customers. This will guide salary and benefit levels as well as provide a standard for raises and reductions.

The worthiness principle also should frame the attitude about compensation held by executives. They should recognize workers are compensated because of the important contributions they make to the company's success. That is, productive employees earn good compensation because they deserve it. This ensures that a corporation will not treat its workers as beggars, and employees will have a positive attitude about the gifts, talents, and skills they bring to the job, resulting in morale-building self-esteem.

5. *The Equality Principle*: One of the Bible's most remarkable stories is that of Onesimus, the runaway slave. It is remarkable because Paul's counsel to Philemon, Onesimus's employer, demonstrated an entirely new paradigm in the Roman world, where slaves were often viewed as subhuman.

Apparently Paul and Onesimus had met in Rome, where Onesimus had fled. Perhaps through their relationship, Onesimus became a follower of Christ. The decision was made that he would return to Philemon, also a Christ follower. Onesimus carried a letter from Paul, advising Philemon how to treat Onesimus. Paul wrote,

> My plea is that you show kindness to Onesimus. I think of him as my own son because he became a believer as a result of my ministry here in prison. Onesimus hasn't been of much use to you in the past, but now he is very useful to both of us. I am sending him back to you, and with him comes my own heart. I really wanted to keep him here with me while I am in these chains for preaching the Good News, and he would

have helped me on your behalf. But I didn't want to do anything without your consent. And I didn't want you to help because you were forced to do it but because you wanted to. Perhaps you could think of it this way: Onesimus ran away for a little while so you could have him back forever. He is no longer just a slave; he is a beloved brother, especially to me. Now he will mean much more to you, both as a slave and as a brother in the Lord. So if you consider me your partner, give him the same welcome you would give me if I were coming. (Philem. 10–17 NLT)

We can learn much from Paul's Spirit-inspired instructions to Philemon that will guide us in forming the best human resource practices for today's companies. First, employees, even the underperformers (as Onesimus apparently had been), must be seen as human beings. Second, workers are to be regarded as equal in human value to the owners and top executives of the company and treated accordingly. Third, when an employee fails, if at all possible management should seek to restore the worker and provide him or her with another chance.

6. *The Responsibility Principle*: Paul bluntly stated the responsibility principle when he wrote, "Whoever does not work should not eat" (2 Thess. 3:10 NLT). The problem Paul was immediately addressing was that some in the church at Thessalonica had become so stricken with "Second Coming fever" that they had left their jobs to wait for Christ's return. They had become a burden to others, who had to feed them.

The attitude is expressed in modern culture in the form of egalitarianism. Many wrongly equate egalitarianism with equality. However, here's the subtle and vital difference: equality means all human beings deserve the same *opportunity* to succeed in life; egalitarianism holds that all people deserve the same *outcomes*, irrespective of what they have done with the opportunities extended to them.

In the workplace it's important that equality not deteriorate into egalitarianism. A company that treats its employees by the principles we've found in the Bible should also be able to expect its employees to be responsible in their work, behavior, and attitudes.

Businesses can survive Globequake-induced turbulence when the culture is built on solid values that form not only their relationships with their customers but also their treatment of their employees.

Costs

Executive leadership will discover solid, stabilizing principles for cost-effectiveness in the Bible's ancient wisdom. These principles include the following:

QUALITY: "Cheap" isn't a part of a sound cost-control strategy.

We learn this principle from a man who was destined to become a leader of one of history's greatest enterprises. He had made a critical error of judgment that brought disaster on people looking to him for leadership. The leader desperately needed counsel from higher authority and knew what to do to get it.

King David had taken a census of the people of Israel to boost his own sense of importance. David's true significance came from God, not from the bigness of the nation he led. David's action impeded his close relationship with God and cut off blessing to the people. David was led to make a sacrifice to God to show his acknowledgment of his error, along with his repentance. The king chose for his place of sacrifice an ideal property owned by a man named Araunah, who offered the land to King David at no cost. David answered,

"No, but I will surely buy it from you for a price, for I will not offer burnt offerings to the LORD my God which cost me nothing." So David bought the threshing floor and the oxen for fifty shekels of silver. David built there an altar to the LORD and offered burnt offerings and peace offerings. Thus the LORD was moved by prayer for the land, and the plague was held back from Israel. (2 Sam. 24:24–25)

David's finances were stressed, but he didn't allow his economic condition to block him from doing his best. "Cheap" was not an option.

Achieving cost-efficiency must never be attempted at the price of quality. King David's reputation for excellence—with the exception of his sin with Bathsheba—stands across history and struck fear in his "competitors." Executives who seek to control cost by reducing the quality of products and services are trying to get something for nothing and risk losing the good brand name they have worked hard to establish.

FUTURITY: Cost-efficiency strategies that ignore the future cause a company to be like a railroad without a destination.

Jesus drove home this point when He talked about the importance of follow-through: "For which one of you, when he wants to build a tower, does not first sit down and calculate the cost to see if he has enough to complete it? Otherwise, when he has laid a foundation and is not able to finish, all who observe it begin to ridicule him, saying, 'This man began to build and was not able to finish'" (Luke 14:28–30).

REALITY: A company living in delusion will plunge into insanity.

Proverbs 28:20 states that "a faithful man shall abound with blessings, but he who makes haste to be rich [at any cost] shall not go unpunished" (AMPLIFIED BIBLE). Businesses that try to scheme their way into cost-effectiveness are not facing reality. "Business units lose focus when they fail to determine whether a contribution is truly incremental and when they fail to account for all associated costs," says John Whitney, a former Harvard Business School associate dean and business turnaround specialist.[1] Further, he notes, companies get in trouble when they are not realistic about their goals, especially as they impact budgets. Goals, he believes, should be high, but budgets must be realistic: "When high goals are expressed in stretch budgets, expenses and working capital requirements tend to rise more quickly than revenues and margins."[2]

RESPONSIBILITY: Management and employees succeed in cost-effectiveness when they refuse the easy answers and take on the hard work.

The Bible provides a sound principle highlighting the importance of responsibility as a key element of cost-efficiency: "Wealth from get-rich-quick schemes quickly disappears; wealth from hard work grows" (Prov. 13:11 NLT).

These are foundational best practice elements for effective cost control in a shaky world. It takes not only courageous management to apply them but also wise executive leadership.

In fact, under Globequake conditions, executive leaders must be something akin to prophets. The "sons of Issachar" mentioned in 1 Chronicles 12:32 were described as "men who understood the times." Cost-effectiveness amid the turbulence of today's business environment will require men and women who know what's going on and what to do about it.

Understanding the times can be depressing. Some experts believe the heightened need for therapy and medications in our culture is that people have too much information. Also, the enormity of stabilizing the spheres as we have seen in this and the other chapters in part 2 is intimidating and seems impossible.

People are driven to scramble in the search for hope. Some, as we will see, travel the wrong roads or ride the wrong craft in the quest for hope. Many arrive not at hope but at hopelessness.

There is, however, a quality of hope so sturdy that not even the worst blasts of the Globequake can destroy it. The light radiating from this hope cannot be doused, even if the Globequake rips apart all the power plants!

PART 3

HOPE

Hope does not disappoint, because the love of God has been poured out within our hearts through the Holy Spirit who was given to us.
—Romans 5:5

CHAPTER 18

HOPE SOUGHT, HOPE FOUND

*Yellow brick roads and yellow submarines
won't get you there*

"Reunite Pangea! Stop man-made continental drift now! Restore one world utopia now!" So reads a coffee mug I spotted.

"Man-made continental drift" is created by all the divisive people throughout the world, goes the argument. Their foolish belief systems dig deep fault lines between the blissfully peaceful regions of Pangea. If only humanity could rediscover the holistic way of thinking and living that Pangea symbolizes, utopia would be restored, the Pangeans believe. In the words of a college student in a rapturous paper about Pangea, it is the "utopia that must exist internationally in the minds of all free thinkers." Pangea is to be "free from all governments, free from all social and geo-political boundaries." Contemplating the one great continent that theoreticians say existed before tectonic shifts and earthquakes severed them, the student rhapsodizes,

Oh, how South America snuggles with Africa, and Antarctica sleeps at their feet keeping them warm, Pangaea [*sic*], where our world is peacefully united. Pangaea is John and Oko, Pangaea is Texas, Pangaea is world peace, Pangaea embraces all, unifies all, Pangaea the impossible. . . . Yet it exists. Pangaea, like Paris, London is in all of our minds.[1]

One can almost hear Judy Garland singing, "Somewhere over the rainbow"! The Kansas farm girl character she played in *The Wizard of Oz* dreamed of utopia too. Thanks to an accommodating tornado, she got there. Soon the child, accompanied by a cowardly lion, a brainless scarecrow, a heartless tin man, and the dog Toto, was on the yellow brick road to find the Emerald City and the genius behind this glorious utopia. At the end of the journey was nothing more than a runty, wrinkled old man behind a curtain, speaking into a contraption that made his voice sound like a god's.

The yellow brick road never has led to hope. Yet people across history keep trying to build it. Nimrod hacked out its route and dug the original course along which the bricks would be laid. "He was the first to be a mighty man on the earth," reports Genesis 10:8 (AMPLIFIED BIBLE). *Mighty*, in the Hebrew of the Old Testament, refers to a dominant figure, a tyrant.

UTOPIANS WITH US ALWAYS

Utopians, the descendants of Nimrod, are with us always. They build Babels and Babylons and always the yellow brick road. They offer us flowers and tea. But the stalks of the flowers are swords, and the tea is the bitter gall of oppression. Like their ancestor, Nimrod, they always become tyrants. Sometimes their tyrannies are subtle and high sounding, and sometimes they are gun-in-your-face blunt and direct.

They surge at us from right and left. From the extreme right wing come the Fascists of history. They promise if we will turn ourselves, our churches, our homes, our schools, and our businesses over to the state and its leaders (*Der Fuhrer* in World War II Germany, *Il Duce* in

Italy), we will inhabit utopia. Hitler determined to make Europe Pangea. He wanted to pull together the politically divided plates of all the European countries—and ultimately the world itself—into a Pangea in which everyone was unified under the swastika. Blitzkrieg would be his strategy. He started with Austria, Czechoslovakia, and Poland. Anyone who was not of the proper racial stock or refused the Nazis' generous offer to join Pangea would be executed.

The left-wingers have their own visions of Pangea. "Workers of the world unite!" scream Marxists everywhere. Private property, freedom of thought and expression, and worship of a God people dare to believe is supreme over the party, the philosophy, the state, and the bureaucracy—the *nomenklatura*—are the dynamics that have severed the Pangea of Marxism. To create their utopia, they must kill the landowners, even if—as Ho Chi Minh did in Vietnam—those private property owners are peasant farmers. They must put locks on the human mind and vocal cords. Above all, the Marxist Pangeans will have to impose state atheism because nothing can be greater than the party and the bureaucracies. Add to the list of leftist utopian Pangean tyrants, along with Ho Chi Minh, North Korea's Kim, Fidel Castro of Cuba, and all their socialist allies. With one great voice they sing the anthem of their version of Pangea:

> *No saviour from on high delivers*
> *No faith have we in prince or peer*
> *Our own right hand the chains must shiver*
> *Chains of hatred, greed and fear*
> *E'er the thieves will give up their booty*
> *And give to all a happier lot.*
> *Each at the forge must do their duty*
> *And we'll strike while the iron is hot.*
> *So comrades, come rally*
> *And the last fight let us face*
> *The Internationale unites the human race*[2]

The utopians of right and left know how to build concentration camps, gulags, torture chambers, and efficient execution devices. They also share a humanism stark and cruel in its godlessness, and the idolatry of the state.

As I write, the banner of the Pangean quest, having been dropped by the Nazis and the Communists, has been picked up by the radical Islamicists (among others). A global caliphate, ruled over by sharia, will bring the world to its utopian condition. The continents must be forced back together. The methods are the same as in all other forms of Pangean utopianism. Religious police prowl the sandy streets of cities in countries under the power of the radicals. Criticizing Islam must be outlawed, churches burned, and the critics silenced. Anyone unwilling to come in to this Pangea must be taken out brutally so examples can be set.

Also in our time Darwinism has expanded its Pangean quest. Inspired by the Enlightenment—age of reason-*cum*-romantic idealism that quaked across eighteenth- and nineteenth-century Europe, Charles Darwin saw progress everywhere. Evolution became the great hope. At first it was narrowed down to biology. But now the Pangean utopians have taken over, and it's Darwinism everywhere. Marx and his followers were social Darwinians. Ayn Rand, the radically libertarian author, preached Darwinian individualism. Margaret Sanger, founder of Planned Parenthood, and her optimistic band of racialists—including Hitler—were eugenic Darwinians. Richard Dawkins, biologist and anti-belief-in-God crusader, along with other militant atheists, are philosophical Darwinians.

They remind me of the island builders of Singapore. Mighty hotels and housing estates stand on land that didn't exist a decade ago. New zones are made of mud scooped constantly from the sea. The island nation grows ceaselessly. So all the Pangea builders are sweaty with the work of constructing their great one continent. The Pangean-Utopian-Darwinians are among the most energetic. Refuse to move to their Pangea and you lose your job in the scientific establishment, your tenure in an academic institution, publishing contracts in establishment media, and certainly a chance at walking across a gilded stage watched by royalty to receive one of the grand prizes by which the Pangeans credentialize one another.

Even theologians fall into the Pangean stupor. Followers of the social gospel believe human institutions will usher in the kingdom of God and global unity. Universalists teach that ultimately all will dwell in a sweet Pangea by-and-by because a loving God would never stick someone on a floe drifting apart from the great one continent, no matter how great his or her evil. And then there was Teilhard de Chardin. I was fascinated by this Catholic theologian-scientist when I was a college student. There was not only a biosphere embracing all of life but also a *noosphere* consisting of pure thought, he believed. Teilhard taught the end of all things would be Christogenesis, the ultimate of evolution, which, he thought, is the progressive journey toward Christ.

The ultimate Pangean passion will beat in the heart of Antichrist. Bringing the whole earth under his ruthless dominion is the objective. Deluded individuals naive enough to believe all we need is the reassembly of a spiritual and social Pangea have swallowed the bait. Everywhere and in every generation people have been panting for Pangea. Alfred Wegener, the early twentieth-century scientist whose theories gave us the word *Pangea*, would be surprised to hear what a postmodern college student in Maine and many others have done with his concept.

The yellow brick road to Pangea is like a narrow street I wound up on once in Germany. My wife and I, along with an American friend, were in a hurry to get back to Nuremberg from Heidelberg. We decided to take a shortcut. The shorter the cut, the more confused we were. Finally we asked directions in our broken—no, shattered—German. We held a small conclave in the car to determine the translation of the directions we had been given in German. Convinced we had it right, I headed the car straight ahead. The road compressed into a dirt track, then a one-lane alley into a cemetery—which is where the yellow brick road always leads. The Nazis and their Axis partners launched a war that killed sixty to eighty million human beings. *The Black Book of Communism* totaled the numbers of deaths caused directly by Marxism's tyrants in various nations and came up with the staggering sum of ninety-four million. Terrorism adds to the total daily.

Despite all this, there are many who still pant for Pangea. They believe the best hope in the Globequake era of accelerated continental drift is the return to Pangea. For multitudes of politically correct secularists, this is the "blessed hope."

THE YELLOW SUBMARINE

And then there was Atlantis.

Pangea suffered tectonic *shift*, but Atlantis needed tectonic *lift*. If the search for Pangea is a futile journey on the yellow brick road, then the hunt for Atlantis is a wasted trip on a yellow submarine.

Twenty-three hundred years before Alfred Wegner gave the world the theory of the vast one continent, Plato, in 360 BC, introduced the idea of Atlantis. Ancient records, Plato wrote in his dialogue, *Timaeus*, reported that once "there lay an island which was larger than Libya and Asia together." Plato, in his dialogue, *Critias*, described the end of Atlantis:

> . . . nine thousand was the sum of years which had elapsed since the war which was said to have taken place between those who dwelt outside the Pillars of Heracles and all who dwelt within them; this war I am going to describe. Of the combatants on the one side, the city of Athens was reported to have been the leader and to have fought out the war; the combatants on the other side were commanded by the kings of Atlantis . . . which was an

island greater in extent than Libya and Asia, and when afterwards sunk by an earthquake, became an impassable barrier of mud to voyagers sailing from hence to any part of the ocean.[3]

So before the Pangean quest there was the Atlantean quest, and it continues. The passion some feel to find Atlantis, like the Pangean quest, is as much spiritual, mental, and emotional as it is—for a few at least—physical. W. H. Auden captured the ethos of the Atlantis hunters in a poem:

> *Stagger onward rejoicing;*
> *And even then if, perhaps*
> *Having actually got*
> *To the last col, you collapse*
> *With all Atlantis shining*
> *Below you yet you cannot*
> *Descend, you should still be proud*
> *Even to have been allowed*
> *Just to peep at Atlantis*
> *In a poetic vision:*
> *Give thanks and lie down in peace,*
> *Having seen your salvation.*[4]

Many are not satisfied with a mere "peep" in a "poetic vision." They want to probe the depths of Atlantis and raise the whole continent off the sea bottom. Edgar Cayce, an occultist, even predicted Atlantis would rise on its own about 1968 or 1969. The Nazis, mesmerized by the dark side, got into the Atlantis quest even while feverishly trying to restore their warped version of a Pangea. Heinrich Himmler, the sinister chief of the SS, actually led an expedition to the Himalayan region to look for the descendants of the Atlanteans, assuming them to be the Aryans.

Hardly anyone, however, pined over Atlantis like Ignatius

Donnelly, a nineteenth-century American politician and writer. He wrote that Atlantis "was the true Antediluvian world; the Garden of Eden; the Garden of Hesperides; the Elysian Fields; the Gardens of Alcinous; the Mesomphalos; the Olympos; the Asgard of the traditions of the ancient nations; representing the universal memory of a great land, where early mankind dwelt for ages in peace and happiness."[5]

Humans must have hope. We cannot live without it. When hope dies, we die. If we cannot find hope at the top of the earth, in Pangea, we will try to dredge it up from the bottom of the sea. The yellow submarine won't take us to the top. The only hope that truly lifts us as the Globequake threatens to sink us is God's variety.

CONFUSING HOPE AND WISH

The Pangean and Atlantean utopians don't really have hope; they have only a wish. For hope as genuine and solid as God, you have to go to Him and His Word. Paul wrote,

> For the grace of God has appeared, bringing salvation to all men, instructing us to deny ungodliness and worldly desires and to live sensibly, righteously and godly in the present age, looking for the blessed hope and the appearing of the glory of our great God and Savior, Christ Jesus, who gave Himself for us to redeem us from every lawless deed, and to purify for Himself a people for His own possession, zealous for good deeds. (Titus 2:11–14)

"Hope" is *elpis* in the Greek original. The term means "expectation," not "aspiration." A gambler buys a ticket for the multistate gonzo lottery and hopes to win. She doesn't expect to get a check for millions, but she aspires to it. She wishes she might win. On the other hand, a man with a hefty load of baggage steps from a gangplank onto an ocean liner and jokes to a porter trying to carry all the luggage that he hopes it won't sink. In reality, the seagoing passenger knows the huge ship won't founder under the weight of his suitcases, trunks, and boxes. Biblical hope is like the latter. We can throw all our "baggage" on Christ, and we know He won't drop under the weight.

Such hope is blessed because it is the early sign of Christ's appearing and the arrival into this Globequake-shaking domain of the kingdom that cannot be shaken. This is the true Pangea, when "all the earth will be filled with the glory of the LORD" (Num. 14:21), when

> the wolf will dwell with the lamb,
> And the leopard will lie down with the young goat,
> And the calf and the young lion and the fatling together;
> And a little boy will lead them.
> Also the cow and the bear will graze,
> Their young will lie down together,
> And the lion will eat straw like the ox.
> The nursing child will play by the hole of the cobra,
> And the weaned child will put his hand on the viper's den.
> They will not hurt or destroy in all My holy mountain,
> For the earth will be full of the knowledge of the LORD
> As the waters cover the sea.
> (Isa. 11:6–9)

and when people

> hammer their swords into plowshares
> And their spears into pruning hooks;
> Nation will not lift up sword against nation,
> And never again will they train for war.
> (Mic. 4:3)

Purely humanist Pangea panters scoff at such prophecies, dismissing them as idealism, mysticism, and pie-in-the-skyism. They prefer their own spooky ideas, like the Aryanism and Nietzschean-Wagnerian never-never land of the Nazis, or Hegelian mysticism behind Marxism's theory of history. They accuse people who embrace the biblical vision of the future hope as being "so heavenly minded they are no earthly good" or so focused on a "dreamy someday" they can't live in the present.

The reality is men and women who see the future as the *blessed hope* live in a *blessed present*. Not that they aren't feeling the tremors along with everyone else in the Globequake age. But note Paul's linkage between the future hope and living in the present. We are "to deny ungodliness and worldly desires and to live sensibly, righteously and godly in the *present age*" (Titus 2:12, italics added).

The more we focus on the Lord in His future coming, the more we will be like the Lord in our present moment. Thus, "we all, with unveiled face, beholding as in a mirror the glory of the Lord, are being transformed into the same image from glory to glory, just as from the Lord, the Spirit" (2 Cor. 3:18). Sanctification is the true evolution. It is the increasing conformity of the existential human being to the image of the Lord who has come, is come, and will come. It is the progressive setting apart of every facet of one's being unto Him. It is the enlightening of the eyes of the heart by which we know "the hope of His calling" (Eph. 1:18).

BEGGING FOR UPHEAVAL

People anchored in such hope directed toward the future are steadied in the present because they understand what's going on. This is not smug Gnosticism because they don't want the truth about history to be a secret. Thinking the thoughts of God and beating in the rhythm of His heartbeat, they want the whole world to know what they know, namely, *the cosmos begs for upheaval, and all the tectonic movements and their tremors and turmoil lead ultimately to the fulfillment of hope*. This is the point of Romans 8:18–25:

> I consider that the sufferings of this present time are not worthy to be compared with the glory that is to be revealed to us. For the anxious longing of the creation waits eagerly for the revealing of the sons of God. For the creation was subjected to futility, not willingly, but because of Him who subjected it, in hope that the creation itself also will be set free from its slavery to corruption into the freedom of the glory of the children of God. For we know that the whole creation groans and suffers the pains of childbirth together until now. And not only this, but also we ourselves, having the first fruits of the Spirit, even we ourselves groan within ourselves, waiting eagerly for our adoption as sons, the redemption of our body. For in hope we have been saved, but hope that is seen is not hope; for who hopes for what he already sees? But if we hope for what we do not see, with perseverance we wait eagerly for it.

Hop on the ark with Noah, and you will understand. The Flood brings down everything. There is catastrophe as the water surges from the quaking earth. But after all the heaving, the torrents above and below subside and Noah, his family, and the animals walk out into a new world, one cleansed of the old chaos. However, it took a Globequake in the form of the Flood to get there.

The world cries for renewal. The forests will erupt in flame, burning off the dross of the old. Snakes shed their skin—and so do humans—so the fresh will canopy their bodies. Old wineskins and garments must go so new ones can handle the new forms that will fill them. The renewing times are always experienced as Globequakes. People who see with the eyes of God, by opening their vision to Him, behold what He's up to. They know in every

Globequake, no matter how great the pain, there is the eagle wing of hope, soaring above the upheaval like the birds that remain airborne while a tsunami scourges the land below.

"The early Christians did not believe in progress," wrote N. T. Wright. "They did not think the world was getting better and better under its own steam—or even under the steady influence of God. They knew God had to do something fresh to put it to rights."[6] That required the most intense Globequake of all times, one that would put the upside-down world right side up.

No mayhem has ever been greater than Calvary. Matthew tells us,

> Jesus cried out again with a loud voice, and yielded up His spirit. And behold, the veil of the temple was torn in two from top to bottom; and the earth shook and the rocks were split. The tombs were opened, and many bodies of the saints who had fallen asleep were raised; and coming out of the tombs after His resurrection they entered the holy city and appeared to many. Now the centurion, and those who were with him keeping guard over Jesus, when they saw the earthquake and the things that were happening, became very frightened and said, "Truly this was the Son of God!" (Matt. 27:50–54)

How appropriate that the earth quaked at the Lord's crucifixion, for it was the greatest Globequake the world will ever experience—and the most renewing. It took the quake for a Roman soldier to come into the new life Christ died to secure for us all. It took the Globequake of Calvary and its cross to make renewal possible for the whole world.

In God's hands the turmoil becomes constructive. The veil of the temple is split from top to bottom as Jerusalem's ground shakes that afternoon. Tombs are opened, and the dead walk through the trembling streets. Just days after the turmoil of Golgotha, a grave is opened, and Jesus Christ walks out. The grand renewal of all things has begun, and God has used the Globequake to accomplish His purpose for His image bearers and the world they inhabit.

If anyone was an expert on Globequakes and the passion for hope amid the upheaval, it was the apostle Paul. His physical, mental, and emotional seismograph rarely settled. Those at Corinth who questioned his authority as an apostle got an earful. Paul didn't want to brag, but they needed to know that as a follower of Christ, he had been tossed around a time or two. He wrote,

> I know I sound like a madman, but I have served him far more! I have worked harder, been put in jail more often, been whipped times without number, and faced death again and again. Five different times the Jews gave me thirty-nine lashes. Three times I was beaten with rods. Once I was stoned. Three times I was shipwrecked. Once I spent a whole night and a day adrift at sea. I have traveled many weary miles. I have faced danger from flooded rivers and from robbers. I have faced danger from my own people, the Jews, as well as from the Gentiles. I have faced danger in the cities, in the deserts, and on the stormy seas. And I have faced danger from men who claim to be Christians but are not. I have lived with weariness and pain and sleepless nights. Often I have been hungry and thirsty and have gone without food. Often I have shivered with cold, without enough clothing to keep me warm. Then, besides all this, I have the daily burden of how the churches are getting along. Who is weak without my feeling that weakness? Who is led astray, and I do not burn with anger? (2 Cor. 11:23–29 NLT)

Despite all this, at times Paul seemed intoxicated with hope. He referred to hope fifty times from Romans to Philemon. Paul's hope, however, didn't come from a foaming brew. He preferred the filling of the Spirit to being drunk on wine (Eph. 5:18). Paul's hope wasn't something he cooked up in a hyperfantasizing mind. Paul was as choleric as they come and had a hard time suffering fools. He wasn't given to dreamy speculations. Paul wasn't likely to go skipping down a yellow brick road or hopping aboard a yellow submarine.

Paul's hope was not intrinsic to himself. He had been an angry Pharisee. His manner was as soft as steel wool. Paul was a grumpy old man from his youth. No, hope was not native to the soil of Paul's soul. So where did it come from? Here are four keys to Paul's unshakeable hope as the Globequake of his times rocked everything around him.

1. Paul had the right "spine."

"Christ in you, the hope of glory," he wrote (Col. 1:27, italics added).

Sturdy foundations are crucial in anchoring the Statue of Liberty so it can resist the hefty wind loads racing through New York Harbor. The other part of that stabilizing system is Miss Liberty's spine of steel. The sculptor Frederic-Auguste Bartholdi partnered with Gustave Eiffel, the famous tower builder, to raise the 151-foot statue. Eiffel designed a spinal system of four massive columns, to which a metal framework is attached. Three hundred copper sheets give Lady Liberty her external shape. Without the spine and strong interior, Miss Liberty would be three hundred sheets to the wind—literally.

Christ is the spine of hope! Without Him, the mighty thrusts of the Globequake would fragment us. We would disintegrate into fear, despair, and confusion without the sturdy reality of Christ and His hope in the core of our lives. Christ's presence in Paul through the Holy Spirit transformed Paul's way of looking at the world. Through Christ, Paul experienced the renewing of the mind (Rom. 12:1–2). The sourpuss became a smiling saint who loved the word *joy* as much as he did *hope*. But Paul's joy was grounded in his hope, which was anchored in Christ.

2. Hope framed Paul's worldview.

In Romans 5:1–5, he wrote,

Having been justified by faith, we have peace with God through our Lord Jesus Christ, through whom also we have obtained our introduction by faith into this grace in which we stand; and we exult in hope of the glory of God. And not only this, but we also exult in our tribulations, knowing that tribulation brings about perseverance; and perseverance, proven character; and proven character, hope; and hope does not disappoint, because the love of God has been poured out within our hearts through the Holy Spirit who was given to us.

Paul knew "that God causes all things to work together for good to those who love God, to those who are called according to His purpose" (Rom. 8:28). For Paul, "to live is Christ" (Phil. 1:21), and so the "purpose" toward which God works "all things" to "good" is Christlikeness in the individual's life (Rom. 8:28). In fact, "those whom He foreknew, He also predestined to become conformed to the image of His Son, so that He would be the firstborn among many brethren; and these whom He predestined, He also called; and these whom He called, He also justified; and these whom He justified, He also glorified" (Rom. 8:29–30).

Paul was confident that turmoil, tribulation, shaking, and scariness were knocking off the ugly stuff, refining the profile, reestablishing the beautiful image of God marred by sin. "But we all, with unveiled face, beholding as in a mirror the glory of the Lord, are being transformed into the same image from glory to glory, just as from the Lord, the Spirit," he wrote (2 Cor. 3:18).

Nobody said transformation is easy. Every caterpillar knows about Globequakes. Your average hardworking grub couldn't give you rhyme or reason about why it has a powerful impulse to imprison itself in a sticky tunnel called a chrysalis. Inside that cocoon the bug starts going to pieces, literally. Then there are rebuilding, reforming, reshaping. Had caterpillars a well-developed nervous system so they could feel acutely the rending change of metamorphosis, hikers in the deep woods would probably hear shrieks and screams coming from every tree.

But if caterpillars who have been earthbound or confined to a tree limb knew the end of the harrowing process of transformation would be their emergence as a glorious butterfly able to soar out over the forest, they would be giddy with hope!

The joy of people whose worldview is framed by Christ as they ride the roiling tsunamis spurred by the Globequake is not because they live in denial or simply don't know what's going on. They do know, at a level the rest of the world doesn't. While many people try to deny the existence of evil and sin, people whose worldview is set on Christ acknowledge sin's corrosive power in their own lives and world and know Christ has dealt with its penalties in His work of justification, and the Holy Spirit is restructuring the redeemed individual through sanctification.

3. Hope gave Paul understanding of the linkage of the Globequake and the successful execution of his mission.

The Philippian Christians were distressed about Paul's imprisonment in Rome toward the end of his life. They sent an emissary, Epaphroditus, to check up on him. Paul got to Rome under the hardest of circumstances. He sailed through a winter storm, got shipwrecked, and was snakebit. Once in Rome he was confined, harnessed to a soldier 24/7. What about your mission, Paul? Aren't you the apostle to the Gentiles?

Paul reported to the Philippian church that the ruckus, turbulence, and hardship

> have turned out for the greater progress of the gospel, so that my imprisonment in the cause of Christ has become well known throughout the whole praetorian guard and to everyone else, and that most of the brethren, trusting in the Lord because of my imprisonment, have far more courage to speak

the word of God without fear. Some, to be sure, are preaching Christ even from envy and strife, but some also from good will; the latter do it out of love, knowing that I am appointed for the defense of the gospel; the former proclaim Christ out of selfish ambition rather than from pure motives, thinking to cause me distress in my imprisonment. What then? Only that in every way, whether in pretense or in truth, Christ is proclaimed; and in this I rejoice. (Phil. 1:12–18)

It has been almost four decades now, but I still remember a man named Dennis who chose to view cancer through the lens of Christ's hope. Dennis, his wife, and two small sons joined our church. This thirtysomething man was so exuberant that not even a grump could stay grim in his presence. Dennis was a salesman, one of those amazing people who could sell bamboo to jungle dwellers.

About a year after I first met Dennis, health issues cropped up. After a series of tests, he got the diagnosis: aggressive leukemia. But it couldn't erase his smile or the glimmer in his eye. I visited Dennis frequently at home and in the hospital. I always left Dennis buoyed up and inspired. On one of the visits he was grimacing with pain. "How do you endure this?" I asked. I'll never forget Dennis's reply. "I am called to the ministry of leukemia," he told me. "Because I am in this hospital, doctors and nurses come into my room all the time, and I am able to tell them about Christ."

Dennis's hope wasn't fixed on a quickie prayer or denial of his sickness any more than Paul denied he was in dank Roman confinement. Dennis had the dual gifts of evangelism and encouragement. Confinement in a hospital bed with suffering intense enough for everyone to see enabled him to execute the mission and exercise his gifts. Dennis lived in hope and he died in hope.

One day I had to go to his home and tell the little boys their daddy had moved to a new place. At six and seven, they had a hard time wrapping their minds around death. But the attitude of their dad had rubbed off on them and their mother, who kept Dennis's hope in Christ wonderfully vibrant in her little reshaped family circle.

4. Paul's hope in Christ gave him an appreciation for the dynamics of brokenness.

Globequakes break things. "Good!" said Paul, at least with respect to those things that are useless until they are broken. That was the apostle's point in 2 Corinthians 4:7–12:

> We have this treasure in earthen vessels, so that the surpassing greatness of the power will be of God and not from ourselves; we are afflicted in every way, but not crushed; perplexed, but not despairing; persecuted, but not forsaken; struck down, but not destroyed; always carrying about in the body the dying of Jesus, so that the life of Jesus also may be manifested in our body. For we who live are constantly being delivered over to death for Jesus' sake, so that the life of Jesus also may be manifested in our mortal flesh. So death works in us, but life in you.

HOPE'S THUMBS-UP

One night in the 1970s, on a flight from Singapore to the United States, I had to change planes in Tokyo, where I had a two-hour layover. I got off the flight from Singapore and walked around the vast pod in the airport. Suddenly I spotted a long line of people waiting to board a Northwest Orient plane to Seattle. Many wore T-shirts emblazoned with red crosses. As I drew closer, I could see other indications they were Cambodians from a refugee camp in Thailand. I tear up when I remember the look in their eyes. Hope danced; expectancy and anticipation shouted. They were ribbon thin and some were haggard, but joy was all over them. At the very end of the line was a young man, maybe seventeen years old. He looked at me, recognized me as an American, and exploded in a huge smile. I gave him a thumbs-up, which he returned quickly.

I knew what he was about to experience. Our church in Alabama had adopted a group of more than one hundred Cambodian refugees. Irene and I, along with our kids, became close to one of the refugee families consisting of a widowed mother and her three children. Cha-Rok, her fifteen-year-old son, was the only person among the Cambodian group who could speak English conversationally. Over the months, as he relaxed with us, Cha-Rok told of how he and his brother had hidden high in a tree and watched Khmer Rouge—the horribly cruel Communist insurgency that overran Cambodia— hack their father to death with a machete. Miraculously, the family survived and managed to get to America.

Through the years, Irene, Lauri, Travis, and I watched Cha-Rok and his family take solid root in their new world. They worked menial jobs because they wanted to support themselves. They learned to speak English. The three children enrolled in high school, where all were inducted into the National Honor Society, and Cha-Rok was elected president of the student body. He went on to become a physician.

The Globequake of the war in Southeast Asia brought tragedy to many, but it propelled others into a new life and into hope. Because of what I knew about Cha-Rok and his family, there was great meaning in my thumbs-up to the young man that night in the Tokyo airport!

Globequakes make us all refugees, leaping from severed continent to severed continent. Our forebears began the trek that got us to where we are from the region of Ararat. And even that wasn't the original home of the human race. In the most distant past, we are all refugees from Eden, and we hunger to go home. The continents move across the face of earth, and so do their people. Ultimately we all look for the same thing—hope.

Thus, the Pangean and Atlantean quests are ultimately a search for hope that one can find safety, sanity, and stability in a world gone wild. But travelers on the yellow brick road or riders on the yellow submarine never find hope. The yellow brick road keeps circling, always winding up at the same dismal starting point. The real road to hope, however, is not a circuit. It's a straight line, like those flights the refugees took from Tokyo. The real road to hope leads not to a dreamy, mystical counterfeit, like Pangea, but to the unshakeable kingdom.

And the yellow submarine searches the bottom, but always at the wrong place. The hearts of those aboard flutter when they see images sticking from the sand, thinking they might be the lost ruins of Atlantis. Then their hope sinks when the yellow submarine gets close enough to reveal just one more cluster of seaweed.

But the hope that can sustain us through the Globequake does exist. Millions have found it. They left the yellow brick road, or disembarked from the yellow submarine, and looked into the depths of God and His kingdom.

And there they found the hope that comes from living in the unshakeable kingdom while the world falls apart.

ACKNOWLEDGMENTS

On my journey of writing, I have had the joy of many encouraging, insightful companions. They have reviewed, critiqued, and provided valuable information that has greatly enhanced my efforts.

Irene, my wife of more than fifty years, as you have read in these pages, has shared experiences and given me many insights regarding issues presented in this book. Her discernment, wisdom, faith, and courage are mighty stabilizers for our whole family as we all experience the upheavals of the Globequake.

Both our daughter, Lauri, and our son, Travis, have made significant contributions. Lauri is an educator, and Travis is a vice president of a large multinational corporation. I gained much insight through discussions with their spouses, Jim Rushing and Linda Henley, each of them corporate executives as well. My sister, Linda Moon, also an educator, gave insights that strengthened discussions regarding that sphere. My dear grandchildren were always in view as I wrote and considered the impact of the Globequake on their futures.

Ed Young is my pastor, boss, mentor, and dear friend. He has inspired and encouraged me throughout this process. His generosity, leadership, tenacity, courage, and knowledge are exceptional.

I am grateful for the Headwaters Leadership Institute team and the way they have shared and contributed to this vision—Brad Hays,

Acknowlegments

Hugh Willis, Bob Warren, Bobby Hillin, Charley Stewart, Dean Fox, Bill Blessing, and Judge Jim Squier are dear friends and wise counselors.

Linda Willis, my administrative assistant, has made it possible for me to write through her efficient administration of responsibilities we have at Second Baptist Church.

The Globequake Business Brain Trust made valuable contributions that got this project rolling. The team included Professor John Whitney, David Bearden, Steve Carlin, David Drowley, Brad Hays, Ed Lambert, Keith Okano, Michael Pinckert, Travis Henley, Mike Kinney, Mike Rome, Roger Wernette, Dr. Leslie Haugen, Judge Jim Squier, Professor Mohan Kuruvilla, Professor Ernest Liang, Keith Miller, Jim Rushing, and Christine Williams.

I am grateful to my agent, Joel Kneedler, and the team at Alive Communications. Joel wouldn't let this project go, and his constant encouragement and sharp ideas helped me move forward.

It's an honor and privilege to work with Joel Miller and the team at Thomas Nelson. Renee Chavez, Dimples Kellogg, and Janene MacIvor provided sharp substantive and editorial insights. Jennifer Keller, Kristi Henson, Brenda Smotherman, and the marketing and graphics team presented a well-designed book to the marketplace. The Thomas Nelson team's drive for quality sets high standards for authors, and I appreciate their guidance through the publishing process.

Fellow staff and members of our church have also played a major role, especially those who reviewed chapters—Tonya Riggle, Toni Richmond, Angel Texada, Keith Carmichael, Steve Seelig, Beverly Gambrell, Chris Hopf, Mark Sepulveda, Charley Townsend, Melody Wren, Chris Cox, Judge Jim Squier, David Drinnon, and Scott and Lori Ann Belin took time to read and respond with helpful suggestions.

Thanks to all of you, dear friends. This book would be greatly diminished without your spiritual gifts, professional wisdom, and keen insights.

Wallace Henley

NOTES

Chapter 1: The Globequake and the New Normal

1. Huntington (1927–2008) was a Harvard professor who wrote extensively on nations and their cultures. His book *Clash of Civilizations* was a brilliant and farsighted look at the shifts occurring in the geopolitical landscapes. In *Who Are We?* Huntington probed the importance of national identity and the impact of its loss.
2. Rich Lowry, "Coming Apart at the Seams," *National Review*, April 12, 2011.
3. Alexander Solzhenitsyn, *The First Circle* (New York: Harper and Row, 1968), 116.
4. Victor Davis Hanson, "America's Nervous Breakdown," *National Review Online*, October 2, 2008, http://www.nationalreview.com/articles/225848/americas-nervous-breakdown/victor-davis-hanson.
5. Will Durant, *The Greatest Minds and Ideas of All Time*, comp. John Little (New York: Simon and Schuster, 2002), 90.
6. Peter Apps, "After the Crisis, a Worldwide Rise in Unrest?" Reuters, February 28, 2011, http://www.reuters.com/article/2011/02/28/us-global-unrest-idUSTRE71R3M420110228.
7. Cited in *New York Magazine*, February 24, 2009, and other publications and sites.
8. Hugh Hefner was the founder and editor of *Playboy* magazine. In its pages, he wrote extensively about the "new morality" in an attempt to legitimize adultery and fornication. Timothy Leary was a clinical psychologist who pioneered psychedelic, mind-altering drugs that he claimed enhanced spiritual experience.
9. Peter Drucker, *Management Challenges for the 21st Century* (New York: Harper Business, 1999).
10. Wendy McAuliffe, "Hawking Warns of AI WorldTakeover," ZDNet UK, September 3, 2001, http://www.zdnet.co.uk/news/application-development/2001/09/03/hawking-warns-of-ai-world-takeover-2094424/.
11. Ibid.
12. "The Speed of Information," *The Technium*, 2006.
13. Ibid.

14. Ibid.
15. G. K. Chesterton, *Orthodoxy* (Garden City, NY: Image Books, 1959), published originally, 1924.
16. Joseph Brandon Ford and Michel Paul Richard discuss Sorokin's concept of the "sensate stage" in their book *Sorokin and Civilization* (Transaction Publishers, 1995), 69.
17. Christopher Orlet, "The Look-at-Me Generation," American Spectator, March 2, 2007, http://spectator.org/archives/2007/03/02/the-look-at-me-generation.
18. E. Fuller Torrey and Judy Miller, *The Invisible Plague* (New Brunswick, NJ: Rutgers University Press, 2002).
19. Robert Whitaker, "Anatomy of an Epidemic," *Ethical Human Psychology and Psychiatry* 7, no. 1 (Spring 2005).
20. Samuel P. Huntington, *Who Are We? The Challenges to America's National Identity* (New York: Simon and Schuster, 2004), 21.
21. Chesterton, *Orthodoxy*.

Chapter 2: How Time Works

1. *Greek-English Lexicon Based on Semantic Domain* (New York: United Bible Societies, 1988).
2. For readers not familiar with the term *Antichrist*, it refers to a person and movement that will arise in the last days, seeking to displace the rule of Christ and His kingdom. *Anti* is the Greek word carrying two meanings: that of opposing something or someone, and that of occupying a position or office held by someone else. Therefore, the Antichrist's objectives regarding Christ are *opposition* and *imposition*.
3. Thayer and Smith, "Kairos," in *The New Testament Greek Lexicon*, http://www.searchgodsword.org/lex/grk/view.cgi?number=2540.
4. Georg Hegel was a nineteenth-century philosopher who believed social and political history moved from one foundational worldview to its opposite and then back to a synthesis of the two. This was described as the "dialectic": thesis-antithesis-synthesis. Marx was uncomfortable with Hegel's dialectical *idealism* and, in concert with Friedrich Engels, developed the idea of dialectical *materialism* (a term coined by the socialist philosopher Joseph Dietzgen in 1887). The status quo of bourgeois class and wealth would be confronted by the revolutionary proletariat, leading to the synthesis of a truly classless and socialistic society. Marx and his followers believed that history was on the side of communism and that ultimately communism would triumph.
5. William Strauss and Neil Howe, *The Fourth Turning: An American Prophecy* (New York: Broadway Books, 1997).
6. Jay Winik, 502.

Chapter 3: The Unshakeable Kingdom

1. *Patriot Sage*, ed. Gary L. Gregg and Matthew Spalding (Wilmington, DE: ISI Books, 1999), 79.
2. Paul Johnson, *A History of the American People* (New York: Harper Perennial, 1997), 160.
3. Ron Chernow, *Washington: A Life* (New York: Penguin, 2010), 324.
4. Cited in Brookhiser, 33.
5. *Winston Churchill: His Wit and Wisdom* (London: Hyperion, 1965), 16–17.

Chapter 4: Standing Like a Stone Wall

1. *International Standard Bible Encyclopaedia* (Biblesoft, 1996), electronic database.
2. Lewis Carroll, *Alice in Wonderland*, Project Gutenberg edition. Retrieved from http://www.cs.cmu.edu/~rgs/alice-table.html.
3. Allan David Bloom, *The Closing of the American Mind* (New York: Simon and Schuster, 1987), 26.
4. Stanley L. Jaki, *Science and Creation* (New York: Academic Press, 1974), 278; cited in Kenneth D. Boa and Robert M. Bowman Jr., *20 Compelling Evidences That God Exists* (Tulsa: RiverOak Publishing, 2002), 175.
5. *Times of London Online*, December 27, 2008.
6. "Economists Want to Know: Do Europeans Work Less Because They Believe Less in God?" Joshua Burek, *The Christian Science Monitor*, February 22, 2005. Retrieved from http://www.csmonitor.com/2005/0222/p12s01-woeu.html.
7. The Madison and Webster quotations are cited in Boa and Bowman, *20 Compelling Evidences*, 181–82.

Chapter 5: The Kingdom and the Spheres

1. *Thayer's Greek Lexicon* (Biblesoft, 2003), electronic database.
2. *McClintock and Strong Encyclopedia* (Biblesoft, 2003), electronic database.
3. *Greek-English Lexicon Based on Semantic Domain* (New York: United Bible Societies, 1988).
4. Ibid.
5. Retrieved from http://www.goodreads.com/author/quotes/385896. Abraham_Kuyper.
6. Alex Preston, "God's Bankers: How Evangelical Christianity Is Taking a Hold of the City of London's Financial Institutions," *Independent*, April 24, 2011.
7. *Keil and Delitzsch Commentary on the Old Testament*, new updated ed. (Hendrickson Publishers, 1996), electronic database.
8. See, for example, "Prince Charles of Arabia," by Ronni L. Gordon and David M. Stillman, *The Middle East Quarterly*, September 1997, 3–7.

Part 2: Stabilizing the Spheres

1. W.E. Vine, *Vine's Expository Dictionary of New Testament Words* (Nashville: Thomas Nelson Publishers, 1996).

Chapter 7: Safe and Secure in Your "Amness"

1. "Invictus," by William Ernest Henley. Retrieved from www.poetryfoundation.org/poem/182194.
2. We will not list goals for each sphere since they will be determined within the context of the specific institutions within the respective spheres.
3. This is a mere sampling. There are many more!
4. Tom Blackwell, "Toronto Parents Hide Child's Gender in Bid for Neutral Treatment," Gazette/Montreal Gazette.com, http://www .montrealgazette.com/life/Toronto+parents+hide+child+gender+neutral+ treatment/4837762/story.html.
5. *Greek-English Lexicon Based on Semantic Domain* (New York: United Bible Societies, 1988).

Chapter 8: The Rock-Solid Church

1. Russell Kirk, "Can Our Civilization Survive?" (address, Heritage Foundation, July 24, 1992).
2. This does not imply, of course, equivalency—for example, that all these "churches" are the authentic church.
3. Philip Jenkins, "The Next Christianity," *Atlantic*, October 2002.
4. Alexis de Tocqueville, abridged edition by Scott A. Sandage, *Democracy in America* (New York: HarperCollins Publishers, 1969, introduction copyright 2007), 253.

Chapter 9: When the Globequake Puts the Lights Out

1. Helen Kennedy, "Haiti Earthquake: Port-au-Prince Rocked by 7.0 Quake; Buildings Collapse, Hundreds Feared Dead," *New York Daily News*, January 12, 2010.
2. Malcolm Muggeridge, *The End of Christendom* (Grand Rapids: Eerdmans, 1980), 52–56.
3. "The Defence of Freedom and Peace," a speech by Winston S. Churchill, October 16, 1938. From *Churchill, Into Battle* (London: Cassell, 1941), 83–91. Retrieved from www.winstonchurchill.org/learn/speeches/ churchill/524-the-defence-of-freedom-and-peace.
4. Robert Nisbet, *The Twilight of Authority* (Indianapolis: Liberty Fund, 2000).
5. Ethan Cole, "Tim Keller: 'Mushy Middle' in Religion Is Disappearing,"

Christian Post, April 25, 2011, http://www.christianpost.com/news/tim-keller-mushy-middle-in-religion-is-disappearing-49983/.

6. David Wells, *God in the Wasteland* (Grand Rapids: Eerdmans, 1994), 6, italics in original.

7. Ibid., 22.

8. For an excellent discussion of this issue see Robert W. Ferris, "The Role of Theology in Theological Education," https://www.applyweb.com/apply/ciu/review_article.pdf.

9. Edward Farley, *Theologia: The Fragmentation and Unity of Theological Education* (Philadelphia: Fortress Press), cited by Ferris, "Role of Theology."

10. Tim Stafford, "Historian Ahead of His Time," *Christianity Today*, February 8, 2007, italics added.

11. "What Is Joshua Project?" http://www.joshuaproject.net/joshua-project.php.

12. "World Evangelization—AD 2000 and Beyond," http://www.adopt-a-people.org/articles/world_evangelism.pdf.

13. Ibid.

14. Ralph D. Winter and Steven C. Hawthorne, eds., *Perspectives on the World Christian Movement*, 3rd ed. (Pasadena: William Carey Library, 2004), 75.

Chapter 10: Indestructible Families

1. Pat Ammons, "Pre–Civil War Log House Survives Tornado, Protects Family in Harvest," Huntsville Times, May 14, 2011, http://blog.al.com/breaking/2011/05/pre-civil_war_log_house_surviv.html.

2. *Greek-English Lexicon Based on Semantic Domain* (New York: United Bible Societies, 1988).

3. *Biblesoft's New Exhaustive Strong's Numbers and Concordance with Expanded Greek-Hebrew Dictionary* (Biblesoft, and International Bible Translators, 2003).

4. *McClintock and Strong Encyclopedia* (Biblesoft, 2003), electronic database.

5. Rebecca Hagelin, *Home Invasion: Protecting Your Family in a Culture That's Gone Stark Raving Mad* (Nashville: Thomas Nelson, 2005), 3.

6. Andree Aelion Brooks, *Children of Fast-Track Parents* (New York: Viking, 1989), 67–68.

Chapter 11: Designing the Forever House

1. Kathryn Jean Lopez, "Billy Ray Knows Best," *National Review Online*, February 21, 2011.

2. Ibid.

3. Hagelin, *Home Invasion*.

4. See, for example, 1 Corinthians 7:12–16.

5. Lopez, "Billy Ray Knows Best."

6. Patrick Fagan, "The Real Root Causes of Violent Crime,"

Notes

Heritage Foundation Backgrounder, March 17, 1995,
http://www.heritage.org/Research/Reports/1995/03/
BG1026nbsp-The-Real-Root-Causes-of-Violent-Crime.

Chapter 12: Sane Education

1. Duncan Williams, *Trousered Apes*, from the foreword to the American ed. (New York: Dell).
2. *Greek-English Lexicon Based on Semantic Domain* (New York: United Bible Societies, 1988).
3. Rich Milne, "The Christian Mind: Does It Really Matter?" http://www.northave.org/MGManual/xnmind/xnmind3.htm.
4. Harry Blamires, *The Christian Mind* (Ann Arbor: Servant Books, 1978), 67–68.
5. Thomas D. Williams, "Values, Virtues, and John Paul II," *First Things* 72 (April 1997): 29–32.
6. Ibid.
7. "The Study of God," a speech by Thomas Paine. Retrieved from www.wallbuilders.com/libissuesarticles.asp?id=81.
8. Samuel P. Huntington, *Who Are We? The Challenges to America's National Identity* (New York: Simon and Schuster, 2004), 175.

Chapter 13: Rebuilding the Educational Rubble World

1. Romain Leick, Matthias Schreiber, and Hans-Ulrich Stoldt, "Out of the Ashes: A New Look at Germany's Postwar Reconstruction," *Der Spiegel*, August 10, 2010, http://www.spiegel.de/international/germany/0,1518,702856,00.html.
2. Ibid.
3. These same theories were being promoted in the United States by Margaret Sanger, founder of Planned Parenthood and a proponent of the eugenics theories the Nazis would use to justify eradication of the Jews.
4. Botting, 284.
5. Mona Charen, "It's Education, but Higher Is a Misnomer," *National Review Online*, June 3, 2011.
6. From the title of a book by Rick Godwin.
7. A. Dixon, "Parents: Full Partners in the Decision-Making Process," *NASSP Bulletin* 76 (April 1992): 15–18.
8. Larry Elliott, "Decline and Fall of the American Empire," *Guardian*, June 6, 2011, http://www.guardian.co.uk/business/2011/jun/06/us-economy-decline-recovery-challenges, italics added.

Chapter 14: The Cracked Dome

1. Rob Moll, "Rx for Recidivism," *Christianity Today*, November 2006.

2. The Papers of General Washington documents to verify: http://gwpapers.virginia.edu/documents/revolution/profanity_1.html. It is administered by the University of Virginia. Wording shown here from the author appears in Wiki. Copy cited in this extract was issued to Continental Army then at New York, August 3, 1776.
3. *The Christian Science Monitor*, March 24, 2010.
4. Edward J. Erler, "Moral Ideas for America: The Progressive Income Tax and the Progressive Attack on the Founding" (Claremont, CA: Claremont Institute, 1998).
5. Milton Viorst, "Sudan's Islamic Experiment," *Foreign Affairs*, May/June 1995, 46.
6. A. Daniel Frankforter, *A History of the Christian Movement* (Chicago: Nelson-Hall, 1978), 131.
7. Cited in Charles Colson with Ellen Santilli Vaughn, *Kingdoms in Conflict* (Grand Rapids: Zondervan, 1987), 141.
8. *Selected Works*, 3:322, as cited in Jean Esmine, *The Chinese Cultural Revolution* (Garden City, NY: Doubleday, 1973), 8.

Chapter 15: Strategic Equilibrium

1. Agnes Newton Keith, *Bare Feet in the Palace* (Boston: Little Brown, 1955). Thanks to Ed Young for making me aware of this book.
2. Mark Zandi, *Financial Shock* (Upper Saddle River, NJ: FT Press, 2009), 64.
3. Cited in Russell Kirk, *The Conservative Mind* (Washington, DC: Regnery, YEAR???), 483.
4. Rufus King, *The Life and Correspondence of Rufus King*, ed. Charles R. King editor (New York: G. P. Putnam's Sons, 1900), Vol. VI, 276, to C. Gore on February 17, 1820. Retrieved from http://www.wallbuilders.com/libissuesarticles.asp?id=111.
5. Seymour M. Hersh, *The Dark Side of Camelot* (Boston: Little, Brown, 1997), 295.
6. Thomas C. Reeves, *A Question of Character* (New York: Free Press, 1991), 95.

Chapter 16: Business in Upheaval

1. *Guardian*, June 2, 2009.
2. John Zogby, *The Way We'll Be* (New York: Random House, 2008), 198.
3. Ibid., xi.
4. Ibid., 115.
5. Samuel Huntington, *Who Are We? The Challenges to America's National Identity* (New York: Simon and Schuster, 2004), 7.
6. Derek Scissors, "Deng Undone," *Foreign Affairs* 88, no. 3 (May/June 2009).
7. Zogby, *The Way We'll Be*, xi.

8. *Our Global Neighborhood: The Report of the Commission on Global Governance* (Oxford: Oxford University Press, 1995), 7.

9. Ibid., 342–43.

10. Jay R. Galbraith, Edward E. Lawler et al., *Organizing for the Future: The New Logic of Managing Complex Organizations* (San Francisco: Jossey-Bass, 1993), 9.

11. Sarah Jane Gilbert, "Social Network Marketing: What Works?" *HBS Working Knowledge*, July 27, 2009.

Chapter 17: Globequake-Proof Business

1. John Whitney, "Strategic Renewal for Business Units," *Harvard Business Review*, 1996.

2. Ibid.

Chapter 18: Hope Sought, Hope Found

1. http://machias.edu/Pangaea.html.

2. From "The Internationale," composed originally in 1871 by Eugene Pottier, a member of the Paris Commune, and sung by Communists, socialists, and anarchists.

3. *Critias*, by Plato, translated by Benjamin Jowett. Retrieved from http://www.classicallibrary.org/plato/dialogues/18_critias.htm.

4. "Atlantis," by W.H. Auden. From *A Selection of British Poetry*. Retrieved from http://www.daimi.au.dk/~sorsha/lit/WHAuden.html.

5. Ignatius Donnelly, *Atlantis*, 7th ed. (New York: Harper & Brothers, 1882), 1–2.

6. N. T. Wright, *Surprised by Hope* (New York: HarperCollins, 2008), 93.

INDEX

ABOUT THE AUTHOR

"Wallace Henley has one of the most diverse experiences of leadership of any Christian leader writing today. His grasp of Scripture, understanding of human nature, and familiarity with the intricacies of leadership are obvious and apparent in every paragraph," says Gary Thomas, author of *Sacred Marriage*. Wallace has worked as a newspaper reporter and editor, an aide at the White House, a congressional chief of staff, and a pastor. He is a leadership consultant to churches and government agencies, and he has worked in more than twenty countries. Wallace is a pastor at the 56,000-member Second Baptist Church of Houston, led by Pastor Ed Young, who says Wallace has "keen insight into popular culture coupled with biblical wisdom." Wallace is the author of more than twenty books.